ASIAN/OCEANIAN HISTORICAL DICTIONARIES
Edited by Jon Woronoff

Asia
1. *Vietnam*, by William J. Duiker. 1989
2. *Bangladesh*, second edition, by Craig Baxter and Syedur Rahman. 1996
3. *Pakistan*, by Shahid Javed Burki. 1991
4. *Jordan*, by Peter Gubser. 1991
5. *Afghanistan*, by Ludwig W. Adamec. 1991
6. *Laos*, by Martin Stuart-Fox and Mary Kooyman. 1992
7. *Singapore*, by K. Mulliner and Lian The-Mulliner. 1991
8. *Israel*, by Bernard Reich. 1992
9. *Indonesia*, by Robert Cribb. 1992
10. *Hong Kong and Macau*, by Elfed Vaughan Roberts, Sum Ngai Ling, and Peter Bradshaw. 1992
11. *Korea*, by Andrew C. Nahm. 1993
12. *Taiwan*, by John F. Copper. 1993
13. *Malaysia*, by Amarjit Kaur. 1993
14. *Saudi Arabia*, by J. E. Peterson. 1993
15. *Myanmar*, by Jan Becka. 1995
16. *Iran*, by John H. Lorentz. 1995
17. *Yemen*, by Robert D. Burrowes. 1995
18. *Thailand*, by May Kyi Win and Harold Smith. 1995
19. *Mongolia*, by Alan J. K. Sanders. 1996
20. *India*, by Surjit Mansingh. 1996
21. *Gulf Arab States*, by Malcolm C. Peck. 1996
22. *Syria*, by David Commins. 1996
23. *Palestine*, by Nafez Y. Nazzal and Laila A. Nazzal. 1997
24. *Philippines,* by Artemio R. Guillermo and May Kyi Win. 1997

Oceania
1. *Australia*, by James C. Docherty. 1992
2. *Polynesia*, by Robert D. Craig. 1993
3. *Guam and Micronesia*, by William Wuerch and Dirk Ballendorf. 1994
4. *Papua New Guinea*, by Ann Turner. 1994
5. *New Zealand*, by Keith Jackson and Alan McRobie. 1996

New Combined Series (July 1996)

Historical Dictionary of Brunei Darussalam

D. Ranjit Singh and Jatswan S. Sidhu

Asian/Oceanian Historical Dictionaries, No. 25

The Scarecrow Press, Inc.
Lanham, Md., & London
1997

SCARECROW PRESS, INC.

Published in the United States of America
by Scarecrow Press, Inc.
4720 Boston Way
Lanham, Maryland 20706

"Table 1: Exports of Oil/Gas, 1993" was first published in the article "Brunei Darussalam, After a Decade of Independence" by Pushpa Thambipillai in *Southeast Asian Affairs 1995*, p. 118. Reproduced here with the kind permission of the publisher, Institute of Southeast Asian Studies.

British Library Cataloguing in Publication Information Available

Library of Congress Cataloging-in-Publication Data

Singh, D. S. Ranjit, 1944–
    Historical dictionary of Brunei Darussalam / D.S. Ranjit Singh and Jatswan S. Sidhu.
        p.   cm.—(Asian/Oceanian historical dictionaries ; no. 25)
    ISBN 0-8108-3276-3 (cloth : alk. paper)
    1. Brunei—History—Dictionaries.   I. Sidhu, Jatswan S., 1962–   .   II. Title.   III. Series.
    DS650.5.S56   1997
    959.55'003—dc21   96-52065
                                                                                          CIP

ISBN 0-8108-3276-3 (cloth : alk. paper)

∞ ™ The paper used in this publication meets the minimum requirements of American National Standard for Information Sciences—Permanence of Paper for Printed Library Materials, ANSI Z39.48–1984.
Manufactured in the United States of America.

For our parents

Contents

Editor's Foreword

Brunei Darussalam is small. Even on a map of Southeast Asia, let alone the world, it is just a speck (actually, two specks). And it ranks among the smaller countries by population. But Brunei Darussalam is far from insignificant. In a list of oil producers, its standing is impressive and this boosts its ranking in per capita GNP and income as well. Brunei also possesses other sources of wealth and is using its oil revenues to develop its economy, expand its infrastructure and improve its educational system and welfare provisions. This clearly gives Brunei increasing influence in Southeast Asia and Islamic groupings. These are good reasons to know more about Brunei.

Brunei is also an intriguing place. Its history is far deeper and richer than might be expected and its domains were once extensive, before it fell prey to nearby rivals and British colonialism. The "white rajahs" episode made it stand out even in colonial times. Today, as an independent state, it is ruled by a Sultan whose powers exceed those of most of his peers abroad and whose wealth is certainly greater than theirs. While Brunei is gradually modernizing, it remains a mixture of old and new. For most countries, this is a trite cliché aimed at tourists. There, it is a reality. These various sides of the country, the historical and political, economic and social, the old and new, are all reflected in the chronology, introduction and entries of this *Historical Dictionary of Brunei Darussalam*. They are further supplemented by maps, tables and appendixes as well as a substantial bibliography.

Fairly isolated until recently, and even now a bit remote, Brunei is not an easy place to know. And there are not many who know the country well. So, it is fortunate that this volume was written by two of the leading authorities. D. S. Ranjit Singh and Jatswan S. Sidhu both teach at the University of Malaya and specialize in Brunei. The former covers especially history and politics, the latter the economic and social aspects. Both have lectured and written extensively. Dr. Singh is the author of, among other things, *Brunei, 1839–1983, The Problems of Political Survival*, and Mr. Sidhu is the author of, among other things, *Sejarah Sosioekonomi Brunei, 1906–1959* (Socioeconomic History of Brunei,

1906–1959). They have joined forces to write this historical dictionary, which should prove extremely useful to all those who want to know more about *Negara Brunei Darussalam.*

Jon Woronoff
Series Editor

Acknowledgments

We would like to thank our families for their encouragement and support while we prepared this dictionary. Our thanks are also due to the libraries of the University of Malaya; British Library, London; Public Record Office, London; and Rhodes House, Oxford. They gave us facilities and assistance toward the accomplishment of this project.

D. S. Ranjit Singh
History Department
University of Malaya

Jatswan S. Sidhu
International Studies Programme
University of Malaya

Note on Language and Names

A new spelling system has been adopted by Malaysia and Indonesia: thus Malacca has become Melaka and Moluccus is Maluku. We have used the new spellings in this work. However, although Malaysia adopted the new spelling for *kampung* (village), which was originally *kampong*, for Brunei, the latter spelling has been retained because it is currently in use in Brunei. Similarly, Brunei uses *ayer* (water), although in Malaysia it is spelt as *air*.

A brief note on the arrangement of Bruneian names and titles may also be useful here. Malays carry only personal names. For bibliographical purposes, therefore, Malays are normally indexed by the full personal name, for example, Metussin Omar or Abdul Latif bin Haji Ibrahim. Note should also be made of two insertions that frequently occur in Malay names: *bin* (son of) and *haji* (which indicates that the person has performed the hajj). Prominent Malays may also carry honorifics, notably "Dato Seri Laila Jasa Awang," "Dato." For Chinese names, the family name appears first, followed by the given name(s): thus Chua Sui Gim. Indian names in this bibliography are arranged with the first name (personal name) followed by the name of the person's father: Pushpavathi Thambipillai. Concerning the use of titles, there are two points to note. The first is that titles appearing in the Malay language commonly used in Brunei and Sarawak appear in the higher case. The second point concerns the title of the white rulers of Sarawak. The spelling for this title is "Rajah" and not "Raja." This spelling had been officially used by all the three white rulers of Sarawak.

British spelling is used throughout this volume in view of the long history of British involvement with Brunei.

Common Abbreviations and Acronyms

ACB	Anti-Corruption Bureau/Biro Mengenah Rasuah
APB	Angkatan Pemuda Brunei/Brunei Youth Front
ASEAN	Association of Southeast Asian Nations
BAP	Brunei Alliance Party
BARA	Barisan Rakyat Brunei/Brunei People's Front
BARIP	Barisan Pemuda Brunei/Brunei Youth Front
BCG	Brunei Coldgas
BFSP	Brunei's Freedom Struggle Party
BIA	Brunei Investment Agency
BIMP-EAGA	Brunei, Indonesia, Malaysia & the Philippines-East Asian Growth Area
BLNG	Brunei Liquefied Natural Gas
BMA	British Military Administration
BMPC	British Malayan Petroleum Company
BNBC	British North Borneo Company
BNDP	Brunei National Democratic Party/Parti Kebangsaan Demokratik Brunei
BNO	Brunei National Organisation
BNSP	Brunei National Solidarity Party
BOGA	Brunei Oil and Gas Authority
BPIP	Brunei People's Independence Party/Parti Barisan Kemerdekaan Rakyat (PBKR)
BRUFICO	Brunei Film Production Company
BSP	Brunei Shell Petroleum
BULF	Brunei United Labour Front/Barisan Buruh Bersatu Brunei
BUP	Brunei United Party
CHOGM	Commonwealth Heads of Government Meeting
DACs	District Advisory Councils
EC	Emergency Council
EDB	Economic Development Board
EIC	English East India Company
EPU	Economic Planning Unit
ESCAP	Economic and Social Council for Asia and Pacific

FMS	Federated Malay States
GRU	Gurkha Reserve Unit
IBB	International Bank of Brunei
ICAO	International Civil Aviation Organization
IDB	Islamic Development Bank
IDB	Island Development Bank
IMO	International Maritime Organization
ISA	Internal Security Act
ISESCO	Islamic Education, Scientific and Cultural Organization
JKD	Jawatankuasa Kerja Darurat/Emergency Executive Committee
JMBRAS	Journal of the Malayan/Malaysian Branch, Royal Asiatic Society
JSBRAS	Journal of the Straits Branch, Royal Asiatic Society
JSEAS	Journal of Southeast Asian Studies (Singapore)
KMB	Kesatuan Melayu Brunei/Union of Brunei Malays
KUBU	Kesatuan Buruh Umum/General Labour Union
LNG	Liquefied Natural Gas
MD	Majlis Darurat/Emergency Council
MIB	Melayu Islam Beraja/Malay Muslim Monarchy
MPMK	Majlis Perundingan Mukim dan Kampong (Consultative Council for Mukim (subdistrict) and Kampong (villages)
MUTU	Persatuan Murid Tua/Old Pupils Association
NBB	National Bank of Brunei
NDPs	National Development Plans
OIC	Organization of Islamic Conference
PAKAR	Parti Kemajuan Rakyat/Peoples Progressive Party
PBKR	Parti Barisan Kemerdekaan Rakyat/Brunei Peoples Independence Party
PGGMB	Persekutuan Guru-Guru Melayu Brunei/Federation of Brunei Malay Teachers
PLO	Palestine Liberation Organization
PRB	Parti Rakyat Brunei/Brunei Peoples Party
PRM	Parti Rakyat Malaya/Malayan Peoples Party
RBA	Royal Brunei Airlines
RBAF	Royal Brunei Armed Forces
RBMR	Royal Brunei Malay Regiment
RBMRR	Royal Brunei Malay Reserve Regiment
RBPF	Royal Brunei Police Force
SBK	Syarikat Buruh Kerajaan/Government Employees Union
SBM	Syarikat Buruh Minyak/Oil Company's Employees Union

SITC	Sultan Idris Training College, Tanjung Malim, Malaysia
SS	Straits Settlements
TAIB	Tabung Amanah Islam Brunei/Brunei Islamic Trust Fund
TNI	Tentera Nasional Indonesia/National Army of Indonesia
TNKU	Tentera Nasional Kalimantan Utara/National Army of North Kalimantan
UBD	Universiti Brunei Darussalam/University of Brunei Darussalam
UMNO	United Malays National Organization
UN	United Nations
UNCTAD	United Nations Conference on Trade and Development
UNTAC	United Nations Transition Authority in Cambodia
UPU	Universal Postal Union
US	United States of America
WHO	World Health Organization
WMO	World Meteorological Organization
ZOPFAN	Zone of Peace, Freedom and Neutrality

Chronology

Prehistory Up To Around 500 B.C.

38,000 B.C.	Earliest remains of man in the area: Niah, Sarawak.
8,000 B.C.	Prehistoric culture in the Malay Archipelago (Hoabinhion and Neolithic).
300 B.C.	Earliest signs of Bronze and Iron Age cultures in the Malay Archipelago.
200 B.C.	Start of trading contacts between the Malay Archipelago and India and China.

Early Polities in the Malay Archipelago, 500 B.C.–A.D. 1400

100 B.C.–A.D. 200	Emergence of trading kingdoms in the Isthmus of Kra.
A.D. 500–800	Development of local trading points in the Malay Archipelago with Hindu-Buddhist orientation.
7th–10th century	Emergence of the Sri Vijaya empire.
13th–15th century	Emergence of the Majapahit empire.
1400–1511	Emergence of the Melaka empire.

The Emergence of Brunei, c. 1360s to late 15th Century

1363	Alak Betatar installed as first Sultan of Brunei in Temasik (Old Singapore).
1365	The *Nagarakertagama*, written by the court poet Prapanca, lists Brunei as a vassal state of the Majapahit. Brunei was then referred to as Buruneng.
1370	A Chinese record states that a Sultan of Brunei known as "Mo-ha-mo-sha" sent tribute to China. "Mo-ha-mo-sa" is a transliteration of Muhammad Shah, the first Sultan of Brunei.
1405	Admiral Cheng Ho visited Brunei.
1408	Sultan Ahmad ascended the throne as the second Sultan of Brunei.

1426	The third Sultan of Brunei, Sultan Sharif Ali, ascended the throne.
1432	Sultan Sulaiman installed as fourth Sultan.
1485	Sultan Bolkiah ascended the throne as the fifth Sultan.

The 16th and 17th Centuries

1521	Antonio Pigafetta, the chronicler of Ferdinand Magellan's expedition, visited Brunei.
1524	Sultan Abdul Kahar installed as sixth Sultan.
1524	Jorge d'Albuquerque, Captain of Melaka, sent a mission to Brunei under Antonio de Pinta.
1530	Goncalo Pereira, the Portuguese Captain-designate of the Maluku (Molucuss) visited Brunei.
1535	The seventh ruler, Sultan Saiful Rijal installed.
1578	Spaniards attacked Brunei and captured the capital on 14 April. Mission was led by Francisco de Sande, Governor of the Philippines. Spaniards were forced to retreat due to disease.
1580	Second Spanish attack on the Brunei capital led by Captain Don Juan Arce de Sadornil. The attack was unsuccessful.
1581	Sultan Shah Brunei installed as the eighth Sultan.
1582	Sultan Muhammad Hassan, the ninth Sultan, ascended the throne.
1597	The tenth ruler, Sultan Abdul Jalilul Akbar, installed.
1659	Sultan Abdul Jalilul Jabbar ascended the throne as the 11th Sultan.
1660	Sultan Haji Muhammad Ali installed as the 12th ruler.
1661	A civil war broke out at the capital in Brunei. The *Bendahara,* Abdul Mubin killed the 12th Sultan of Brunei, Sultan Muhammad Ali. Abdul Mubin usurped the throne as the 13th ruler with the title Sultan Abdul Hakkul Mubin.
1673	Sultan Muhyiddin installed as 14th Sultan.
1690	The 15th ruler, Sultan Nasruddin, installed.

The 18th to 20th Centuries

1710	The 16th ruler, Sultan Husin Kamaluddin, ascended the throne.

1730	Sultan Muhammad Aliuddin installed as the 17th Sultan.
1740	The 18th ruler, Sultan Omar Ali Saifuddin I, installed.
1774	John Jesse, an agent of the English East India Company from its outpost at Balambangan, visited Brunei to negotiate for trade in pepper.
1795	Sultan Muhammad Tajuddin installed as the 19th Sultan.
1804	Sultan Muhammad Jamalul Alam I ascended the throne as the 20th Sultan, but died the same year. The 19th ruler, Sultan Muhammad Tajuddin, is installed.
1807	A civil war broke out at the capital in Brunei between two contending factions when Sultan Muhammad Tajuddin died. The heir to the throne who later became Sultan, Omar Ali Saifuddin II, was still an infant. War started by Omar Ali Saifuddin's maternal grandfather, Muhammad Kanzu Alam, who succeeded in making himself the 21st Sultan.
1824	Discovery of high grade antimony ore in Upper Sarawak. Mining of antimony became an important activity in Old Sarawak. Development of lucrative trade between Sarawak and Singapore. Brunei assumed direct control over old Sarawak and sent Pengiran Indera Mahkota as Governor. Oppressive policies of Indera Mahkota.
1826	The 22nd ruler, Sultan Muhammad Alam, installed.
1828	Sultan Omar Ali Saifuddin II installed as 23rd Sultan.
1835	Outbreak of the Sarawak rebellion led by Sarawak Malay aristocracy and Land Dayaks. Raja Muda Hassim, the *Bendahara* of Brunei, sent to suppress the uprising.
1839	James Brooke's first visit to the Sarawak River. Cordial reception by Raja Muda Hassim.
1840	Second visit of James Brooke to Sarawak. The forging of a political alliance between Raja Muda Hassim and James Brooke. Raja Muda Hassim requested Brooke's help in suppressing the rebellion in return for the governorship and

	trade of Sarawak. Raja Muda Hassim personally anticipated Brooke's support for reinstatement as *Bendahara* at the capital. Brooke succeeded in ending the rebellion.
1841	Preliminary agreement between Raja Muda Hassim and James Brooke appointing the latter as Governor of Old Sarawak.
1842	Official document by Sultan appointing James Brooke as Governor of Sarawak on 31 July.
1844	Raja Muda Hassim returned to the capital with Brooke's support. Resumed his Bendaharaship. Aroused resentment of the Sultan and other *pengirans*. Emergence of anti-Hassim faction.
1845	USS *Constitution* visited Brunei offering protection for exclusive trading rights. Brunei refused in view of impending treaty with Britain.
1846	Raja Muda Hassim and his entire family wiped out by rival faction.
1846	Labuan ceded to British as crown colony. James Brooke obtained Sarawak in perpetuity from the Sultan. Declared Sarawak as independent and proclaimed himself as an independent Rajah.
1847	Treaty of Friendship and Commerce between Brunei and Britain.
1850	Treaty of Friendship and Commerce between Brunei and the United States.
1852	Sultan Abdul Mumin ascended the throne as the 24th Sultan.
1853	Beginning of expansion of Sarawak. James Brooke obtained the Samarahan, Batang Lupar, Sadong, Saribas, Lingga, and Rejang rivers from the Sultan of Brunei.
1860	The Mukah crisis erupted with Sarawak having a strong hand in the affair, the whole episode being part of Sarawak's policy to usurp more of Brunei's *jajahans* (dependencies).
1863	James Brooke obtained the Mukah and Bintulu.
1865	Arrival of Charles Lee Moses as first United States Consul to Brunei. Lease of territory in Sabah to Moses.
1868	Charles Brooke succeeded his uncle as the second Rajah of Sarawak upon the death of the latter. In addition, Sarawak attempted to annexe

	the Baram. The Sultan appealed to the British government and the latter imposed a ban on all further expansion by Sarawak.
1874	The Kayans of the Baram River rebelled against Brunei rule due to excessive oppression and taxation imposed by Brunei.
1877	The Overbeck-Dent Syndicate is leased an area in Sabah by the Sultan of Brunei.
1881	British North Borneo Company (BNBC) granted a charter by the British government.
1882	The British government sanctioned the annexation of Baram by Sarawak. Brunei loses all the rivers from Kidurong to Baram.
1882	W.C. Cowie obtained a concession to mine coal at Muara Damit from the Sultan of Brunei.
1884	The British North Borneo Company obtained a lease of the Padas-Klias region for an annual payment of $3,000 to the Brunei government.
1884	The BNBC obtained the Tuaran and Putatan.
1885	Sultan Abdul Mumin died and is succeeded by Temenggong Hashim Jalil-ul-alam, son of Sultan Omar Ali Saifuddin II. Hashim, the 25th Sultan, was known as Sultan Hashim Jalilul Alam Aqamaddin.
1885	Sultan Hashim approved the Trusan cession.
1887	The Sultan approved the Padas-Damit cession.
1887	Sir Frederick Weld visited Brunei.
1888	Brunei became a British protectorate with the signing of the Protectorate Agreement on 17 September. Under this agreement, Brunei handed over the conduct of her foreign relations to Britain. In addition, W.C. Cowie sold his concession in Muara Damit to Charles Brooke.
1890	Rajah Charles Brooke, the second white Rajah of Sarawak, annexed the district of Limbang from Brunei.
1899	The first oil well to be drilled in Brunei at Ayer Bekunchi, near Bandar Seri Begawan, was unsuccessful.
1903	Oil discovered at Charles Brooke's coal mine in Pulau Berembang near Muara Damit.

The Residential System, 1906–1959

1906	Introduction of the British Residential system

with the signing of the Supplementary Agreement of 1905 and 1906 where the British appointed a British adviser-styled Resident who was to assist the Sultan in the administration of the State. This treaty was a success in that it preserved what was left of Brunei.

1906	Sultan Muhammad Jamalul Alam II installed as the 26th Sultan of Brunei.
1906	First post office in the state established in Brunei Town.
1908	Rubber introduced to the state.
1914–1918	World War I.
1914	Oil found at Labi in the Belait District.
1914	First Malay school in the state established in Brunei Town.
1916	First Chinese school in the state established in Brunei Town.
1917	Charles Vyner Brooke, eldest son of Rajah Charles Brooke, ascended the throne of Sarawak as the third and last white Rajah of Sarawak.
1924	Sultan Muhammad Jamalul Alam II died at the young age of 35 due to malaria and was succeeded by his son Sultan Ahmad Tajuddin Akhazul Khairi Wadin, who was only 11 years old. Sultan Ahmad Tajuddin was the 27th Sultan.
1924	The first automobile introduced to Brunei in February. It was owned by the British Resident, E. E. F. Pretty.
1929	Large reserves of oil found in Seria.
1929–1932	The Great Depression.
1931	First English school in the state established in Kuala Belait.
1932	Oil exported for the first time.
1941	Japanese forces attacked Kuala Belait on 16 December and quickly occupied Seria and Brunei Town.
1945	Allied Forces landed at Muara Damit to end three and a half years of Japanese occupation of Brunei.
1946	The British North Borneo Company surrendered North Borneo (Sabah) to the British government. Rajah Charles Vyner Brooke did the same for Sarawak. Both Sabah and Sarawak be-

	came Crown Colonies until 1963, when both joined Malaysia and achieved independence.
1950	Sultan Omar Ali Saifuddien III, father of the present Sultan ascended the throne on 6 June. Reigned till 1967, when he abdicated and was succeeded by Sultan Hassanal Bolkiah, the present Sultan.
1953–1958	First Five-Year Development Plan.
1954	Brunei obtained its first modern airport at Berakas, near Brunei Town.
1956	The Parti Rakyat Brunei (Brunei Peoples Party) was formed on 22 January with A. M. Azahari as its President. In February of that year, the party applied for registration but was denied.
1959	On 29 September, the Sultan promulgated a new constitution when a treaty, the 1959 Brunei Agreement, was signed with Britain. Britain granted internal self-government to Brunei, the 1906 Agreement being revoked. The Residential System was withdrawn.

The Post-Residential System Period, 1959–1983

1961	The Malaysia proposal made by the Malayan Prime Minister, Tunku Abdul Rahman, on 27 May.
1961	The Royal Brunei Malay Regiment (RMBR) is formed on 31 May.
1962–1966	Second Five-Year Development Plan.
1962	Brunei held its first ever elections to the District Councils on 30 and 31 August with the Parti Rakyat Brunei (PRB) winning 54 out of the 55 seats.
1962	Brunei revolt by the PRB led by A. M. Azahari broke out on the Saturday morning of 8 December. The revolt was short-lived for it was crushed within a week.
1963	The first offshore oil concessions were granted to Brunei Shell Petroleum.
1963	Sultan Omar Ali Saifuddien III announced, in July, that Brunei will not join Malaysia.
1963	Malaysia formed on 31 August with the Federation of Malaya, Singapore, Sabah, and Sarawak.

1965	General elections to the Legislative Council held in March.
1967	Brunei issued its own currency on 12 June.
1967	Sultan Omar Ali Saifuddien III abdicated in favour of his son, Hassanal Bolkiah, on 4 October.
1968	The coronation of the 29th Sultan, Hassanal Bolkiah on 1 August.
1970	The capital, Brunei Town, was renamed Bandar Seri Begawan in honour of the 28th Sultan, Omar Ali Saifuddien III, on 4 October.
1971	The 1959 Agreement between Brunei and Britain was amended on 23 November.
1973	The world's largest LNG plant is opened in Lumut on 4 April.
1975–1979	Third National Development Plan.
1975	Royal Brunei Airlines took to the air on 14 May.
1979	Brunei signed the Treaty of Friendship and Cooperation with Britain on 7 January. Britain to grant Brunei independence by late 1983.
1980–1984	Fourth National Development Plan.
1981	Sultan Hassanal married Mariam binti Abdul Aziz, who became his second wife on 28 October.
1983	Date of independence officially announced in Brunei, being 1 January 1984.

Post-Independence Period, 1984–

1984	Brunei received its independence on 1 January and became a member of the Commonwealth.
1984	Brunei became the sixth member of ASEAN on 8 January.
1984	Brunei joined the Organization of Islamic Countries (OIC) on 16 January as its 45th member.
1984	The Legislative Council was dissolved on 13 February and in its place a Cabinet was formed.
1984	Brunei celebrated its first National Day on 23 February.
1984	On 21 September, Brunei became the 159th member of the United Nations.
1984	Sultan Hassanal declared the concept of *Melayu Islam Beraja* (Malay Muslim Monarchy) as the state philosophy.

1985	Brunei established full diplomatic relations with Jordan in March. Also in the same month, West Germany and Pakistan opened their embassies in Bandar Seri Begawan and British Prime Minister Margaret Thatcher visited Brunei.
1985	The Brunei National Democratic Party (BNDP) was officially registered in May, and at the same time Brunei became a full member of the World Health Organization (WHO).
1985	West German Foreign Minister Dr. Hans-Dietrich, visited Brunei in July.
1985	Sultan Hassanal Bolkiah purchased the Dorchester Hotel in London.
1985	King Birendra Bir Bikram Shah Dev, the King of Nepal, visited Brunei in September.
1985	Brunei's first and only university, the University of Brunei Darussalam (UBD), established at Gadong near Bandar Seri Begawan on 28 October.
1986–1990	Fifth National Development Plan.
1986	Brunei hosted the 21st Meeting of the Southeast Asian Ministers of Education Council (SEAMEC) in January.
1986	France established an embassy in Brunei and the first French ambassador to Brunei was appointed in February.
1986	A Belgian trade mission led by Crown Prince Albert visited Brunei in March.
1986	King Hussein of Jordan visited Brunei in March-April.
1986	George Shultz, the United States Secretary of State, visited Brunei in June.
1986	Sultan Haji Omar Ali Saifuddien III, the 28th Sultan of Brunei and father of the present Sultan, died on 7 September.
1986	Sultan Hassanal reshuffled and expanded the Cabinet, which was announced on 20 October.
1987	The Malaysian Prime Minister, Dato' Seri Dr. Mahathir Mohamad, and the *Yang di-Pertuan Agong* of Malaysia visited Brunei, both in early April.
1987	Sultan Hassanal went on a state visit to Indonesia on 10 September. Sultan Hassanal purchased the Beverly Hills Hotel in Los Angeles for a re-

	ported sum in excess of US$200 million, also in September.
1987	Lee Kuan Yew, Prime Minister of Singapore, visited Brunei together with his son Brigadier-General Lee Hsien Loong.
1987	Sultan Hassanal attended the Commonwealth Heads of Government Meeting (CHOGM) in Vancouver in October.
1988	The Royal Brunei Malay Reserve Regiment (RBMRR) is formed.
1988	The Brunei National Democratic Party (BNDP) deregistered on 27 January and its leaders, Abdul Latif Hamid and Abdul Latif Chuchu, were detained.
1988	General Benny Murdani, the Indonesian Defence Minister, visited Brunei in February. This was followed by Ali Alatas, Indonesia's Foreign Minister, who visited Brunei in April.
1988	Thailand's Deputy Foreign Minister, Prapas Limpabandhu, visited Brunei in June.
1988	Prince Mohamed Bolkiah, Brunei's Foreign Minister, attended the 21st meeting of ASEAN Foreign Ministers in Bangkok in July.
1988	President Corazon Aquino of the Philippines made an official visit to Brunei in late August.
1988	The Royal Brunei Armed Forces (RBAF) held a military exercise with forces from Great Britain from 22 August to 4 September. This was its first exercise with a Western power as earlier exercises involved only Malaysia and Singapore.
1989	The Foreign Minister of Djibouti visited Brunei in January.
1989	The Prime Minister as well as the Foreign Minister of Thailand visited Brunei in mid-February.
1989	President Arap Moi of Kenya visited Brunei in late February.
1989	British Minister of State for Foreign Affairs visited Brunei in March.
1989	Brunei hosted the 22nd ASEAN Ministerial Meeting in July.
1989	Ugandan Deputy Prime Minister visited Brunei in mid-September.

1989	French President François Mitterrand visited Brunei in December.
1990	The MIB concept is implemented vigourously.
1990	Brunei sent its first economic mission to Europe in March. This is in line with Brunei's plan to diversify the country's economy by attracting foreign investments. The delegation was headed by Brunei's Minister for Industry and Primary Resources.
1991–1995	Sixth National Development Plan.
1991	Japanese Prime Minister Toshiki Kaifu, visited Brunei in April.
1991	Brunei hosted the Executive Committee Meeting of the Regional Islamic Da'wah Council of Southeast Asia and the Pacific (RISEAP) in June.
1991	Sultan Hassanal visited the Philippines in September.
1991	Brunei established diplomatic relations with the People's Republic of China (PRC) in September, and in October it established official relations with the former Union of Soviet Socialist Republics (USSR). Brunei was the last ASEAN country to establish formal relations with the PRC and the former USSR. Also in October, Brunei forged official ties with Mexico and Qatar.
1991	Brunei along with 19 other signatories signed the Peace Accord on Cambodia in Paris in October. It also donated US$1 million for the rehabilitation and reconstruction of Cambodia.
1991	Sultan Hassanal attended the Festival of Islamic Culture in Jakarta in June and the Organization of Islamic Countries (OIC) Convention held in Dakar, Senegal, in December.
1992	The year was the Silver Jubilee of the ascension to the throne of the reigning monarch, Sultan Hassanal Bolkiah.
1992	Sultan Hassanal undertook a five-day official visit to Malaysia in February. At the same time, the Sultan was conferred an honorary doctorate degree in law by the University of Malaya, Kuala Lumpur.
1992	Brunei and Vietnam established diplomatic ties

	when Vietnamese Prime Minister Vo Van Kiet visited Brunei in early March. This was the first official visit by a Vietnamese leader to Brunei, and in July Brunei sent a delegation led by Deputy Foreign Minister Mohamed Ali, for a five-day visit to Vietnam.
1992	Singapore's Prime Minister Goh Chok Tong, visited Brunei on a two-day goodwill visit at the end of June. He was accompanied by members of the Singapore business community.
1992	Brunei joined the Non-Aligned Movement (NAM) on 28 August.
1992	Sultan Hassanal announced a personal donation of US$1 million for the Muslims of Bosnia-Herzegovina on 6 October.
1992	In November, Brunei sent a group of 12 personnel from the Royal Brunei Police Force, accompanied by three observers from the Brunei Royal Armed Forces to participate in the peacekeeping process in Cambodia under the supervision of the United Nations Transitional Authority in Cambodia (UNTAC).
1993	Japanese Prime Minister Kiichi Miyazawa, visited Brunei in January.
1993	In April, Sultan Hassanal donated US$10 million to the newly created Islamic Studies Centre established at the University of London.
1993	Lee Kuan Yew, the former Prime Minister of Singapore, visited Brunei twice, in April and again in October.
1993	Prince Mohamed Bolkiah, Brunei's Foreign Minister, met United States Secretary of State, Warren Christopher in Singapore in July to discuss a Memorandum of Understanding (MoU) regarding U.S. Navy visits to Brunei.
1993	Malaysian Prime Minister Dato' Seri Dr. Mahathir Mohamad, visited Brunei in August.
1994	The Sultan led a delegation to attend the tenth Non-Aligned Movement (NAM) summit held in Jakarta in early September.
1994	Brunei established diplomatic ties with Albania, Bosnia-Herzegovina, Lebanon, Ivory Coast, Costa Rica, Bulgaria, Guinea-Bissau, and Uruguay, bringing the total number of countries

	with whom Brunei has diplomatic relations to 94 by the end of September.
1994	The Davao Agreement signed in March between Brunei, Indonesia, Malaysia, and the Philippines for the creation of an East ASEAN Growth Area (BIMP-EAGA), a subregional approach to economic cooperation.
1994	Official relations between Brunei and Palestine came into force with the signing of an agreement by their respective ambassadors to Malaysia in Kuala Lumpur in May.
1994	Brunei assumed the chairmanship of the ASEAN Standing Committee in July.
1994	Sultan Hassanal met John Major in London where a Memorandum of Understanding on defence cooperation in the fields of training, infrastructure development, and weapons purchase was signed in mid-December.
1995	Sarawak sent a trade mission to Brunei led by Sarawak's Industrial Development Minister Datuk Abang Haji Johari Tun Openg on 27 and 28 March.
1995	Brunei's first development bank, Bank Pembangunan Brunei (BPB) was opened in April.
1995	Brunei's Minister of Industry and Primary Resources, Pehin Haji Abdul Rahman led an entourage of 100 businessmen to visit Sarawak in June.
1995	Prince Mohamed Bolkiah met U.S. Secretary of State, Warren Christopher in July to discuss ways to enhance cooperation between both countries. The meeting was held in Washington, D.C.
1995	The Royal Brunei Navy and the U.S. Seventh Fleet conducted a training exercise in Brunei, codenamed CARAT, in July.
1995	A major natural gas discovery was made by Brunei Shell near its Selangkir-1 well in July.
1995	Brunei hosted the 27th ASEAN Economic Ministers Meeting (AEM) in Bandar Seri Begawan in September.
1995	Brunei and Malaysia signed a Memorandum of Understanding in Kuala Lumpur, to combat oil

	spills in the South China Sea and Brunei Bay on 7 November.
1995	Brunei held its first East ASEAN Growth Area (EAGA) trade exposition in November which attracted some 100,000 visitors.
1995	Prince Jefri Bolkiah purchased Aspreys of London, also known as "The Queen's Gift Shop" for a reported sum of US$378 million in November.
1995	Malaysian Deputy Prime Minister Dato' Seri Anwar Ibrahim, who is also Finance Minister, met Brunei's Finance Minister Pengiran Muda Jefri Bolkiah, in Kuala Lumpur on 4 December, where both held talks on promoting bilateral investments.
1996–2000	Seventh National Development Plan.
1996	Bandar Seri Begawan is chosen as the Secretariat for the Brunei, Indonesia, Malaysia, the Philippines-East ASEAN Growth Area (BIMP-EAGA) on 10 January.
1996	Brunei hosted the 6th ASEAN-Australian Economic Cooperation Programme Joint Planning Committee meeting between 18–19 January.
1996	Sultan Hassanal Bolkiah celebrated his 50th birthday in July. Some US$25 million was spent to celebrate the occasion and amongst his guests was the Prince of Wales. To entertain Bruneians, the ceremony also saw three concerts performed by Michael Jackson on which some US$15 million was spent.
1996	The Sultan, in early 1996, ordered the drafting of a new constitution undertaken by a committee headed by Prince Mohamed Bolkiah. This was probably done due the continuous demands for a representative government by the BNSP. Until late 1996, the Sultan was still studying the document.

Maps

Map 1   Southeast Asia

Source: Brunei Darussalam in Profile. Bandar Seri Begawan: The Government of Brunei, 1989, 9.

Map 2   Brunei Darussalam: Major Towns and Communications

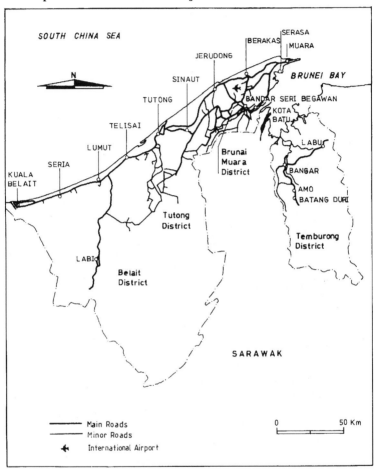

Source: Brunei Darussalam in Profile, 152.

Map 3 Brunei Darussalam: Population Density according to *Mukims*, 1992

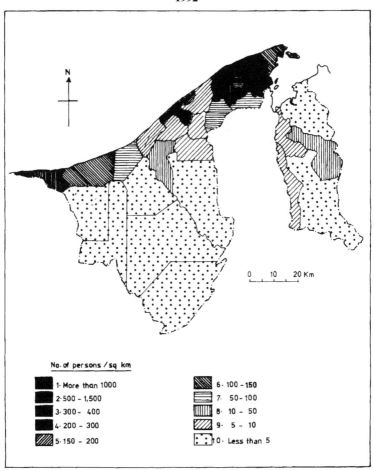

No. of persons / sq km

1· More than 1000
2·500 - 1,500
3·300 - 400
4·200 - 300
5·150 - 200
6· 100 - 150
7· 50 - 100
8· 10 - 50
9· 5 - 10
10· Less than 5

Source: K. U. Sirinanda. "Biophysical Environment of Brunei," Abu Bakar bin Haji Apong, Dato Seri Laila Jasa Awang Haji (ed.), *Sumbangsih UBD, Essays on Brunei Darussalam.* Gadong, Brunei: Akademi Pengajian Brunei: Universiti Brunei Darussalam, 1992, 256.

Map 4   Brunei Darussalam: Generalized Geology and Stratigraphy

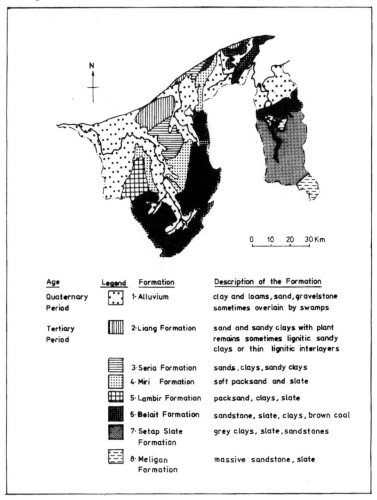

Age	Legend	Formation	Description of the Formation
Quaternary Period		1· Alluvium	clay and loams, sand, gravelstone sometimes overlain by swamps
Tertiary Period		2· Liang Formation	sand and sandy clays with plant remains sometimes lignitic sandy clays or thin lignitic interlayers
		3· Seria Formation	sands, clays, sandy clays
		4· Miri Formation	soft packsand and slate
		5· Lambir Formation	packsand, clays, slate
		6· Belait Formation	sandstone, slate, clays, brown coal
		7· Setap Slate Formation	grey clays, slate, sandstones
		8· Meligan Formation	massive sandstone, slate

Source: Sirinanda. "Biophysical Environment of Brunei," 240.

Map 5   Brunei Darussalam: Landforms

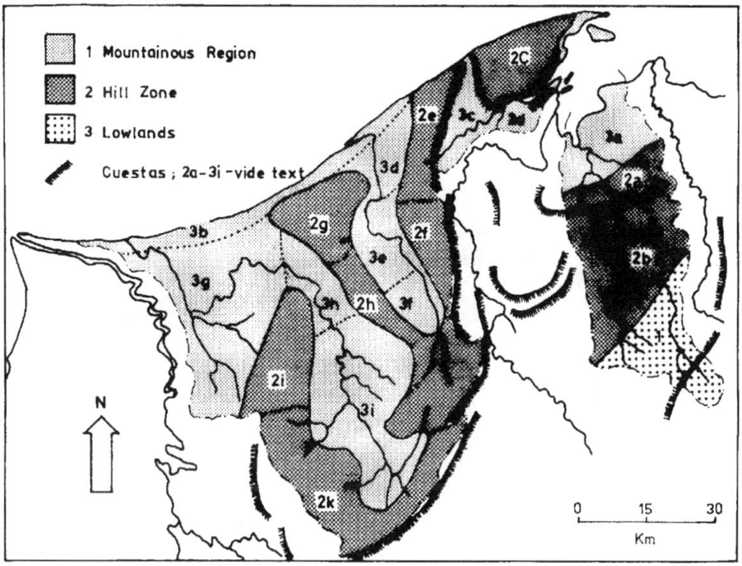

Source: Sirinanda. "Biophysical Environment of Brunei," 242.

Map 6 Brunei Darussalam: River Basins

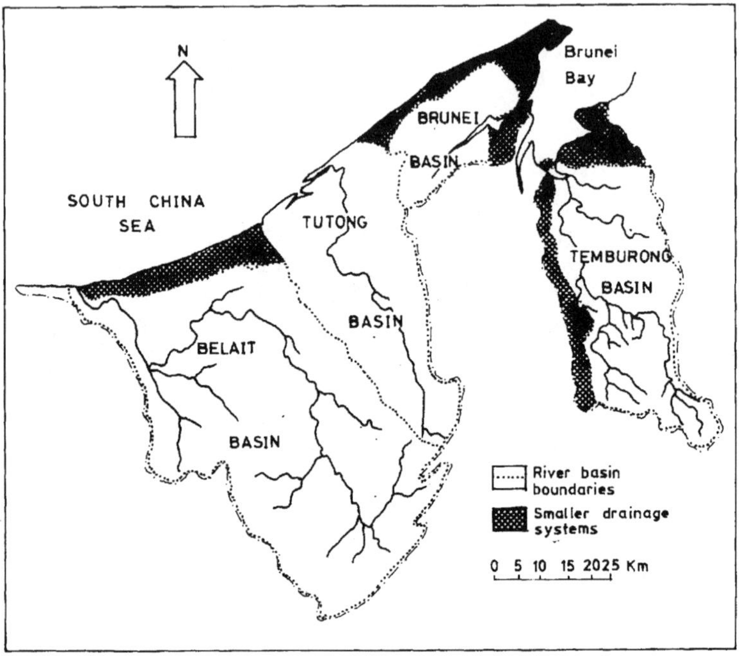

Source: Sirinanda. "Biophysical Environment of Brunei," 243.

Map 7   Brunei Darussalam: Topography and Soils

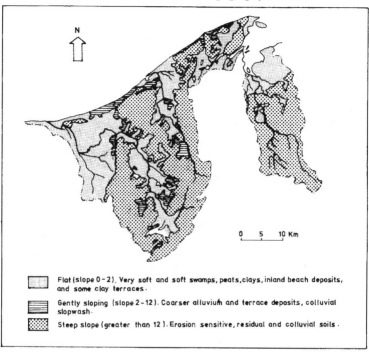

N

0   5   10 Km

Flat (slope 0-2). Very soft and soft swamps, peats, clays, inland beach deposits, and some clay terraces.

Gently sloping (slope 2-12). Coarser alluvium and terrace deposits, colluvial slopwash.

Steep slope (greater than 12). Erosion sensitive, residual and colluvial soils.

Source: Sirinanda. "Biophysical Environment of Brunei," 245.

Map 8   Brunei Darussalam: Natural Vegetation

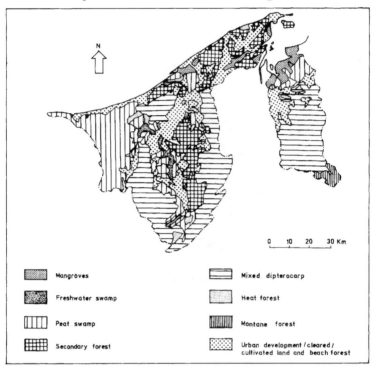

Source: Sirinanda. "Biophysical Environment of Brunei," 246.

Map 9   Brunei Darussalam: Mean Annual Rainfall (mm)

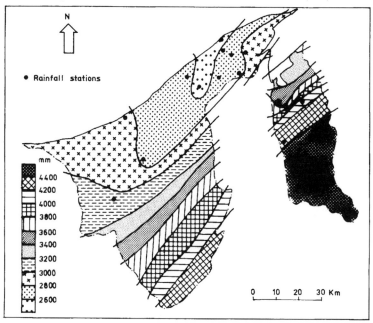

Source: Sirinanda. "Biophysical Environment of Brunei," 251.

Introduction

The modern state of Negara Brunei Darussalam (Abode of Peace) achieved its independence from the British on 1 January 1984 after being a British protectorate for about 96 years since the 1888 Treaty of Protection. The state is run by a royal family that established a kingdom in Brunei some 630 years ago, when the first Sultan, Muhammad (Alak Betatar), was installed in c.1363. The present ruler, Sultan Hassanal Bolkiah, is the 29th Sultan from the lineage and is the world's richest man. Although called a ministate, Brunei is well known around the world because her population enjoys one of the highest per capita incomes in the world, an average of US$25,000 a year.

Geographical Location

Covering an area of some 5,765 square kilometres in two noncontiguous wedged-shaped pieces of land, Brunei is situated on the northwest coast of the island of Borneo and is about 442 kilometres north of the equator between east longitudes 114°23′ and north latitudes 4° and 5°5′. It is surrounded by the Malaysian states of Sabah in the north and northeast and Sarawak to the south and southeast, which divides Brunei into two parts. Brunei is divided into four districts, namely the Brunei-Muara District, Tutong District and Belait District, all situated on the larger southern enclave of the state, and the Temburong District, which is separated from the earlier enclave by the District of Limbang in Sarawak.

Climate and Rainfall

Brunei's climate has high temperatures throughout the year, ranging from 23°C to 35°C. Humidity averages between 67 per cent and 91 per cent. Annual rainfall can be as high as 7,500 mm in the interior, but only about a third is recorded along the coast, most of it occurring between September and January.

The Physical Environment

Much of the state is low-lying alluvial land with often extensive areas of mangrove fringing the coastal belt. To the west the terrain is hilly lowland rising to about 300 metres inland. Farther east, beyond the wide coastal plain, is a mountainous region rising to about 1,184 metres above sea level. Inland, the Tutong, Teraja and Temburong Highlands form a largely inaccessible border area with Sarawak. Most of the country is covered by primary and secondary rainforest especially the Temburong District, which has large areas of forest rich in flora and fauna. Forests, classified into five main types, namely mangrove, heath, peat swamp, mixed dipterocarp and montane, cover about 1,679 square miles, or 75 per cent of Brunei's total land area. Forests reserves constitute approximately 818 square miles, or 37 per cent of the total land area. Only a relatively narrow coastal strip from Bandar Seri Begawan in the north to Kuala Belait in the south is cultivated. Its coastline along the South China Sea is 161 kilometers long. Geologically, Brunei is highly complex with rapid lateral and vertical changes in rock type. Of particular importance are depositional deposits laid down since the Miocene. A series of basins contain the major oil-, gas- and coal-bearing sediments that constitute the wealth of the country. Alongside the extensive hydrocarbon deposits, a range of other resources are available. There are extensive gravel deposits in the Temburong District that have been heavily quarried, as have beach and river deposits. In addition, there are also important silica sands in the Temburong District, which could provide for the glass-making industry. Coal is found in the Belait District and around the Brunei River but has not been mined for some decades now.

Population

The population of Brunei is predominantly Malay, accounting for about 68 per cent of the total population, which was estimated at 256,500 in 1990. In addition to the Malays, other indigenous groups are namely the Kedayans, Bisayas, Penans, Muruts and Ibans (the latter are of insignificant numbers and live in the upper reaches of the Belait and Temburong rivers). According to statistics of 1990, these non-Malay indigenous communities represent some 5 per cent of Brunei's total population. Of the migrant communities, the Chinese are the majority, accounting for some 18 per cent of Brunei's total population in 1990. Other migrant communities are Indians and Eurasians. The Indian ethnic groups are mainly the Tamils, Malayalese, Punjabis and Sindhis. In addition, there are also the Nepalese and Ceylonese. Brunei's population can be divided into two major categories, namely residents and nonresidents. The non-residents are mainly the foreign workforce such as Filipinos, Malaysians, Indonesians, Europeans and Indians. In 1988, there were some 20,000 expatriates working in Brunei.

Language

The official language of Brunei is Bahasa Melayu Brunei (Malay language), one that is very similar to the language spoken by the Malays in Malaysia as well as some other indigenous groups in Indonesia, namely those living in Sumatra. In addition to Bahasa Melayu, English is spoken quite widely in Brunei and this is mainly due to the fact that Brunei was, prior to 1984, a British protectorate. Amongst the Chinese in Brunei there are some Chinese dialects such as Hakka, Hokkien and Teochew, while the Indians speak mainly Tamil, Malayalam and Punjabi.

Religion

The official religion of Brunei Darussalam is Islam with the Sultan as the head of the faith in the country. The majority of the Malays are Muslims following the Shafeite form of Islam. The other indigenous minorities are either Muslims, or Christians with some animist. The majority of the Kedayans are Muslims while the other indigenes like the Bisayas, Muruts, Ibans and Penans are either animist or Christians. In addition to Islam, Brunei's constitution also provides religious freedom to other minorities. The Chinese are either Buddhist or Christians while the Indians are mainly Muslims, Hindus, Christians or Sikhs.

History

Brunei is one of the oldest existing polities in Southeast Asia, with a rich historical heritage. It also boasts of being the longest surviving sultanate in the region. Brunei has had its share of glory and difficulties. From the position of a small vassal state in the sixth century A.D., Brunei rose to emerge as a great empire in the 16th and 17th centuries. From then on began a slow decline until the 19th century, when its very existence was threatened. Through the ages in its ups and downs, Brunei acquired an astute sense in the use of international diplomacy. The monarchy especially made effective use of this tool to steer the kingdom out of very tight situations, and in the process, has managed not only to save and preserve the identity of the state, albeit a very reduced one, but to bring it to the status of a full sovereign nation with its rightful place in the family of nations. In the 20th century, two other factors have helped preserve its survival: British protection, 1906–1984; and the wealth from the hydrocarbon industry. To give a more meaningful treatment to its past, the history of Brunei may be studied along the following major phases, namely: The Pre-Sultanate Period, 6th–14th centuries A.D.; The Golden Age, 15th–17th centuries; Decline, Dismemberment and Survival, 18th–19th centuries; Salvation through British Protection, 1906–1959; The Period of Political Change, 1946–1963; The Consolidation of Absolute Monarchism, 1963–1984; and The Post-Independence Era, 1984–1995.

The Pre-Sultanate Period, 6th–14th centuries A.D.

Brunei's rich historical experience can be gleamed through the centuries to the time when it was a young emerging polity in the sixth century A.D. From the very beginning, Brunei, then known as *Po-ni* by the Chinese, sought to establish relations with big powers to obtain protection and thus security. Naturally, the first power she turned to for protection was the Middle Kingdom. Tribute missions were sent by *Po-ni* from the sixth century to about 1424, when the Chinese began to withdraw from active involvement in overseas affairs. The early close relations with the Chinese helped Brunei consolidate itself politically, and laid the foundations for the commercial base that later made Brunei into a great emporium in the Borneo region. Brunei was also acutely aware of the political power balance nearer home in the Southeast Asian region. The powers that rose and fell in the region at the time, Sri Vijaya, Majapahit and Melaka (Malacca), not infrequently menaced the existence of weaker states, and Brunei, in her diplomatic tradition, changed the course of her foreign relations from time to time to maintain her political viability. It is not surprising therefore to find that while Brunei maintained tributary relations with China on the one hand, it also entered into relationships of vassalage first with Sri Vijaya and later Majapahit.

In the late 14th and early 15th centuries, fresh winds of change brought independence, the new religion of Islam and the establishment of the present dynastic line. These transformed Brunei from a small kingdom to a great emporium and empire. The 16th and 17th centuries, thus, witnessed the flowering of the golden age of Brunei. It is unfortunate that historians have seldom recognised Brunei as a great traditional Southeast Asian power whose fame and greatness was equal to that of Sri Vijaya and Majapahit, if not Melaka itself. The emergence of Brunei as an independent state in late 14th or early 15th centuries may be related to two events:

1. The conversion of its ruler Alak/Kalak/Khalak Betatar to Islam. This occurred in Temasik (Old Singapore) when Alak Betatar was invited by the ruler of Temasik to marry his daughter. It is assumed that the ruler of Temasik was a Muslim. Alak Betatar was converted and took the name of Sultan Muhammad Shah.
2. The decline of Majapahit, which followed the death of its Chief Minister, Pateh Gajah Mada, in the 1380s. Brunei, which was a dependency of Majapahit till then, broke away and became independent.

It may be erroneous to conclude that the conversion of Alak Betatar and the assertion of Brunei's independence occurred at the same time. According to the evidence available, Sultan Muhammad Shah was probably converted in the early years of the 1360s. On the other hand, it would be more plausible to suggest that Brunei became independent of Majapahit in the early decades of the 15th century.

The Golden Age, 15th–17th centuries

Sultan Muhammad Shah, having returned to his capital from Temasik, set about consolidating his kingdom. Sultan Muhammad began to lay the basis of the Islamic faith in Brunei and this provided the kingdom with a new revitalizing theological and political philosophy. The royal family itself began to assume a cosmopolition character when strands of Chinese and Arab blood were introduced into its composition. This happened when the second Sultan, Ahmad, took on a Chinese wife who supposedly came from a Chinese settlement in the Kinabatangan in Sabah. The second Sultan is said to have no son but a daughter, who was later married to Sharif Ali, who came from Taif in Arabia. He became the third Sultan and further consolidated the Islamic faith in the state. The introduction of new blood from these ethnic strands also meant the enrichment of Brunei culture and the ferment of new ideas. The international political scene in the region too benefited Brunei. Melaka was captured by the Portuguese in 1511, and many of the displaced Indian-Arab Muslim merchants who were looking for new trading bases turned to Brunei. With this cultural, political and commercial infrastructure, Brunei began to emerge as a great power, and by the time Antonio Pigafetta visited the Brunei capital in 1521, she was reputed to have exercised control over the whole island of Borneo and even as far as Manila. The expansion of Brunei into an empire is credited to the dynamic rule of the fifth Sultan, Bolkiah. He was popularly known as *Nahkoda Ragam* (the singing king) and is described in Brunei tradition as a great navigator and warrior. This was the golden age of Brunei. When Pigafetta visited the capital, he calculated that the city, known as

Kampong Ayer (city on water), had 25,000 families residing in it. The court boasted of magnificence, with elephants to welcome visitors, and gold plates being used to serve food.

In addition to the fall of Malaka, two other factors helped to raise Brunei to eminence. One was trade with China. As has been noted earlier, Brunei had established tributary relations with China as early as the 6th century A.D. In addition to the protection she gained from China, Brunei also benefited greatly from the tributary trade. Moreover, the Chinese were great consumers of Southeast Asian products such as spices, bird's nests, shark's fins, *tripang* (a fish), *agar-agar* (jelly) and a host of other sea and jungle produce. From early times, Chinese traders established settlements at Santubong (Sarawak), Brunei and parts of Sabah. However, as Brunei established hegemony over the whole area, the Chinese traders began to look to Brunei as one of their main headquarters for trading activities. The coming of Islam too had a significant impact on Brunei. In addition to providing a theoretical and spiritual basis for the structure of the governmental setup, it also made Brunei, like Melaka in the 15th century, a commercial amd missionary base. That Brunei did develop into a great Islamic missionary base in the 16th century is shown by the fact that the Spanish authorities in the Philippines were forced to launch punitive attacks on Brunei in 1578 and 1580 for her refusal to end Islamic missionary activity in what Spain claimed to be her sphere of influence, namely the Luzon-Sulu region.

During the period of its golden age, a sophisticated socioadministrative structure evolved in Brunei. As in the Peninsular Malay States, society was strictly divided into a ruling and a subject class. There was, however, an important trading class as well, the *nakhoda*. Generally speaking, Brunei was a sultanate based on the Hindu-Islamic concept of a hierarchic cosmos applied to society. At the apex was the Sultan, or the *Yang Di-Pertuan* (officially installed as king), who was attributed with supernatural powers and *daulat* (majesty). Below him was a hierarchy of officials of various orders divided into noble and non-noble officials corresponding to the social division. Nobles were generally referred to as *pengiran*. The most important officials of state were called the *Wazir* (Vizier), and they came from the core of the nobility. In the 16th century there were only two *wazir*, the *Pengiran Bendahara* (Chief Minister) and the *Pengiran Temenggong* (lord of the sea). In the late 17th century, however, Sultan Muhammad Hasan, the ninth Sultan, added two more posts, that of the *Pengiran Pemancha* (home minister) and the *Pengiran Di-Gadong* (lord of the treasury). The second category of state officials were called *cheteria*, who also came from the nobility. The rest of the centrally appointed officials came from the subject class and were generally known as *menteri*. At the lowest rung of the administration were the village headmen who did not come into the category of centrally appointed officials.

Since the empire was so large and sprawling, Brunei invented a unique decentralised system of administration whereby rivers (dependencies) and their inhabitants were divided into three categories. While ultimate sovereignity resided in the Sultan, de facto control was shared as follows: certain *sungai* (rivers/dependencies) and their *hamba* (inhabitants) were referred to as *sungai kerajaan* and *hamba kerajaan*, respectively. These were the appanages of the office of Sultan and therefore not the private property of the incumbent. On the death of a particular Sultan, they remained with the office and were inherited by whosoever became the next Sultan. The second category were the appanages of the four *wazir* and were styled *sungai kuripan*. Likewise they were appanages of office, reverting to the next officeholder. Other rivers constituted the third category known as *sungai tulin*. These could be owned by the Sultan, the *wazir* or the leading *pengiran* in their private capacity. Nevertheless, the cession of any of these rivers required the official consent of the Sultan and one or two of his *wazir*.

Decline, Dismemberment and Survival, 18th–19th Centuries

Brunei reached the pinnacle of its power in the 17th century, but even before this, the process of decline had set in. Both internal and external factors combined to produce a gradual decline over the centuries till, by the late 19th century, the very spectre of her total elimination loomed in the horizon.

The first major challenge to Brunei's supremacy came from the Spaniards. After having conquered most of the Philippine islands, the Spaniards sought to extend their influence to the south, namely, the Sulu islands. Brunei's hegemony in the area was an obvious obstacle and the Spaniards sought to destroy the political, economic and religious power of Brunei. Having made contact with dissatisfied elements in the Brunei court, they invaded the capital twice, in 1578 and 1580. Though Brunei survived these attacks, her very foundations were shaken. Moreover, Spain's activities in the Philippines, especially her occupation of Luzon and her restrictive trade policies meant, in the final analysis, that Brunei's sphere of influence and trade domination in the area was greatly constricted.

Spanish campaigns to subdue Sulu produced another interesting result. While Brunei was weakened by the Spanish attacks, Sulu rose in the face of these incursions. Thus from Brunei's point of view, there appeared yet another power as an active contender for supremacy in the Sabah-Sulu region. Paradoxically, internal events in Brunei were themselves, to a large extent, responsible for the creation of this situation. Brunei was engulfed in a long drawn-out war of succession from 1662 to 1674, and one of the contenders to the throne, Muhiddin, sought Sulu assistance. For having assisted him in defeating his rival (Abdul Hakkul Mubin) at Pulau Chermin, Sultan Muhyiddin is purported to have ceded the area now known as Sabah. Brunei authorities, however, soon denied ever having ceded the territories, with the result that the area became the focus of dispute for the next three centuries between the two powers. The spillover has resulted in the present-day Philippines' claim over Sabah. The immediate consequence for Brunei was that the ascendency of Sulu, and its de facto control of parts of Sabah delivered a blow from which Brunei was unable to recover.

Spain and Sulu were not the only powers that were causing Brunei's decline. In the south, Pontianak, Banjarmasin and Sambas had emerged as independent sultanates by the early decades of the 17th century, when the Dutch first arrived on the scene. The activities of the Dutch East India Company, which only amounted to establishing a theoretical supremacy over the southwestern part of Borneo in the 17th century, resulted in the establishment of Dutch paramount control beginning from the second half of the 19th century. Thus the political divisions of the Brunei Empire into what subsequently became portions of present-day Indonesia, Malaysia and the Philippines, was given the character of permanency by European expansionist activities.

Brunei suffered not only territorial encroachments; she encountered commercial competition and as a result, economic decline. The establishment of Spanish rule in the Philippines and the rise of Sulu effectively destroyed Brunei's trade in the Luzon-Sulu area. The Dutch policy of monopoly delivered yet another blow. Though Brunei herself did not come directly under the Dutch system, her markets, real or potential, were almost completely wiped out with the exception of China with whom she still carried on a small trade in pepper in the 1770s.

In the 19th century, Brunei was to face commercial competition from yet other quarters, namely the Bugis and the English. The English, mainly to obtain Southeast Asian produce for their lucrative China trade, established themselves at Balambangan in 1773, with the aim of attracting local traders away from Sulu and Brunei. With a declining economy, and with no other means of supplementing the revenues of an ever-increasing nobility, it is not surprising that a large number of *pengiran* turned to oppression and piracy.

To add to the dilemma, Brunei was plagued from 1807 to 1852 by the rivalry of two royal factions. In 1807, when Sultan Muhammad Tajuddin died, the heir, his paternal grandson, Omar Ali Saifuddin II, was still an infant. The struggle for power was started by Saifuddin's maternal grandfather, Muhammad Kanzu Alam, who succeeded in becoming Sultan till 1826. But Saifuddin's mother was able to prevent her father from being appointed the *Yang Di-Pertuan* (officially installed as king). After Muhammad Zul Alam's death, his son Raja Api (Pengiran Muda Muhammad Alam) conducted a bitter struggle against his sister's faction for the throne, culminating in his elimination around 1824. Omar Ali Saifuddin II was installed Sultan, but resentment and hatred between the two factions persisted. Raja Api was survived by his brothers, the most famous being Raja Muda Hassim, who, in classic Asian style, courted the British and James Brooke, probably with the hope of obtaining their support in the palace power struggle. Raja Muda Hassim's "flirtations" with James Brooke, together with his official appointment as the heir to the throne, induced Sultan Omar Ali Saifuddin II to launch a bloodbath in 1846, when Raja Muda Hassim and his entire family were wiped out. After Saifuddin's death in 1852, though there was no major domestic upheaval among the members of the royal family, the rivalry persisted till the end of the 19th century.

Thus, at a crucial period in her history, when Brunei began to experience increasing European encroachments, the sultanate was also internally weak. The kingdom was left to decay, with the ever-increasing depredations of the nobility on the *rakyat* (subjects). It is therefore not surprising that throughout the 19th century, many outstation chiefs became de facto independent, while oppressed dependencies rose to rebellion, Sarawak being one of them.

Hemmed in by the Spaniards and the Sulus in the north, and by the Dutch in the south, faced with the prospect of declining trade and dwindling revenues, and plagued by internal strife and recalcitrance, Brunei in her diplomatic tradition began to turn to Britain to obtain protection for its crumbling empire. The 19th century provided a classic example of how an Asian state (Brunei) used diplomacy to preserve her political survival. Faced with rapid disintegration, Brunei turned to Britain for protection, believing that such a course would regenerate the political and economic viability of her remaining empire. Relations with the British in the initial stage, however, transformed the need merely to arrest disintegration to one of survival. The Bruneians, however, held on rigidly to their belief, and despite the odds, disappointments, setbacks and heartaches, continued in their quest. Finally, in 1906, they were rewarded when Britain introduced the Residential System with a total commitment to protect Brunei. By then, however, Brunei had lost most of its territories, owing to British uncertainty, but had, through her persistence and diplomacy, prevented total partition, which had become a stark reality in the 1880s and the 1890s. It can be thus said that preservation and political survival became Brunei's major problem in the 19th century, salvation through British protection was her objective, and the use of diplomacy her means.

As early as 1774–1775, and again in 1803–1805, Brunei had tried in vain to seek protection from the English East India Company (EIC). Having failed in these two attempts, Brunei seized the opportunity of utilising the services of a British national, James Brooke, in 1841, with the hope ultimately of getting the British government involved. It was generally believed in Brunei circles that James Brooke was a representative of the British government. James Brooke in his initial interviews with the Brunei nobility had himself given this impression and had even indicated, though vaguely, that the British government would come to the aid of Brunei in case of Dutch interference. Here was a golden opportunity to play one European power off another. In some respects, Brunei diplomacy in employing James Brooke achieved some results, for James Brooke became an active proponent of British involvement. He was, to a large degree, instrumental in the British decision to open a naval base at Labuan in 1846. In the next year, he again played a major role in bringing about the conclusion of a Treaty of Friendship and Commerce between Brunei and Britain. By these two events, the British may be said to have made a major shift in their policy toward Borneo. Having adopted a policy of aloofness towards Borneo since the Anglo-Dutch Treaty of 1824, they now became committed in the Brunei region. The British, however, were still cautious and restrained, and refrained from getting directly involved in the affairs of Brunei. The Treaty of 1847, therefore, did not give Brunei anything more than moral protection from Britain.

In other respects, the employment of James Brooke proved to be a political blunder. For Brooke, instead of helping to consolidate the empire, initiated a policy of recalcitrance and expansion at Brunei's expense. Taking advantage of Brunei's helplessness, he began to nurture his own ambitions of establishing himself as an independent ruler in Sarawak. By the use of "gunboat" diplomacy, he induced the Sultan to sign a series of agreements by which he emerged as de facto ruler of Sarawak by 1853. He assumed the title of Rajah (king) and subsequently founded a dynasty of independent white Rajahs who were to govern Sarawak till 1946. This was not all. Soon he launched an aggressive policy aimed at undermining Brunei's authority in the neighbouring rivers of Sarawak. Having further weakened Brunei's authority in these areas, he employed various means, including threats, the withholding of annual cession monies and even open aggression, to acquire these rivers from the Sultan of Brunei. In 1853, the Sultan was thus forced to cede the Samarahan, Sadong, Lingga, Batang Lupar, Saribas and Rejang.

Alarmed and helpless, Brunei appealed to the British government for intervention, but to no avail. The British government either took an ambivalent attitude or quietly acceded to Sarawak expansion. Brunei had to turn to other avenues, one of which was to exploit the rivalry that existed between the Governors of Labuan and the Sarawak government in such a way as to obtain the sympathies of the Labuan Governors to advance the Brunei cause. Brunei resorted to this course when James Brooke intervened in the Mukah in 1860 with the intention of annexing the river and Bintulu. The Brunei authorities appealed to the Governor of Labuan, George Warren Edwardes, to investigate the Mukah affair and protect Brunei interests. Edwardes was of the opinion that Britain was honour-bound by the Treaty of 1847 to extend protection to the Sultan. Edwardes conducted a very fair investigation into the Mukah affair and found that the Sarawak government was openly aggressive and were bent upon annexing the river under any condition. It was only when Edwardes warned that in attacking Mukah the Sarawak force would have to fire at the British flag, that the latter withdrew.

The Sultan through his diplomatic action, had saved Mukah and Bintulu, but only temporarily. He was soon to be disappointed for the Foreign Office disapproved of Edwardes's action on the ground that he had interfered in a local dispute. The Bruneians became ever more apprehensive that the James Brooke's government was all-powerful, that nothing could check their imperialistic aims, now that even the British government supported their action. In 1863, the Sultan was advised by the new Consul General for Borneo, Spenser St. John, that some arrangement would be made to relieve him of all further troubles in the Mukah. The Sultan, finding nowhere to turn, realised that further resistance was useless. In 1863, he signed an agreement with Sarawak ceding Mukah and Bintulu for an annual payment of $4,500.

The Brunei authorities, however, did not give up their diplomatic efforts. In 1868, the Tuan Muda of Sarawak (Regent), Charles Brooke, attempted to take the Baram. The Sultan refused to cede and appealed to the Governor of Labuan, John Pope-Hennessey, for help. Charles Brooke applied economic pressure by imposing a fine of $4,000 on the Sultan for breach of dignity. Thus only one third of the annual tribute money due to the Sultan was paid. Pope-Hennessey, on the other hand, wrote to the Foreign Office, which led to a ban on all further expansion by Sarawak. The Bruneians had for once succeeded in their diplomatic effort. But this success had not come about purely due to their manoeuvre of playing the Labuan Governors against the Sarawak government. In 1850, they had signed a Treaty of Friendship and Commerce with the United States of America. In 1865, when the first United States Consul, Charles Lee Moses, arrived in Brunei, the Sultan gave him a large concession in Sabah for ten years. In the face of British disinterest and open Sarawak aggression, the Brunei authorities wanted to draw the United States into their political affairs in an attempt to introduce a counterweight to Sarawak expansion. At the same time, they hoped that Britain, out of jealousy of the United States, would be aroused to action. Their manoeuvre had the desired results. The British government was quite alarmed and enquired from the United States about its aims in Borneo. Though the latter denied having any political aims in Borneo, the British nevertheless began to pay more attention to the Sultan's rights on the one hand and to their own position on the other. Thus, an immediate about-turn in policy occured when Charles Brooke tried to annex Baram in 1868.

The Brunei authorities should have been satisfied with the British ban on Sarawak expansion, but owing to persistent fear of Sarawak, they continued to seek further counterweights to check Sarawak's designs. Realising that the United States of America was not interested in getting involved in Sabah, the Brunei authorities leased the area to the Overbeck-Dent Syndicate in 1877. Alfred Dent, the major shareholder of the syndicate realised that the best way to develop Sabah was to establish a British joint-stock company and obtain British governmental patronage by securing a royal charter. After much diplomatic effort and lobbying, Alfred Dent and his influential associates succeeded in obtaining a royal charter for their association, which was renamed the British North Borneo Company (BNBC). This development, however, created a very delicate and fluid situation in the Borneo region. On the internal scene, the recognition of the BNBC's lease in Sabah by the British government meant that the ban on Sarawak expansion could no longer be justified. This led to a removal of the ban, which in turn led to a fierce rivalry between BNBC and Sarawak for more Brunei territories, so much so that the ancient kingdom was rapidly carved away.

Following the new policy, the British government sanctioned the acquisition of the Baram by Sarawak in 1882. The Sultan was unwilling and reluctant, but the new Consul General for Borneo, Peter Leys, applied diplomatic pressure. In 1884, the BNBC obtained a lease of the Padas-Klias for $3,000 a year. The *Temenggong*, who was the chief owner (*tulin* rights) did not favour it and refused to affix his seal to the document. In the same year, the *Temenggong* ceded the Trusan and the Limbang to Sarawak, but these cessions did not have the Sultan's approval and seal and were therefore invalid. In Sabah, the BNBC was bent upon acquiring the independent intermittent rivers to make its holdings a solid block of contiguous territory. These rivers, which were situated on the west coast of Sabah, were usually held by Brunei *pengiran* as their *tulin* property. Nevertheless, the question of Brunei's sovereignty was involved. By negotiations or sometimes the use of force, these rivers were acquired one by one: the Putatan and the Tuaran in 1884; the Kawang in 1885; and the Padas-Damit in 1888, to mention a few. Thus, while the BNBC and Sarawak were trying to outbid each other in a mad scramble to possess more Brunei territory, the Sultan and his *wazir* were at loggerheads, trying to outbid each other in selling their possessions. The remaining *pengiran* were left in the cold without any leadership, direction or protection. In utter hopelessness, some of them sold their *tulin* rivers. Others were braver and willing to fight to protect their rights, but in the face of the Company's strength and the weakness of their own government, they capitulated in no time, though often after a heroic struggle.

In February 1885, Sultan Abdul Mumin tried to halt further sales by ordering the Brunei *pengiran* to swear an oath called the *amanah*. However, he died shortly after in the same year. Temenggong Hashim, who succeeded him, made an attempt to save the rest of Brunei. While he was *Temenggong*, he had acted in a reckless manner by offering the Trusan and the Limbang to Sarawak. After his accession to the throne, however, he showed remarkable responsibility and tried all means to recover the Padas, the Trusan and the Limbang. He also tried to prevent the *pengiran* from selling their territories by binding them to the sacred *amanah*. His attempts to recover the three rivers, however, were frustrated by external pressure. Strong intervention by Consul General Leys, the BNBC and Charles Brooke finally led him to approve the Trusan cession in 1885 and the Padas cession in 1887, but he stubbornly refused to approve the Limbang cession. Leys even suggested the total partition of Brunei, with the Sultan retaining only the capital and Muara.

The degenerating internal conditions of the Brunei empire could have led to dire international implications. The British government was particularly worried about the possibility of German and French intervention, especially in light of the increased tempo of European imperialism during the period. The Colonial Office suggested the total partition of Brunei, the union of Sarawak and North Borneo and the proclamation of an overall protectorate. William Hood Treacher, the Governor of North Borneo, however, suggested the preservation of Brunei with the appointment of a British Resident. The British government decided to send a mission under Sir Frederick Weld to study the situation and make recommendations.

Weld found that the Sultan was firm and would not even listen to the possibility of partition and reminded Weld of the sacred *amanah*. Weld himself was sympathetic to the Brunei cause and recommended a protectorate for Brunei with a British Resident to help the Sultan administer the Limbang. The Sultan welcomed the first, but only reluctantly agreed to accept a Resident. The British government, however, rejected the idea of a Resident mainly on financial considerations, but agreed to the establishment of a protectorate over Brunei. The British government also wanted to rectify its unsatisfactory position in both Sarawak and North Borneo. In 1888, therefore, three separate protectorates were established in the three states of Brunei, Sarawak and North Borneo.

The Protectorate Agreement with Brunei was signed on 17 September 1888. By Article I of the Treaty, Brunei gained British protection but retained internal independence whereas, by Article II, Brunei handed over the conduct of her foreign relations to Britain. This was a very important clause because in case of a dispute with other countries, including Sarawak and North Borneo, she had to abide by the British government's decision. Article IV provided for the appointment of British Consular Offices, while Article VII granted extraterritorial rights to British subjects. Article VI prohibited the Sultan from ceding or alienating territory to other powers without the prior approval of the British government. The Bruneians had at last achieved what they believed was the only guarantee for the survival of their kingdom, a solution they had been seeking since 1774.

The Protectorate Agreement of 1888, though preventing the immediate partition of Brunei, proved a great disappointment to the Bruneians. The greatest shock for the Bruneians came when Rajah Charles Brooke annexed the Limbang in 1890. A rebellion had broken out in that district in 1884, but all the efforts of the Sultan to subdue the rebels ended in failure. Sultan Hashim appealed to Charles Brooke to help him restore peace in the area, but the Rajah had intentions of acquiring the river himself and instead encouraged the turbulent state of affairs. Weld's suggestion, in 1887, that a British Resident be appointed to help the Sultan administer the Limbang would have no doubt restored the Sultan's authority as well as thwarted Sarawak's designs, but the Foreign Office gave priority to its own imperial interests. Desirous of preventing other European powers from gaining a foothold in Sarawak, the British government wanted to consolidate its position there by establishing a protectorate. There is reason to believe that the British government gave secret permission to Charles Brooke to occupy Limbang to induce him to accept British protection.

Thus, when in 1890 the Sultan was making final preparations to subdue the rebels, Rajah Charles Brooke made his move and quietly annexed the river. The Brunei authorities were horrified at this blatant aggression and appealed to the British government to intervene. The latter, however, were committed to Sarawak and, in 1891, accepted the annexation as a fait accompli. Charles Brooke was merely ordered to pay the Sultan a yearly compensation of $6,000. The Sultan refused to accept the money or to reconcile himself to the annexation and protested vehemently against the decision of the British government approving of the annexation. He also asked the *Straits Times* (Singapore) to publish his protest. The Brunei *pengiran* too were unanimous and persistent in their protest. Led by the *Bendahara*, they presented a petition to the Sultan, in 1895, urging him not to accept the decision of the British Government or the cession money amounting to $18,000.

The British government's decision was, to say the least, disillusioning for Brunei, indicating either negligence or pure indifference on their part. The damage done to Brunei was irreparable, for Limbang was the richest and most populous of the remaining districts. Moreover, Brunei ceased to be one geographically integrated kingdom, for the annexation of Limbang split the tiny state into two separate parts. The effects of the loss of the district were lasting, for the state, already beset by economic problems, now became almost economically destitute. The *pengiran* deprived of their traditional sources of income with the rapid loss of their territories, began to squeeze the remaining districts. Acting Consul, J. Weld, observed in 1898 that the loss of Limbang caused great damage to Brunei, for many of the *pengiran* lost their only source of revenue. The population, destitute and oppressed, either migrated to other areas or rose in rebellion. With British apathy and reluctance to improve the state of affairs, anarchy and rebellion once more set in, with the result that within seven years of the Protectorate Agreement, the "Brunei question" erupted with greater vehemence.

This happened when serious revolts broke out in 1899, in two of the remaining districts of Brunei, that is, Tutong and Belait. The rebels wanted Sarawak rule; and with Charles Brooke ever willing to make political capital out of such incidents, the future survival of Brunei was really bleak. It is surprising that she survived at all. It was in these hopeless circumstances that the Bruneians put to good use the only means left at their disposal, diplomacy. Sultan Hashim's first move was to establish cordial relations with the Consul General, Arthur Keyser. His steadfastness and sincerity won Keyser to his side, a development that was to stand him in good stead. Hashim readily agreed to Keyser's suggestion that he send a written request for assistance and that he take no repressive measures. Keyser sincerely wanted the preservation of Brunei and the only course he saw open was for British intervention in the internal affairs of Brunei. He suggested strong British action, even to the extent of deposing some of the corrupt ministers to increase the power of the Sultan. He felt that it was unavoidable for the British government to go beyond the terms of the 1888 Treaty and suggested strong intervention.

Sultan Hashim also sought help from other interested parties to support his cause. In response to his efforts, Governor Ernest Woodford Birch of North Borneo wrote to Frank Swettenham, the High Commissioner for Borneo, opposing any cession to Sarawak. He recommended the Residential System for Brunei and even suggested the reopening of the Limbang case. The Directors of the BNBC too supported the preservation of the ancient kingdom, if not for its instrinsic value at least to serve as a buffer state between North Borneo and Sarawak. The Sultan's diplomatic efforts were creating quite a stir. It embarrassed the British government for having shown lack of responsibility in its commitments to Brunei. As a consequence, the British sent Malcolm Stewart

Hannibal McArthur as Acting Consul on a special fact-finding mission. McArthur made a thorough study of the situation and proposed the Residential System for Brunei. The British government had awakened to the fact that it should discharge its obligations to Brunei. Two other factors also changed the British government's stand from supporting total partition to the preservation of Brunei. One major factor was the discovery of oil in Brunei, which Consul G. Hewett had reported in 1903. Brunei at once became important in the eyes of the British government. In 1903, the Colonial Office wrote to the Foreign Office that influence should be exercised on the Sultan so that concessions for working the oil would not fall into the hands of third parties. The other development was that the Sultan showed signs of turning to other powers to preserve his kingdom, especially Turkey and the United States.

Thus on 9 November 1905, D. Campbell and McArthur were instructed to negotiate with the Sultan for the appointment of a British Resident. After difficult negotiations, the Sultan and his *pengiran* agreed to sign the treaty on 3 December 1905. In January 1906, Sir John Anderson, the High Commissioner for Borneo, visited Brunei and signed the agreement on behalf of the British government. Thus the Bruneians' search for British protection as a means of political survival ended after almost 130 years of endeavour.

Salvation Through British Protection and the Residential System, 1906–1959

With the introduction of the Residential System, Britain extended full protection to Brunei and thwarted all further attempts by Sarawak to buy her out. As Britain scrupulously prevented further encroachments on Brunei territories, the political and territorial viability of the ancient kingdom was ensured, thus ending her long search throughout the 19th century for effective British protection. The period 1906 to 1941 was a transitional period that saw British administrative practices supplanting the traditional administrative system. The early Residents encountered many difficulties, but by the end of the period, a British-type of administration was firmly established. The end of the period, however, saw the outbreak of the devastating Pacific War, which in turn set into motion a chain reaction of political events that was to throw the whole of Southeast Asia into political turmoil.

From 1906 onward, the internal politico-administrative system began to experience significant changes as British practices and procedures were introduced by the British Residents. A system of administration similar to the one existing in the Federated Malay States evolved. The most significant feature of the Supplementary Agreement was the appointment of the British Resident whose advice was to be taken and acted upon on all matters other than those concerning Islam. Article I of the treaty thus gave the Resident wide sweeping powers. It is significant that the Resident's jurisdiction extended over even the questions affecting Malay customs. This was in contrast to the Treaty of Protection signed with Perak in 1874, where the Resident's powers legally did not cover questions affecting Malay customs.

As far as its international status was concerned, Brunei remained a protectorate in contradiction to a colony, but the difference was merely a technical one. For all practical purposes, it lost internal independence, for government and power passed into the hands of the British Residents. Traditional policy-making institutions and offices, though retained, lost much of their former functions and powers. The traditional State Council assumed a more formal and definite format, consisting of ten members, including the British Resident with the Sultan as president. The council's sanction was required for all important legislation and policy decisions. In theory, therefore, the Sultan-in-Council was the supreme authority in the state, but in practice it was the Resident who exercised actual powers. Brunei was closely tied administratively to the Straits Settlements (SS) and the Federated Malay States (FMS). The Governor of the SS was the High Commissioner for Brunei, and correspondence connected with the administration of Brunei was done through his office. The Resident himself was an officer of the Malayan Civil Service. Moreover, the heads of the various departments in the SS and the FMS regularly visited Brunei to offer advice and undertake inspection.

The first British Resident was Malcolm Stewart Hannibal McArthur, who was the chief figure in the 1905 negotiations with the Sultan. His immediate tasks were to create a modern civil service and to reorganise the state's revenues along Western lines. As far as the administration of the State was concerned, the Residents made a modest beginning by creating an efficient impersonal civil service. Such departments as the customs, postal, agricultural and public works with their own heads were created in the early years. Gradually as the state revenues increased, more departments such as the police, medical and education departments were added. Administratively, the state was divided into five districts: Brunei, Muara, Temburong, Tutong and Belait. The administration of these districts was entrusted to Malay officer-style magistrates. *Penghulu* and village headmen were appointed in the rice-growing areas with powers and functions of "peace officers." Over the years, Sanitary Boards were formed for the towns of Brunei (1921), Kuala Belait (1929) and Tutong (1931) with responsibilities for sanitation, buildings, markets and streets. With the exception of the examples given above, the local populace was not given much opportunity to participate in the running of the government. In 1918, an insignificant beginning was made when outstanding pupils from Malay vernacular schools were recruited as apprentices in the government service to fill junior posts.

As far as the monarchy was concerned, the 1906 Agreement not only guaranteed its continuance but made it hereditary, thus assuring the preservation of the royal line. The old Sultan, Hashim, who had signed the 1906 Agreement, was concerned about this point. McArthur recalled how Sultan Hashim had queried him on this issue and was relieved by McArthur's reassurances. The Sultan did not survive long; he died on 10 May 1906. He had issued a decree before his death nominating his son, Pengiran Muda Muhammad Jamalul Alam, as his successor.

One of the most pressing problems the Residents faced in the early years was the reorganisation of the revenue system. Brunei not only possessed meagre resources, but whatever there was, was the personal income of the Sultan and of the *pengiran* who obtained it either through cession monies on territories ceded to the Sarawak government and the BNBC, or through payments on revenue farms and trade monopolies given out mainly to the Chinese. The Residents thus had to redeem these cession monies, revenue farms, trade monopolies and existing traditional rights of taxation to create a reasonable state revenue. For this purpose, in 1914, the Brunei government had to take a large loan from the FMS amounting to $439,750. As such, in the same year, the cession monies payable by the Sarawak government and the BNBC were redeemed. All other monopolies, with the exception of the one held by Rajah Charles Brooke at Muara Damit (Brooketon), were also purchased. This latter monopoly was redeemed in 1924 for a yearly payment of $6,418 to the Rajah.

In addition to these measures, a land policy was implemented so that land was properly alienated with grants and titles. In 1909, a Land Code, similar to the one operating in the FMS, was introduced. According to this code, all land not held under title became state land, which could be disposed of by the Resident on behalf of the Sultan. This measure was somewhat revolutionary in the eyes of the local populace, who had owned land by hereditary right and considered unoccupied land as tribal land. Initially, there was opposition to the land reforms, but the matter was settled amicably. The result was that revenue collection not only became more systematic and efficient, but the revenues of the state also began to increase so that by 1910, for the first time, revenue exceeded expenditure. By 1936, the state was enjoying prosperity, mainly as a result of the discovery of a large oil field at Seria in 1929, by the British Malayan Petroleum Company (BMPC). The debt outstanding to the FMS was completely repaid, leaving the state with an accumulated surplus of $541,254.

The second important result was that land was opened up for European investment and a few large European companies began to invest in rubber estates while others engaged in oil exploration. The local populace, especially the nomadic Kedayans, began a more settled pattern of cultivation in place of the earlier practices of shifting cultivation. Trade too began to improve as a result of the removal of restrictive, stifling monopolies. More important were the effects on the social structure: the Sultan and *pengiran* lost their hereditary rights and powers of taxation; the institutions of retainers and slavery began to breakup; free men began to turn more to land for a living and the land reforms ended the hereditary tribal ownership of land.

Another important development was the emergence of the oil industry in Brunei. The presence of oil in the northwest coast of Borneo was known rather early, and since at least 1903 there were hopes of exploiting it. This was one of the attractions that brought the British into Brunei. Soon European companies began to apply for prospecting licences, one of the earliest to obtain it being the Burma Borneo Petroleum Company (BBPC). It obtained a lease in the Belait District in 1911 and struck payable oil at Labi in 1914. By 1924, one of the wells here was producing about 238 tons of oil annually. In the same year, the BMPC obtained and took over the lease from the BBPC and began to expand its operations. The company established a wharf and a wireless station at Kuala Belait in 1928 where a small village soon emerged. In 1929, the company's discovery of a large oil field at Seria turned the fortunes of the tiny kingdom. The oil field turned out to be one of the largest in the Commonwealth, and Brunei was rolling in oil wealth. In 1933, the royalties received by the state government from oil amounted to $230,000, representing two-fifths of the total state revenue. In 1935, the oil royalties accounted for 47 per cent of the total state revenue. The discovery of oil and its economic contribution to the state's revenues provided Brunei with one of the major ingredients for survival: economic viability.

As the revenues of the state improved, better social and welfare services were provided. During the early phase of the Residential System, little attention was given to education. However, by the closing years of the interwar period, the government began to give greater priority to the establishment of Malay schools. The number of Malay vernacular schools increased from one in 1914 to twenty-one in 1938, and the enrollment from a handful of boys to 1,810 children, including 189 girls. In addition, there were four Chinese vernacular schools with an enrollment of 201 boys and 144 girls. The number of private English schools had increased to three, namely, the Kuala Belait English School; the Catholic School, Kuala Belait; and the Catholic School, Brunei Town. The Education Department boasted of a Malay Superintendent of Education, five teachers trained at the Sultan Idris Training College (SITC), Tanjung Malim in Malaya and 40 locally trained teachers. The outbreak of the Pacific War interrupted further development. The results of this good progress in education were observable only after the war when in the 1950s, political leadership was provided by educated and enlightened Bruneians such as Sultan Omar Ali Saifuddien III.

With the outbreak of the Pacific War the whole of Southeast Asia came under Japanese domination. The Japanese forces attacked Brunei on 16 December 1941, landing at Kuala Belait and quickly occupied the towns of Seria and Brunei. As in other places, the period was a harsh one. With the disruption of the economy and shipping, food became scarce, but there was no famine. Resistance to Japanese rule was absent in Brunei. As such, the populace was spared the cruelties inflicted by the Japanese in North Borneo where resistance movements were active.

On 10 June 1945, the Allied Forces landed at Muara and Brunei was taken over by the British Military Administration (BMA). The period immediately after the war was mainly one of reconstruction and rehabilitation. Brunei, however, picked up fast in all fields and soon became embroiled in the political crosscurrents that swept Southeast Asia after the war.

The Period of Political Change, 1946–1963

Since the establishment of the Residential System in 1906, Brunei remained in a sort of political hibernation. After the Second World War, however, the forces of decolonisation, nationalism, communism and federalism broke the political slumber. The desire by the British to decolonise reawakened in the Bruneians intense concern for the future survival of their kingdom. The rise of nationalist activity in Southeast Asia and the emergence of independent nations gave rise to a vociferous nationalism in Brunei. The various schemes of federalism and the rising tide of communism threw Brunei into the midst of international crosscurrents and domestic political conflict. External influences and internal developments led to the emergence of modern political parties in the 1950s, and the first outcry for independence. They were also, to a large extent, responsible for the emergence of two power groups in Brunei: the monarchist-aristocratic group, led by Sultan Omar Ali Saifuddien III, and a mass-based nationalistic group led by Parti Rakyat Brunei (PRB). The monarchist-aristocratic group, though conservative in nature, sought to provide national leadership through a programme of guided democracy following the virtues of paternalistic enlightened despotism. It wanted Brunei to come out of the political backwater status under the Residential System and therefore wished to introduce constitutional changes designed toward the gradual achievement of self-government but one controlled by the Sultan, who alone, by virtue of his despotic will, could bestow whatever democratic institutions he deemed desirable. In this context, the 1950s was a period of fundamental constitutional change for Brunei. The PRB, however, wanted national leadership to pass to the people through rapid democratisation of the governmental institutions, eventually leading to independence.

The orientations of the two power groups were so diametrically opposed that they clashed on most issues confronting the state. As such, the 1950s were also a period of intense internal power struggle. This struggle climaxed in the Brunei Rebellion of 1962, led by the PRB. The monarchist-aristocratic group, however, emerged triumphant and the 1960s saw a further eclipse of the power of modern political parties.

When Sultan Omar Ali Saifuddien III ascended the throne in 1950, he realised that the position of Brunei as a state governed by a British Resident represented an anachronism in an area that was rapidly moving toward independence. To forestall criticism from within and without, and to raise the international status of Brunei, he embarked on a slow programme designed to give Brunei internal self-government and a small measure of parliamentary democracy. He had a personal motive too, namely that he, rather than the British Resident, should wield power in Brunei. Hence, in 1953, he announced his desire to promulgate a new constitution for the state. As a first step, he established an Advisory Committee composed of seven officials to prepare a report on the proposed constitution. The report was ready by 1954, and immediately local councils known as District Advisory Councils (DACs) were set up in the state. Progress, however, was slow, and even by 1958 the Sultan had not fulfilled his promise concerning the new constitution.

Meanwhile, political consciousness dawned among the people. The moving force behind this phenomenon was A. M. Azahari whose political philosophy was shaped by the Indonesian guerrilla movement against the Dutch and the continuing Indonesian revolution under Sukarno. He was also attracted by the socialist movement in the Federation of Malaya and Singapore. Being a self-declared anticolonialist and somewhat of a romantic revolutionary, he formed the first modern political party in the British Borneo region in 1956, called the Parti Rakyat Brunei. The party's manifesto was to oppose all forms of colonialism, support the monarchy and fight for the attainment of self-government.

Unlike the socialist parties in the Federation and Singapore, the PRB was immensely popular with the masses. By early 1957, it boasted a membership of 16,000, which represented about 75 per cent of the adult male population of the state. Bolstered by this mass support, the party became radical in outlook and began to demand immediate elections, the creation of a federation of the British Borneo territories and *merdeka* (independence). It became overtly critical of the feudalistic leadership under the monarchist-aristocratic setup and wanted power to pass into the hands of the people through rapid democratisation of the governmental institutions. Impatient with the slow rate of constitutional change being implemented by the Sultan's conservative government, the party in 1957 began to agitate for speedy constitutional reforms and sent a delegation to London to present an ultimatum on this matter to the Secretary of State for the Colonies. The Sultan was not only embarrassed but aroused to action. In 1958, he gave top priority to the issue, and in 1959 successfully negotiated with the British government on two matters: a new constitution for Brunei, and a new treaty with Britain ending the Residential System.

Under the new treaty, known as the 1959 Brunei Agreement, Britain granted internal self-government to Brunei, and the 1906 Agreement was revoked. The British retained jurisdiction over external affairs, defence and internal security. The post of the Resident was abolished and a High Commissioner was appointed to advise the Sultan and his government. Under the new constitution promulgated on 29 September 1959, supreme executive authority in the state was vested in the Sultan. The old State Council was replaced by the Executive Council and the Legislative Council. The administration was to be run by four important officials: the *Menteri Besar* (Chief Minister), the State Secretary, the Attorney General and the State Financial Officer. The Executive Council was to be the most important body in the State. It was to be presided over by the Sultan, who had to consult it but could disregard its advice by giving written reasons. It would approve annual estimates, meet only when the Sultan wanted and might consider only matters tabled by the Sultan. The Sultan, thus became supreme in Brunei. The Legislative Council was to consist of eight ex officio members, six official members, three unofficial members nominated by the Sultan, and 16 elected members chosen from the district councillors. Elections to District Councils were to be held two years after the date of the promulgation of the new constitution. The constitution as it stood no doubt represented an important step forward for Brunei, in the sense that it gave birth to internal self-government. However, it did not represent a big step toward parliamentary democracy. Power was in the hands of the Sultan; the councils were appointive; and even the Legislative Council was to have a majority of nominated members. Understandably, the PRB denounced the new setup, calling it a "colonial-type administration." It contended that all that Brunei had achieved was "self-administration" instead of self-government. The PRB argued that no provision had been made for a general election to choose a responsible or representative government. Despite the disappointment, the party, however, decided to give the constitution a try and pinned its hopes on the District Councils elections as a stepping-stone for ultimately gaining power.

The PRB consolidated its ranks by aligning itself with the labour movement in Brunei led by the Barisan Buruh Bersatu Brunei (Brunei

United Labor Front/BULF), which was formed in 1960. The government was alarmed at the strength of the PRB and was hesitant to hold elections. Meanwhile, the Malaysia issue had become embroiled in the internal power struggle. The Sultan supported the Malaysia plan as a political strategy, which the PRB did not see. The PRB, on the other hand, rejected the proposal as it was an obstacle for them to taste their own independence. The government tried to delay the promised elections, but open threats of violence by the PRB forced it to hold the elections in August 1962. The PRB won 54 out of 55 seats. The government, fearing that power would pass into the hands of the PRB, was apprehensive about the convening of the new Legislative Council. As such, the inauguration of the body was continously postponed until the PRB became weary of constitutional means and launched an armed uprising.

The Brunei Rebellion broke out on 8 December 1962. The revolt, though swift and well supported, was crushed within a week. The Sultan asked for British assistance and the rebels were no match for the well-equipped, well-trained British soldiers. The Sultan declared an emergency and outlawed the PRB. Azahari, who was in Manila, vowed to wage jungle warfare, but over the years his attempts have fizzled out.

The Consolidation of Absolute Monarchism, 1963–1984

The Brunei Rebellion of 1962, brought about a significant change in the domestic political scene. It wiped out the most vocal, popular and powerful political party, leaving the monarchist-aristocrat group without a strong political contender. In one respect this was good for Brunei for it put an end to an ever-present politically explosive situation. A small state in a changing era could not afford internal conflict. On the other hand, the eclipse of the PRB was a blow to modern nationalism and the further development of responsible government. The monarchist-aristocratic group, once in complete power, had an iron grip on political parties and the labour movement and saw to it that little progress was made toward popular government. As such, the period after 1962 saw the entrenchment and consolidation of absolute monarchism in Brunei. Some of the older pro-Malaysia parties survived, but they were never able to command the popular support that the PRB had obtained. Nevertheless, these parties were soon disillusioned by the fact that despite their loyalty to the Sultan the government showed no intention of collaborating with them. Frustrated and weak, they tried to step into the shoes of the PRB by taking up the same issues that had been championed by that party, but they made little headway toward achieving their aims. Immediately after the 1962 uprising, most of the remaining political parties decided to merge. Thus on 22 January 1962, the Brunei United

Party (BUP), Brunei National Organisation (BNO) and two more small parties merged to form the Brunei Alliance Party (BAP), a name directly copied from the Malayan Alliance Party. Its President, Haji Hasbullah, the former President of the BUP, declared that the BAP would work for Brunei's entry into the proposed Federation of Malaysia, a stand that he hoped would earn continued royal patronage. The Sultan, however, had no intention of working with any political party and completely ignored the BAP, when in February 1963 he sent a six-member official delegation to Kuala Lumpur to negotiate for the terms of Brunei's entry into Malaysia.

Another political organisation in Brunei, the Brunei Peoples Alliance (BPA), echoed the views of the BAP concerning the need to form a democratic government in Brunei. The leader of the BAP called on the government to hold elections immediately so that a democratically elected government could be formed before Malaysia was formed on 31 August 1963. Political parties in Brunei, especially the BAP, experienced a second shock when the second round of Brunei-Malaya negotiations in June failed and when the Sultan at the London talks in July decided to keep Brunei out of Malaysia. Though disappointed, the leaders of the BAP still hoped that Brunei would reverse the decision. They highlighted the danger to Brunei's internal security posed by the supporters of Azahari. However, the real reason was that political parties in Brunei had pinned their hopes on Brunei joining Malaysia, as they were confident the Federal Government would insist on the establishment of responsible government in Brunei. This was also one of the fundamental considerations leading the Sultan to refuse to join Malaysia. As a state in Malaysia, it could not continue to be ruled by a despotic ruler. The Sultan was, however, the least prepared to hand over his jealously guarded powers to the representative of the people. Immediately after his decision not to join Malaysia, the Sultan made some conciliatory but superficial moves toward introducing constitutional reforms. He gave an assurance that the elected element in the Legislative Council would be restored in the near future. In December 1963, he announced that general elections would be held within the space of two years for this purpose. No mention, however, was made of forming a responsible Cabinet.

The Sultan subsequently held discussions with the British government pertaining to the election. Both governments agreed that election to the Legislative Council would be held in early 1965. The council was to consist of 21 members, ten of whom would be directly elected. The rest would consist of six ex officio members and five unofficial, appointed by the Sultan. The proposed reform, therefore, would still maintain an appointed majority. The Executive Council or Cabinet was to consist of six ex officio ministers and four assistant ministers appointed by the Sultan. The British government evidently wanted Brunei to have a fully responsible government in due course and impressed upon the Sultan the need for further changes after the elections in 1965. They apparently extorted a promise from the Sultan that eventually the number of elected members in the Legislative Council would be increased from ten to 20, and that a fully elected Cabinet would be formed. The general elections were held in March 1965. A total of 36 candidates contested, most of them as independents. Many of the ten who won in the contest were thus independents. After the new Legislative Council was sworn in, a ministerial form of government was introduced. A Council of Ministers replaced the old Executive Council. The Sultan again left for London to confer with the British authorities over the composition of the Council of Ministers. The British government clearly showed its impatience over the slow progress toward a responsible Cabinet. It tried to pressure the Sultan into introducing more elected members to the Council, but the Sultan was adamant. Despite the British insistence, therefore, the Sultan agreed only to the former plan of having a Cabinet of six ex officio ministers and four assistant ministers appointed by him. The only concession he made was that of the four ministers two would be elected members of the Legislative Council.

As the political parties in Brunei were not making any headway, they decided to revamp themselves and introduce new blood. Politics in Brunei thus took a sudden turn in August 1966 when all political groups merged to form the Parti Barisan Kemerdekaan Rakyat/PBKR (Brunei's People's Independence Party) led by H. A. Hapidz Laksamana, the former Vice President of the PRB. Suddenly, the old charisma and loyalties of the PRB were revived. It criticised the British for not wanting to grant independence to Brunei and duly sent a memorandum requesting speedy independence. The British government was thus pushed into a corner and out of embarrassment emphatically declared that Britain was ready to grant independence. By this affirmative reply, the British government washed its hands of the whole issue and placed the full burden on the Sultan. A furor developed between the Sultan and the British. The Sultan left for London for talks where a further impasse was created when the British pressed for immediate liberalization of the political system and threatened to withdraw if their demands were not met. Rather than give in to the demands of the British government and thereby weaken the monarchy, Sultan Omar Ali Saifuddien III decided to abdicate on 4 October 1967, in favour of his eldest son, Hassanal Bolkiah. In this way he could continue to exercise power from behind the throne.

The turn of events brought about an easing of pressure from the British government and a cooling-off period in domestic politics. In 1971, the 1959 Agreement with Britain was amended, but with little change in the status quo. In 1978, negotiations were held between both governments and the result was a new treaty dated 7 January 1979, which established that Brunei would become independent in December 1983. However, the date was later changed to 1 January 1984.

On 1 January 1984, when Brunei obtained full sovereign status, a new revised constitution was also promulgated. This further consolidated the power of the monarchy by suspending the parliamentary institutions such as the Legislative Council. The new Cabinet mainly consisted of members of the royal family and nobility, though one or two commoners were also given ministerial portfolios. The Sultan, Hassanal Bolkiah, himself took on the portfolios of Prime Minister, Minister of Finance and Minister of Home Affairs. The important Ministry of Defence was retained by the Sultan's father, Omar Ali Saifuddien III. The Sultan's younger brothers, Pengiran Muda Mohammad Bolkiah and Pengiran Muda Jefri Bolkiah, took on the portfolios of Minister of Culture, Youth and Sports cum Deputy Minister of Finance, and Minister of Law cum Minister of Communications respectively.

The Post-Independence Era, 1984–

With the attainment of independence in 1984, and the ending of British protection, Brunei's main concern remained security, both internal and external. As far as the external dimension was concerned, Brunei had limited options. One was to get itself neutralized through international guarantee. The other was to seek membership in ASEAN. It chose the second option and was admitted as the sixth member of the organisation in the same year. Though ASEAN is not a military grouping, membership in the organisation greatly immunises Brunei from subversion from her neighbours, enhances bilateral and multilateral relations and cooperation with ASEAN members and gives Brunei a role to play in the region, especially in the economic and financial spheres. The relationship between Brunei and ASEAN may be said to be symbiotic. Brunei is confident that it can safeguard its cardinal interests through ASEAN. On the other hand, ASEAN members are very much alive to the sensitivities of the sultanate. ASEAN members therefore have refrained from giving adverse comments on the political system in Brunei, which stands in some contrast to the spectrum of democracies in the region. This stand has become even more pronounced since 1995 when the Republic of Vietnam was admitted as the seventh member of the organisation. Brunei's security and survival, therefore, are to a large extent also ASEAN's responsibility. As historical events have proved elsewhere, destabilising small states can prove disastrous to the region as a whole. Threats to Brunei's security could lead to a sudden and tragic end to the region's Zone of Peace, Freedom and Neutrality (ZOPFAN) concept. ASEAN, therefore, has become wittingly or unwittingly the guardian of Brunei's external security.

A marked degree of improvement in bilateral relations with Malaysia and Indonesia, her two big immediate neighbours, has also brought her added security. Especially from 1987 onward, Brunei has sought to strengthen these ties, which had been rather strained in the past. The economic recession of 1987–1988 afforded a unique opportunity to mend fences. Brunei, for her part, felt that she could play a more positive and constructive role in ASEAN by giving support to the ailing economies of her neighbours, especially Indonesia. Indonesia, for its part, found in the recession a golden opportunity to improve its lukewarm relations with Brunei. Brunei was quick to offer some financial assistance, namely a loan, and also indicated her keen interest in investing in Indonesia. Relations between the two were, in fact, raised to new heights. Brunei achieved a much more important objective: she gained Indonesia's friendship, and an unwritten guarantee for her security. Relations with Malaysia have also improved drastically over the years. In April 1987, both the Malaysian Prime Minister, Dato' Seri Dr. Mahathir Mohamad, and the *Yang di-Pertuan Agong* of Malaysia (Paramount Ruler), Sultan Azlan Shah, made official visits to Brunei. This was followed, in April 1994, by a visit by the Malaysian Deputy Prime Minister, Dato' Seri Anwar Ibrahim, who went to Brunei to resolve the overlapping claims over the Limbang through bilateral discussions. On the global scene, Brunei became a member of the United Nations, the Organization of Islamic Conference (OIC) and the Commonwealth immediately after independence.

Having secured, in some measure, a guarantee against external threats, the Brunei government's concern domestically since independence has been to entrench her position and to see that the population remains quiescent. The monarchy is nevertheless apprehensive of a recurrence of political demands, even another 1962-style revolt. Consequently, she has taken some measures to safeguard herself against such an eventuality. One of these includes the building of a palace costing US$300 million, which is virtually a fortress and possibly contains escape routes. The monarchy also maintains for its own safety a Gurkha Reserve Unit in addition to the presence of British forces.

To woo the majority ethnic group, the Brunei Malays, the government has promised that they will continue to occupy a position of dominance and privilege in the state. While Brunei as a welfare state extends generous welfare schemes to its citizens, the position of its Chinese remains unaltered. In the economic sphere, a new five-year development plan was launched, in January 1986, which stressed increasing food production and reducing dependence on oil and gas for income. There was also a drive to improve the existing infrastructure. The Sixth National Development Plan (NDP 6, 1991–1995) echoed similar objectives such as the creation of a dynamic entrepreneurial Malay class to reduce dependence on government.

In the field of education, a decision was made in 1985 to adopt bilingualism in all government schools under which both Malay and English would be mediums of instruction in schools and institutions of higher learning. This was a bold step since it obviously ran against Malay nationalist sentiments and stood in drastic contrast to the official education policy in the neighbouring Malay states of Malaysia and Indonesia. The government, however, wanted Brunei to be a modern, progressive state, and English would give its citizens the opportunity to acquire modern skills as well as facilitate the sending of students abroad for higher education.

The government makes no secret of its domestic policies. There has been a tight control on political parties, but in 1985 there was a partial relaxation in what appeared to be a second attempt at a "mild dose" of democracy. The move was made apparently to placate the more vocal sections of the people. There was even a promise that a general election would be held in 1987. Subsequently two political parties emerged in Brunei, namely, the Brunei National Democratic Party (BNDP), or Parti Kebangsaan Demokratik Brunei, formed on 30 May 1985; and the National Alliance Party (NAP), or Parti Perikatan Kebangsaan. The BNDP pressed for a representative government. As the party received no reply from the Sultan, it sent a petition to the United Nations Human Rights Commission. The BNDP had earlier issued a challenge to the government to conduct a referendum under the auspices of the United Nations to confirm its contention that the people of Brunei were discontented with absolute rule. It was obvious that the activities of the BNDP were causing uneasiness for the monarchy. In January 1988, some top members of the BNDP were arrested under the Internal Security Act and the party was deregistered.

1986 was an important year in the sense that it marked the passing away of Sultan Omar Ali Saifuddien III (Sultan Seri Begawan). The impact of his death, in September 1986, on the institution of the Brunei monarchy was mixed. Sultan Omar Ali was the greatest proponent of royal absolutism in Brunei and its architect. To a large extent, Sultan Hassanal Bolkiah owes to his father the entrenched position he now commands. Sultan Omar Ali, however, believed that he was the ultimate power in Brunei, despite the fact that he had abdicated in favour of his son in 1967. Consequently, Sultan Hassanal had to bear the brunt of constant interference by his father, leaving him little freedom to assert his own authority. Till the early 1980s, he was relegated to the position of a puppet ruler. Sultan Hassanal, however, resented the interference and many a time revolted against his father. A reconciliation, however, was effected between father and son before the death of the Seri Begawan.

With the Seri Begawan removed from the scene, the responsibility of perpetuating and ensuring the survival of royal absolutism in the country now rested squarely on the shoulders of Sultan Hassanal. To a great extent it has meant that the Sultan has had to shed off his polo image, give up some indulgences and create for himself the new image of a responsible, benevolent ruler, especially if he is to give credence to the state political philosophy of Brunei as a progressive, model Malay-Muslim monarchy. Since 1986, the Sultan has shown great energy in his attempt to rise to the occasion and to live up to new expectations. One of his priorities has been to reorganise the financial system of the state so that Brunei can emerge as a financial centre. Another is industrialisation and diversification of the economy, thus the emphasis on the Fifth and Sixth National Development Plans. To prepare Brunei for the rapid changes ahead, he reshuffled the Cabinet in late 1986, broadening its base and streamlining it. Four new ministries were created, including that of a Religious Ministry and eight new Deputy Ministers were appointed, selected from the civil service. The Sultan's priority seems to be to appoint the educated elite and technocrats in development-oriented ministries, such as the finance and development Ministries, to ensure that the country's development policies are successful. To retain the royal family's hold on the reigns of power, however, key positions were retained by the Sultan and his brothers.

In an endeavour to create the image that he is a "working monarch" and not a mere titular head, and to impress upon the people of Brunei that he has their interest at heart, the Sultan makes a public show of his scrutiny of the work of public servants. He makes visits to the countryside to listen to the views and problems of the common people. In a similar vein, the Sultan prays at different mosques each Friday so as to be more accessible to his subjects. He is reported to be taking a keen interest in the right kind of Islamic teachings that are propagated in the state and has banned the *dakwah* movement to prevent the emergence of Islamic extremism. This portrayal of paternalistic benevolence reflects, to some extent, the Sultan's lingering fear of the spectre of a people's revolution. Many people in Brunei have been lulled by the generous social, economic and welfare benefits extended by the state, but a latent desire for a representative form of government is always there, sometimes dormant, sometimes active. Many people are critical of the manner in which the state finances and reserves are treated as the personal wealth of the royal family. Others are totally disillusioned by the fact that though Brunei became an independent nation in 1984, no attempt has been made to introduce even a modest programme that would move the country toward a representative form of government.

The Sultan partially responded to these criticisms in 1985, but his attempts at limited liberalisation, however, disappointed him just as they did his father in 1962. In 1990, Sultan Hassanal declared the concept of *Melayu Islam Beraja* (MIB), or Malay Muslim Monarchy, as the state philosophy. The MIB concept lays great stress on the uniqueness of the Malay culture in Brunei, on the fact that Brunei is still basically a traditional Malay sultanate and on loyalty to the ruler who has absolute powers. Since 1990, the propagation and institutionalisation of the MIB has taken precedence over many other matters in an effort to retain the hold of the monarchy on the political apparatus of the state.

It is extremely difficult for any historian to predict the future, but basing one's thoughts on past historical developments, some pointers or trends may be suggested. Brunei is one of the few states in Southeast Asia to inherit a long, rich and continuous tradition of historical experience. It is undoubtedly one of the oldest surviving political entities in the region and can proudly boast of having the most ancient Malay dynastic line of rulers. In light of her long tradition and success in maintaining her political survival as a separate entity, it is extremely difficult to see Brunei merging in the future as a member in any federation. In 1957–1958, the Sultan rejected the merger in a Bornean Federation, and in 1963 he refused to make Brunei a member state of Malaysia. It may be argued that Brunei's oil wealth and British protection were good enough reasons for the Sultan to reject the Bornean Federation idea in 1957–58 and for his decision not to join Malaysia in 1963. Some analysts believed that once oil resources were depleted and British protection withdrawn after 1984, the Sultan might have changed his mind. This as we have seen has not been the case. Instead, the monarchy has entrenched itself and the state has become a member of ASEAN and other world bodies. Brunei seems to have obtained and secured internal and external security. There may be, however, some problems internally. Internal politics since the postwar period have shown that the Sultans want to rule as autocratic rulers, that they distrust political parties and popular governments. This trend has manifested itself and becomes clear if one analyses how the popular PRB was maneouvred into a rebellion and finally crushed, why the Sultan finally refused to join Malaysia (the central government would insist on a responsible government), why Sultan Omar Ali Saifuddien III abdicated in 1967 (he refused to give in to British pressure to bring about responsible government), and why little progress was made toward reviving political parties or establishing a responsible government till now, though another attempt was made in 1985 to 1988. Since then, the Sultan has gone very strongly on the MIB concept as a state philosophy. However, the people have always clamoured for power to pass into the hands of elected representatives, and it is almost certain that these demands will be revived. This is one reason why the Sultan still wants to retain the British Gurkhas in Brunei. Though therefore it is quite certain that Brunei in the near future at least will retain her separate identity as an independent state in the family of nations, it is uncertain how an internal reconciliation will be affected, which is vital if internal stability is to be maintained.

The Dictionary

A

ABDUL LATIF BIN CHUCHU, HAJI: Born in 1946, this former school teacher is a well-known political activist and is a successful businessman who currently owns a couple of restaurants, a book shop and a construction company. He was instrumental in the formation of the Brunei National Democratic Party (BNDP) (q.v.) in 1985, but he was arrested in 1988 under the Internal Security Act. Released after five years under detention, Haji Abdul Latif Bin Chuchu was elected President of the Brunei National Solidarity Party (BNSP) (q.v.), which he joined in February 1995. Although he was released from detention in 1990, some six years ago, he spent the last six years convincing the dormant BNSP, the country's only political party, to admit him. Under the BNSP, he had the support of some 500 members and was making another attempt to sell the concept of the will of the people to sceptical citizens through the introduction of a representative government in a state tightly controlled by the ruling Sultan's family. In April 1995, after he was issued a warning by Brunei's Ministry of Home Affairs that he refrain from getting involved in politics, Haji Abdul Latif Bin Chuchu resigned his post as President of the BNSP. See also: BRUNEI NATIONAL DEMOCRATIC PARTY (BNDP); BRUNEI NATIONAL SOLIDARITY PARTY (BNSP).

ABDUL MANAN BIN MOHAMAD: Born in September 1914, he had his early Malaysia vernacular education (q.v.) in Brunei. In 1939, he was sent to the Sultan Idris Training College (SITC) at Tanjung Malim, Malaysia, after which he qualified as a teacher. However, his career in the civil service was most astonishing because before and after World War II, he had been in and out of government service several times. When he was bored, he would leave his job to try his hand in business, failing which he would return to the Government service. In January 1956, he joined the Parti Rakyat Brunei (PRB) (q.v.) and was one of its founding members in the Tutong District (q.v.). However, in 1958, he disassociated himself from the PRB due to some political disagreements. Following this, in 1959, Abdul

Manan became an appointed member for the Tutong District to the newly formed Legislative Council (q.v.). In August 1960, he founded and led the Brunei National Organisation (BNO) (q.v.), a party that was said to have been formed under royal patronage and that supported the formation of Malaysia. In the August 1962 election (q.v.) for the District Councils, Abdul Manan contested for the Pekan Tutong (Tutong Town) seat under the BNO ticket but lost miserably to Mohd. Akip bin Abd. Ghani from the PRB. When the PRB-led 1962 Rebellion (q.v.) broke out, Abdul Manan condemned the PRB leaders for their unconstitutional actions. See also: BRUNEI NATIONAL ORGANISATION.

ABDUL MUMIN (MOMIN), SULTAN (r.1852–1885): He was appointed as a compromise candidate upon the death of Sultan Omar Ali Saifuddin II (q.v.), for the former was not aligned to the two major ruling families, namely those of Omar Ali Saifuddin and Pengiran Raja Muda Hassim (q.v.). As a consequence, he was placed in a rather insecure position and was therefore unable to exert a decisive influence over the destiny of Brunei. It was during his reign that the political survival of Brunei became of paramount importance in view of the encroachment upon Brunei territories by both the Sarawak (q.v.) government and the British North Borneo Company (q.v.) in North Borneo/Sabah. Sultan Abdul Mumin was almost reduced to taking defensive actions; he succeeded in persuading his principal *pengiran* to agree to issue a unilateral declaration in the form of an oath called the *amanah* (q.v.). By this declaration, his *pengiran* solemnly declared not to alienate any more Brunei territory. This oath was, to a large extent, responsible for the preservation of Brunei by the next Sultan, Hashim Jalil-ul-alam, son of Sultan Omar Ali Saifuddin II. See also: AMANAH.

ABDUL RAHMAN PUTERA AL-HAJ IBNI AL-MARHUM SULTAN ABDUL HAMID HALIM SHAH, TUNKU (1903–1990): He was born in Kedah and educated in the United Kingdom, where he qualified as a Barrister-at-Law. He was a leading statesman and the Federation of Malaya's first Prime Minister, when the country achieved its independence from the British on 31 August 1957. He first mooted the idea of Malaysia (q.v.) in 1960, with the view of incorporating the Borneo territories of Sabah (North Borneo), Brunei and Sarawak (q.v.) as well as Singapore (q.v.) into the Federation of Malaya under the Malaysia plan. Although initially Brunei showed keen interest in joining Malaysia, by 1963 the Sultan of Brunei, Omar Ali Saifuddien III, made a decision not to join the the proposed Federation of Malaysia. This was mainly due to some disagreement over oil revenue and the position of the sultan vis-à-vis the other Sultans of Malay States. As such, relations between Malaysia and Brunei were strained at least till the late 1970s. Tunku Abdul Rahman was the Malaysian Premier until 1970, when he was replaced by Tun Abdul Razak as the country's second Prime Minister. See also: MALAYSIA; SARAWAK.

ACEH: When Aceh attacked Aru in 1540, Bruneians were listed, along with Turks, Abyssinians, Malabaris and Gujeratis, among the 4,000 fighting men from countries serving Aceh's forces. Following this, Sultan Muhammad Hasan (r.1582–1597), the ninth Sultan of Brunei, established friendly relations with Aceh in the 16th century. Aceh provided Brunei with many cultural and administrative features. For example, the post of *Pengiran Di-Gadong* and *Pengiran Pemancha*, two of the four *Wazir* (Vizier), were copied from the court of Aceh. Even the etiquette of the Brunei court was modelled on that of the sultanate of Aceh.

ALAK/KALAK/KHALAK BETATAR (c.1363–1402): According to the *Brunei Annals*, Sultan Muhammad, the first Sultan of Brunei, who was installed in Temasik (Old Singapore) was before his conversion to Islam (q.v.) known as Alak/Kalak/Khalak Betatar. Alak Betatar, upon his conversion, was not only given the state regalia, but also inherited five states in Borneo, namely, Kalakah, Saribas, Sadong, Samarahan and Sarawak (q.v.). Having returned to his capital, Sultan Muhammad began consolidating his kingdom. He not only laid the foundation for the emergence of Brunei as an independent sultanate and later an empire, but is also remembered for introducing Islam to the state. Islam provided Brunei with a new revitalizing force as a theological and political philosophy. Thus Alak Betatar or Sultan Muhammad is not only considered the founder of Brunei, he was also the first Sultan from the lineage of the current ruling family.

ALBUQUERQUE, JORGE D': He was Captain of Melaka (Malacca) after its capture in 1511 from the Malay sultanate of Melaka. In 1524, he sent a mission to Brunei under Antonio de Pinta, with a letter to the Sultan of Brunei seeking improved commercial relations with Brunei, to which the latter replied in return. Following this and from 1526 onward, many prominent Portuguese (q.v.) officials, mostly captain-designates of Maluku (Molucass), visited Brunei. See also: PORTUGUESE.

AL-FAYED, MOHAMED: A businessman of Egyptian origin, he was also once considered amongst Sultan Hassanal's (q.v.) closest friends as well as the latter's "fixer" who was given the power of attorney to act on behalf of the Sultan. Al-Fayed got into the circle of being amongst the Sultan's close friends somewhere in the early 1980s. Earlier, Al-Fayed was said to have been a close friend of another of Sultan Hassanal's close friends, Adnan Khashoggi (q.v.), who is said to have helped the former in his early days. However, the relationship between Al-Fayed and Khashoggi turned sour when Khashoggi found out that Al-Fayed was having an affair with his sister, Samira. The relationship between Al-Fayed and Khashoggi became even worse when Al-Fayed divorced Samira, whom he had earlier married on 16 July 1954. As such, both Al-Fayed and Khashoggi became bitter rivals. In fact, it was Al-Fayed who influenced the Sultan not to buy Khashoggi's yacht, *Nabila* as well as a Boeing 747 from Carl Hirschmann, a Swiss who was in the business of managing, refurbishing and personalising aeroplanes. It was also reported, in 1985, that Al-Fayed had bought Britain's largest chain of superstores, House of Fraser (which includes Harrods), with money from Sultan Hassanal. A report prepared by an investigation team appointed by the British government revealed, in 1990, that funds used by Al-Fayed to buy House of Fraser was acquired by the former through his association with the Sultan of Brunei.

AMANAH: It is literally translated as an oath. It was declared in 1885, during the reign of Sultan Abdul Mumin (r.1852–1885) (q.v.) when the former and all his principal *pengiran* solemnly declared not to alienate any more Brunei territory. This declaration gave the next Sultan, Hashim Jalilul Alam Aqamaddin (r.1885–1906), much leverage and manoeuvrability to restrain his *pengiran* or to ward off further demands made by Sarawak (q.v.) and the British North Borneo Company (q.v.). See also: ABDUL MUMIN (MOMIN), SULTAN.

ANTI-CORRUPTION BUREAU (ACB): It is known as Biro Mengenah Rasuah (BMR) in the Malay language. As a measure to wipe out corruption, which was on the increase in the early 1980s, the Brunei government in early 1982 established the ACB. This bureau, which is under the direct control of the Prime Minister's Department, was at that time, headed by Ponniah Rajaratnam, a retired Deputy Commissioner of Police from Singapore (q.v.). Following its establishment, some minor officials were charged, but the Bureau's investigations against higher officials made little headway. In 1984, hardly two years after taking up the post, Rajaratnam was found drowned at a beach near Muara. Although apparently a suicide, the inquest returned an open verdict, for it was alleged that Rajaratnam had been threatened by some senior officials. The incident did create some ill feeling between Brunei and Singapore. Since then, the activities of the ACB had virtually ceased until May 1992 when the government launched a monthlong campaign to raise public awareness of corruption. The nationwide campaign, launched by Sultan Hassanal himself, was aimed at identifying corruption-prone areas in the government and prevention was advanced as a major strategy to deal with corruption in the sultanate. Government officers were asked to ensure that there were no loopholes within their ministries and departments that would allow for corruption. The Sultan, when launching the campaign, reminded the ACB to be fair and thorough in their work before any action was taken for failure in doing so could affect the suspect's dignity and good reputation.

ASSOCIATION OF SOUTHEAST ASIAN NATIONS (ASEAN): It is a regional organisation, which was formed on 8 August 1967, as a result of the Bangkok Declaration. Among its aims was to foster regional cooperation amongst member countries. Its initial members were Thailand, Malaysia (q.v.), Singapore (q.v.), Indonesia (q.v.) and the Philippines (q.v.). Negara Brunei Darussalam became its sixth member on 8 January 1984, a week after achieving her independence from the British (the latest addition is Vietnam, which joined in 1995).

In fact, as early as May 1978, the Malaysian Prime Minister Hussein Onn and President Suharto of Indonesia, during a meeting in Labuan (q.v.), had expressed their desire for Brunei to join ASEAN upon achieving its independence in 1984. Following this and in a meeting in June 1978 between President Suharto and Prime Minister Lee Kuan Yew of Singapore, Lee was asked to convey to Brunei that she would be welcome to join ASEAN. This was done by Lee when he met Sultan Hassanal Bolkiah (q.v.) in March 1979. In addition to these initiatives by several ASEAN leaders, the Head of the British Foreign Office's Southeast Asia Department, Kevin Burns, too expressed London's hope that Brunei would join ASEAN upon achieving her independence. At the 14th ASEAN Foreign Ministers Conference in Manila on 1 June 1981, Brunei's membership was confirmed when ASEAN leaders collectively decided to invite Brunei as ASEAN's sixth member.

For Brunei, membership in ASEAN is important because of her past sour relations with some countries in the region, namely Malaysia and Indonesia, although relations have since turned cordial. By joining ASEAN, Brunei not only enjoys some economic benefits in terms of trade and joint-venture business schemes, but ASEAN also provides some form of political legitimacy especially in terms of her survival as a small state. Amongst the foreign policy (q.v.) makers in Brunei, membership in this regional organisation will not only enhance bilateral relations with countries of the region but also with other regions of the world, especially due to the fact that ASEAN is currently considered as amongst the most successful regional organisations, being only second to the European Union. See also: FOREIGN POLICY; INDONESIA; MALAYSIA; PHILIPPINES; SINGAPORE.

AWANG HAPIDZ LAKSAMANA, H.: He was Secretary-General of the Barisan Buruh Bersatu Brunei or the Brunei United Labour Front (BULF) (q.v.), and Vice President of the Parti Rakyat Brunei (PRB) (q.v.). Hapidz's older brother, Pehin Jawatan Dalam Haji Mohd Noor, was at that time a member of the consultative committee, which was undertaking the formulation of the 1959 Contitution (q.v.). As such, the latter did attempt to discourage Hapidz from becoming active in the PRB, but was unsuccessful and this led to some misunderstanding in the family. In the August 1962 elections (q.v.) to the District Councils, Hapidz contested and won the Sungai Kedayan seat in the Brunei-Muara District (q.v.) on the PRB ticket. Also in 1962, he was appointed Minister of Labour of the Tentera Nasional Kalimantan Utara (TNKU) (q.v.). After the 1962 abortive coup led by the PRB, he formed the Parti Barsian Kemerdekaan Rakyat (PBKR) (q.v.), or the Peoples Independence Party, a merger of a few smaller political parties. The activities of Hapdiz and the PBKR were not much heard of after the installation of Sultan Hassanal (q.v.) in 1967. See also: PARTI BARISAN KEMERDEKAAN RAKYAT (PBKR); PARTI RAKYAT BRUNEI (PRB).

AWANG IBRAHIM BIN MUHAMMAD JAHFAR, PEHIN DATO: Originally from Labuan (q.v.), in 1936 he was appointed Secretary to the British Resident of Brunei. Prior to this, he served as District Officer of the Brunei-Muara District (q.v.). During the Japanese occupation (q.v.) of Brunei, he was Chief Administrative Officer or State Secretary under a Japanese Governor, who assumed the duties of the Resident. In fact, during the war, Sultan Omar Ali Saifuddien III (q.v.) worked under Awang Ibrahim, who was at that time State Secretary.

AZAHARI, SHEIKH AHMAD M. (1929–): The leader and founding member of the Parti Rakyat Brunei (PRB) (q.v.) or the Brunei Peoples Party, he was born in Labuan (q.v.) on 28 August 1929 of a mixed Arab-Malay parentage. His father, Tuan Sheikh Mahmud Sheikh Hamid, was a clerk with the Brunei Customs Department, and in fact, in later years Azahari himself served as a civil servant. During the Japanese occupation (q.v.) of Brunei and at the age of 15, he was sent to the Bogor Agricultural Institute in Indonesia (q.v.) to study veterinary science. He deserted the Japanese to join the anti-Japanese resistance movements in British Borneo and the Netherlands East Indies. After the Japanese occupation, he joined the Indonesian revolutionary forces fighting against the Dutch. In 1950, he left for Singapore (q.v.) to start some business ventures, travelling frequently between Singapore and Brunei.

In mid-1951, he finally returned to Brunei and became politically involved there and tried to organise a political party to demand independence especially through alleged underground activities. In January 1953, Azahari along with seven others, namely, Sheikh Nikam bin Sheikh Mahmud, Sheikh Muhammad bin Sheikh Mahmud, Sheikh Osman bin Sheikh Mahmus, Muhammad Haji Manggol, H. B. Hidup, Awang Tuah Putih and Abdullah Jahfar, were arrested and jailed by the British authorities for six months for organising a political demonstration. Earlier, in October 1952, he formed the Brunei Film Production Company (BRUFICO), which was also used as a platform for his political activities.

On his release in June 1953, Azahari once again became active in his political activities, especially by going underground. He formed the PRB in January 1956, but was denied registration by the authorities until August 1956. When the PRB's abortive rebellion of 1962 took place, Azahari was in Manila and then flew to Jakarta to request political asylum from the Indonesian government. At present, he lives in exile in Bogor, Indonesia. See also: PARTI RAKYAT BRUNEI (PRB); REBELLION OF 1962; TENTERA NASIONAL KALIMANTAN UTARA (TNKU).

B

BANDAR SERI BEGAWAN/BRUNEI TOWN: Brunei Town has been known as Bandar Seri Begawan since 4 October 1970, when its name was officially changed. It was originally named after Sultan Omar Ali Saifuddien III (q.v.), who was also referred to as Sultan Seri Begawan (the retired Sultan). Before 1906, it was mainly centered around the water village comprising a cluster of villages known as Kampong Ayer (q.v.) (literally translated as water village). Efforts to establish a settlement on land was started in 1906 by Malcolm Stewart Hannibal McArthur (q.v.), who was the first British Resident in Brunei. Although the new town did take shape on land, the majority of its Malays, however, still dwell in Kampong Ayer. Today, it can boast of having the best infrastructure in the region and some interesting landmarks such as the Sultan Omar Ali Saifuddien Mosque (q.v.) and the new palace, Nurul Iman (q.v.). See also: KAMPONG AYER; MOSQUE; OMAR ALI SAIFUDDIEN III; NURUL IMAN.

BARAM: It is the name of a river in the present-day State of Sarawak (q.v.) in East Malaysia (q.v.). Baram was once a part of the Brunei empire and an important camphor (*Dryobalanops aromatica*) producer, very much in demand then for Brunei's trade with the Chinese and Arab traders. When the Spaniards (q.v.) attacked and captured the Brunei capital in 1578, the reigning Sultan, Saiful Rijal, fled to the Baram to seek refuge, where he eventually died. Although Sarawak officially annexed this river in 1882, she was in fact controlling it since 1868. As such, the Sultan, Abdul Mumin (r.1852–1885) (q.v.), was initially reluctant to surrender his rights over this river but due to diplomatic preassure applied by the British Consul General in Labuan (q.v.), Peter Leys, Abdul Mumin finally granted the cession for all the territory lying between the Kidurong to Baram. In return, the Sultan was to receive $3,000 per year while his *Temenggong* was to be paid $2,000 a year. During the Japanese occupation (q.v.), Baram was included as part of the Brunei "prefecture" along with Limbang (q.v.), Lawas and Labuan (q.v.).

BARISAN BURUH BERSATU BRUNEI: Also known as the Brunei United Labour Front (BULF), it was formed on 29 May 1960 under the leadership of Jassin Affandy (q.v.), who was also at the same time Secretary General of the Parti Rakyat Brunei (PRB) (q.v.). Its formation was the result of a gathering, in Brunei Town (q.v.), of 100 delegates representing various trade unions in Brunei. While A. M. Azahari (q.v.) was appointed its honorary adviser, Hapidz Laksamana (q.v.), who was also Vice President of the PRB, was elected to become its Secretary General. In fact, all the top posts of the BULF were held by PRB's executive committee members such as Awang Hapidz Laksamana (q.v.), Othman Latif, Abdullah Jahfar, including Ong Wee Ming, a local Chinese who led the Kesatuan Buruh Umum (KUBU). Under the umbrella of this organisation, another three subsidiaries were also formed, namely, the Kesatuan Buruh Umum (KUBU), or General Labour Union; the Syarikat Buruh Kerajaan (SBK), or Government Employees Union; and the Syarikat Buruh Minyak (SBM), or Oil Company's Employees Union.

Although initially it did declare to stay away from politics, this policy was soon discarded. In fact, the BULF was formed mainly to supplement PRB's opposition to the Malaysia proposal. At its first anniversary celebrations in June 1961, it openly pledged support for the unification of the British Borneo territories and for any organisation that was fighting for independence. The support, however, was mutual for the PRB championed the cause of labour while the BULF supported the political aspirations of the PRB. This labour union-political party alliance soon became a solid, united force as retrenchment by Brunei Shell Petroleum (BSP) (q.v.) created labour unrest. By June 1961, the BULF together with the PRB organised a Joint Action Rally where both the organisations produced the following demands of the government: produce a Nationality Bill; announce the date for District Council elections (q.v.); introduce a national wage policy; and solve the unemployment problem created by the retrenchment policy of Brunei Shell Petroleum. In view of BULF's growing strength, the government implemented the Trade Union Enactment and Trade Disputes Enactment on 20 January 1962, as a way to control the political activities of the BULF so that it functions only as a trade union. In fact, this legislation did affect BULF's membership for some of its members left the organisation after the act was implemented. When the PRB-sponsored Brunei rebellion (q.v.) broke out in December 1962, along with the PRB, the BULF too was outlawed. See also: PARTI RAKYAT BRUNEI.

BARISAN PEMUDA BRUNEI (BARIP): The Brunei Youth Front was formed in 1939. Some of its founding members were Jamil bin Omar, Zainal Puteh, Pengiran Hidup bin Pengiran Hashim, Abdul Hamid bin Othman, H. B. Hidup, Abdullah Jahfar, Pengiran Yusof (q.v.) and H. M. Salleh (Salleh Masri) (q.v.), all of whom were teachers and instrumental in the formation of the Persekutuan Guru-Guru Melayu Brunei/PGGMB (Federation of Brunei Malay Teachers) (q.v.). Its first President was Abdullah Jahfar, who held office for only five months and was replaced by H. M. Salleh. It had branches all over Brunei as well as in Labuan (q.v.), Jesselton (Kota Kinabalu) and Papar in Sabah. One of its earliest demands was that the Brunei youth be provided better opportunities to hold important positions in Brunei's bureaucracy. In fact, one of its functions was also attended by Sultan Ahmad Tajuddin (r.1924–1950) in 1947, and it was believed that H. M. Salleh maintained close links with the royal family. It once boasted of having a membership of 15,000, and its branch in Jesselton alone had 1,043 members. It was considered the first organisation with political aims in Brunei and marks the beginnings of nationalism in Brunei. However, it was quite short-lived as by the early 1950s it was considered not very active.

BARISAN RAKYAT BRUNEI (BARA): The Brunei People's Front, which was formed after the March 1965 election (q.v.) to the Legislative Council (q.v.), was founded by Othman Sungguh, once an active member of the Angkatan Pemuda Brunei (APB) or the Brunei Youth Front, and later, in the 1950s and 1960s, Parti Rakyat Brunei (PRB) (q.v.). He was, at the time of the formation of the BARA, an elected member of the Legislative Council. This party was officially registered in February 1966. BARA's membership was open to all races residing in Brunei, and the main objective of this party was to demand for the establishment of a constitutional monarchy in Brunei.

BELAIT DISTRICT: It is one of the four districts of present-day Brunei and is situated at the extreme southwest of the state. It is 2,724 square kilometres in size and with a population of some 53,600 persons (1986), it is the largest of Brunei's four districts. It is today also the centre of business activity in Brunei for the district's rich oil (q.v.) reserves made Brunei by 1929, one of the richest states in the region. Much of its development is mainly due to British Malayan Petroleum Company's (BMPC) (q.v.) oil prospecting and drilling activities. It is considered the second most developed district of Brunei, after the Brunei-Muara District (q.v.). In addition to its oil and gas, which are the backbone of this district's economy, there is also some logging, especially around Bukit Puan and Labi. The Lumut liquefied natural gas plant (LNG), built in 1968, is also situated in this district. The major towns of the district are Kuala Belait, Seria (q.v.) and Lumut. See also: KUALA BALAI; KUALA BELAIT; SERIA.

BISAYAS: It is a non-Malay indigenous group found in large numbers in Sarawak (q.v.) and especially Limbang (q.v.). Although in small numbers when compared with the Brunei Malays and Kedayans (q.v.), they are also to be found in the interior of the Tutong (q.v.) and Belait (q.v.) Districts where they are also sometimes refered to as Belaits and Tutongs. It is believed that they settled in the area in very ancient times. At present, most of the Tutong Bisayas (or Tutongs) are Muslims while the Belait Bisayas (or Belaits) are either animist, Muslims or Christians. Some still practice their ancient old customs and are hill-rice cultivators using the slash-and-burn method.

BRITISH MALAYAN PETROLEUM COMPANY (BMPC): It was formed on 20 July 1922, under the Royal Dutch-Shell group, and registered as a company in the United Kingdom. In the same year, the BMPC bought oil-prospecting concessions from two of Shell's companies, namely, the Anglo-Saxon Petroleum Company and the Asiatic Petroleum Company, thereby giving the former extensive prospecting and mining rights in Brunei. Under the agreement, the BMPC was to pay a royalty of two shillings per ton (or 10 per cent in kind) to the Brunei government as well as an additional one shilling in royalty to the British Borneo Petroleum Syndicate. As such, the formation of the BMPC gave Shell a near monopoly of oil prospecting in Borneo. When the BMPC came to Labi, Brunei in 1922, four wells had been drilled in the area by other companies. Like the earlier companies, the BMPC too was unsuccessful in obtaining large quantities of oil (q.v.) at Labi and thereby began concentrating its efforts in an area stretching between the Seria River and the Bera River where the BMPC eventually struck large quantities of oil at a location now known as Seria (q.v.). By 1949, the BMPC's exploration acreage had already doubled after it obtained concessions to explore in the areas between Seria and Labi, and Tutong (q.v.) and Brunei Town (Bandar Seri Begawan) (q.v.). As the Seria and Jerudong oil fields began levelling off their output, in 1952, the BMPC had began conducting offshore exploratory activities. Further, as a result of the implementation of the Brunei Companies Enactment on 1 January 1957, the BMPC was reorganised and came to be known as Brunei Shell Petroleum (BSP) (q.v.). The BMPC has not only contributed to Brunei's economy but has also played an important role in the development of infrastructure around the Belait District, especially in Kuala Belait and Seria. See also: BRUNEI SHELL PETROLEUM (BSP); KUALA BELAIT; SERIA.

BRITISH MILITARY ADMINISTRATION (BMA): As soon as the Allied forces landed at Muara on 10 June 1945, Brunei was placed under this system of administration, which began the immediate rehabilitation of Brunei's infrastucture. Under this system of administration, the position of Resident was taken over by a Senior Civil Affairs Officer who was Wing Commander K. E. H. Keay. A year later, on 6 July 1946, when law and order had already been established, the administration was handed over to the civil authorities, which saw the return of a British Resident. A similar form of administration was also implemented in Malaya as soon as the Allied Forces recaptured it from the Japanese forces in 1945, and a year later, the administration was handed over to civil authorities.

BRITISH NORTH BORNEO COMPANY (BNBC): The BNBC was incorporated by royal charter issued by the British government in November 1881. The company itself was formed in early 1882. The charter empowered the BNBC to administer territorial concessions obtained by a syndicate from the Sultans of Brunei and Sulu in the northern part of the island of Borneo. These territories were forged into the state of North Borneo, now known as Sabah, as a result of the company's administration. The moving personalities behind the formation of the BNBC were Alfred Dent, an English businessman and Baron von Overbeck, the Austrian Consul General in Hong Kong. The two had formed a syndicate which acquired the concessions from both the Sultans of Brunei and Sulu. Subsequently, Overbeck retired from the venture and Alfred Dent applied for a royal charter from the British government to lend prestige and political support to the company. The BNBC governed North Borneo from 1882 to 1946. The charter ensured that the company was British in character and that its principal adminstrative officers were appointed with the approval of the British government. In 1888, Britain proclaimed a protectorate over North Borneo. A Court of Directors oversaw the company's administration in North Borneo, headed by a Governor. From 1882 to 1946, the company's government slowly set up a viable administrative structure, opened the state to capitalist development and left behind a newly created state, at the expense of Brunei's territories. In 1946, the company went bankrupt and North Borneo became a British colony.

BROOKE, CHARLES (r.1868–1917): He was the second Rajah (King) of Sarawak (q.v.) and was a nephew of James Brooke (q.v.), the founder of modern Sarawak. He was instrumental in the expansion of Sarawak, which was done by annexing *jajahans* (dependencies) then owned by Brunei. Charles Brooke himself was responsible for the annexation of the Baram (1882) (q.v.), Trusan (1884) (q.v.), Limbang (1890) (q.v.) and Lawas (1905). By the time of his death in 1917, the present-day state of Sarawak had already been established. He was succeeded by his eldest son, Rajah Charles Vyner Brooke (q.v.). See also: BARAM; BROOKE, CHARLES VYNER; BROOKE, JAMES; LIMBANG; SARAWAK; TRUSAN.

BROOKE, CHARLES VYNER, RAJAH (r.1917–1946): He was the eldest son of Charles Brooke (q.v.) and succeeded his father to become the third as well as the last white Rajah of Sarawak (q.v.). In 1946, he surrendered the State of Sarawak to the British government, thereby ending more than 100 years of Brooke rule over Sarawak. The cession of Sarawak to the British was due to several factors, such as financial difficulties faced by the Raj to rebuild Sarawak after World War II as well as due to the fact that Vyner did not have a son who could succeed him, for his three children were all daughters. His decision to surrender Sarawak to the British was fiercely opposed by his nephew, Anthony Brooke (son of his younger brother, Bertram Brooke), for he denied the rajaship to the latter. In addition, some local chiefs too opposed the cession of Sarawak to Britain on the grounds that the state would become a colony, and all this provoked the Anti-Cession Movement, which resulted in the assassination of the Governor of Sarawak, Duncan Stewart, in 1949. See also: BROOKE, CHARLES; BROOKE, JAMES; SARAWAK.

BROOKE, JAMES (r.1841–1868): Born in 1803, he was an English traveller who, on his way to Maluku (Molocuss) in 1839, arrived at the Sarawak (q.v.) River (Old Sarawak). There he found a Brunei prince, Pengiran Raja Muda Hassim (q.v.), struggling to suppress a rebellion led by the local Sarawak Malays and Land Dayaks. Raja Muda Hassim requested James Brooke's help in quelling the uprising, whereupon, James was bestowed the governership of the Sarawak River in 1841. Raja Muda Hassim then returned to the Brunei capital to resume his post as *Bendahara* (Chief Minister), but his alliance with James Brooke created suspicion and he together with his family, was exterminated by the Sultan's faction in 1846. As a result, James Brooke declared himself as an independent ruler and initiated a policy of territorial expansion at Brunei's expense. James Brooke's expansionist policies witnessed the annexation of several important rivers, such as the Samarahan, Batang Lupar, Skrang, Saribas, Rejang, Oya, Mukah and Bintulu. As such, he is considered the founder of modern-day Sarawak. On his death in 1868 and due to the fact that James Brooke had no children, the throne of Sarawak was bestowed upon his nephew Charles Brooke (q.v.). See also: BROOKE, CHARLES; BROOKE, CHARLES VYNER; SARAWAK.

BRUNEI ALLIANCE PARTY (BAP): It was formed in January 1963, when two smaller pro-Malaysia (q.v.) parties merged. The two parties were the Brunei United Party (BUP) led by Haji Hasbullah bin Haji Mohammed Daud (q.v.) and the Brunei National Organisation (BNO) (q.v.) headed by Abdul Manan bin Mohamad (q.v.). The merger was a result of the crushing defeat suffered by both the parties at the hands of the Parti Rakyat Brunei (PRB) (q.v.) in the August 1962 District Council elections (q.v.). Haji Hasbullah was appointed President of this new party, which copied its name from the Malayan Alliance Party. The BAP supported the Malaysia proposal, thus identifying itself with Sultan Omar Ali Saifuddien's policy at that time and distancing itself from the outlawed PRB. The Sultan, however, ignored this party, which was not given a place in the Brunei delegation sent to negotiate in Kuala Lumpur in February 1963. The BAP protested, arguing that the people's voice had not been heard and that the government's attitude smacked of feudalism. After the Sultan decided to keep Brunei out of Malaysia, relations between the government and the BAP were further strained. The BAP's continued support for Malaysia was viewed by the Sultan as a mark of disrespect to him and defiance of his decision on the issue. Demands by the BAP for new elections, a responsible government and independence for Brunei also went unheeded. Under the government's iron hold on all political parties in the state, the BAP's demands have come to nothing, and the party practically passed into oblivion. See also: HASBULLAH BIN HAJI MOHAMMED DAUD, HAJI.

BRUNEI CURRENCY BOARD: It was established in 1967, and given the sole responsibility of controlling the circulation of currency (q.v.) as well as ensuring adequate asset levels in local banks in Brunei. In addition, it is also the principal licensing and monitoring body for all the country's banks and finance companies. It also coordinates the functions of the Bank Supervision Unit, a unit within the Ministry of Finance. This board also performs an important role in maintaining currency interchangeability with Singapore, based on the provisions of an agreement signed by the Brunei and Singapore (q.v.) governments in June 1967, whereby the two currencies are interchangeable at par and are accepted in either state. The agreement is important in that it allows banks in Brunei to shift funds into Singapore without running the risks of currency fluctuations. This arrangement has been especially important in managing the huge funds flowing from oil (q.v.) revenues, most of which are channeled through Singapore. See also: CURRENCY.

BRUNEI'S FREEDOM STRUGGLE PARTY (BFSP): It was founded by Arshad bin Marsal, who was earlier a unionist and active member of the Barisan Buruh Bersatu Brunei, or the Brunei United Labour Front (BULF) (q.v.), a left-wing labour movement of the Parti Rakyat Brunei (PRB) (q.v.). In 1962, Arshad resigned from the BULF as a result of the implementation of the Trade Union Enactment and Trade Disputes Enactment of 20 January 1962, when some of its members too disbanded the movement. The BFSP was a small party in terms of its membership and size and did not also have a specific political programme other than to achieve Brunei's independence through joining Malaysia (q.v.). This party was, however, short-lived, for several months after its formation in 1962, members of the BSFP joined the Brunei Alliance Party (q.v.) in January 1963.

BRUNEI INVESTMENT AGENCY (BIA): The BIA was established under the supervision of the Ministry of Finance in July 1983, with the aim of diversifying out of sterling investments, and as a part of the decision to remove most of the investment portfolios from the British Crown Agents. It is responsible for investment strategies for the large accumulated surpluses of the state, which is estimated between US$45 billion and US$50 billion. Due to shortage of local skills and expertise in the field, and in view of the time-consuming process of training local staff, four foreign agencies were appointed to act as investment consultants. These were, namely, the Morgan Guarantee Trust and Citibank of the United States (q.v.), as well as Nomura and Daiwa Securities of Japan (q.v.). These firms, with the exception of Morgan Guarantee Trust, were also the portfolio advisers stationed in Brunei to undertake training of local staff. In addition, the BIA has opened offices in London and New York. Since its formation, the BIA has greatly improved the country's foreign investments performance. Brunei's investments which are widely spread out in the Asia Pacific as well as Europe and America include investments in the hotel industry of Singapore (q.v.); investments in the Australian Willerroo ranch to ensure adequate beef supplies and; investments in the Indonesian (q.v.) cement industry to eleviate the shortage of cement and other construction materials in Brunei. See also: QAF HOLDINGS.

BRUNEI-MUARA DISTRICT: It is 571 square kilometres in size and is the most populous of Brunei's four districts with a population of some 136,000 (1986), although territorially it is in fact the smallest of Brunei's four districts. Whilst the Belait District (q.v.) is the centre for Brunei's major economic activity, the petroleum industry (q.v.); the Brunei-Muara District, on the other hand, is the centre for administration for the country. It is also the most developed district in Brunei, equipped with the most modern infrastructure. The capital of the country, Bandar Seri Begawan (q.v.), is situated in this district. Being the centre of administration of the state, it was given more emphasis when the British Residential System (q.v.) was introduced in 1906. Until 1932, when the oil industry emerged, most of the Resident's efforts to develop Brunei were centered in this district, thereby giving her a lead in development over the other three districts. After the emergence of the oil industry, the Brunei-Muara District continued to receive special attention, mainly due to the fact that she has continued to be the seat of the government.

BRUNEI NATIONAL DEMOCRATIC PARTY (BNDP): A political party that was registered in May 1985, some two decades after the abortive rebellion (q.v.) staged by the Parti Rakyat Brunei (PRB) (q.v.) in 1962. Registration for this party was granted without the approval of Sultan Omar Ali Saifuddien III (q.v.), Sultan Hassanal Bolkiah's (q.v.) father, and this was said to have contributed to the rift between father and son. The founders of this party were mainly Brunei Malay businessmen with close royal family connections. The party was established with the aim of gaining government support for Brunei Malay commercial advancement. Haji Abdul Latif bin Abdul Hamid was elected party President, Mohamad Hatta bin Haji Zainal the Vice President, and Haji Abdul Latif bin Chuchu (q.v.) the Secretary-General. The BNDP expanded rapidly but abruptly lost 70 per cent of its 5,000 members when the government forbade civil servants to join. In late January 1988, Haji Abdul Latif bin Chuchu along with Haji Abdul Latif bin Abdul Hamid were arrested as both were about to fly to Australia and were held under the Internal Security Act, which allows for detention for up to two years without charges being filed. Both were released in 1990, and five years later, in 1995, Haji Abdul Latif bin Chuchu joined the Brunei National Solidarity Party (BNSP) (q.v.), of which he was elected President. See also: ABDUL LATIF BIN CHUCHU, HAJI; BRUNEI NATIONAL SOLIDARITY PARTY (BNSP).

BRUNEI NATIONAL ORGANISATION (BNO): It was formed in August 1960, and led by Abdul Manan bin Mohamad (q.v.). At the time of its registration, the BNO claimed to have support from some 700 members, most of them apparently from the Tutong District (q.v.). The party's membership was open to Malays as well as non-Malays. Initially, it opposed the Malaysia (q.v.) proposal, but in January 1962, the party changed its stand and began to support the Malaysian idea. The BNO wanted Brunei to join the proposed federation for it thought that Indonesia (q.v.) posed a danger to Brunei's security and survival. Many observers believe, however, that Sultan Omar Ali Saifuddien's intervention was instrumental in this change of the BNO's stand and that he was keen to present the BNO as an alternative to the Parti Rakyat Brunei (PRB) (q.v.). In the 1962 District 4Councils elections, the BNO campaigned on a pro-Malaysia manifesto and fielded eight candidates, all in the Tutong District (q.v.), where they all lost miserably to the PRB. See also: ABDUL MANAN BIN MOHAMAD.

BRUNEI NATIONAL SOLIDARITY PARTY (BNSP): It was registered as a political party in early 1986 with some 150 members, most of whom were formally from the Brunei National Democratic Party (BNDP) (q.v.), belonging to the Mohamad Hatta bin Haji Zainal faction, who was Vice President of the BNDP. Haji Jumat bin Haji Idris became BNSP's first Chairman while Mohamad Hatta bin Haji Zainal was appointed its Secretary-General. Unlike the BNDP, this party's membership was not restricted to Brunei Malays alone but was also open to the Chinese (q.v.). However, in early 1988, the government detained most of BNSP's leaders. Abdul Latif bin Chuchu (q.v.) joined this party in February 1995, and got himself elected as President. Following a warning issued by Brunei's Ministry of Home Affairs, Haji Latif Chuchu resigned his post as party President in April 1995. Haji Latif Chuchu's resignation is a clear indication that thus far the ruling monarchy does not want to entertain any demand for representative government in Brunei. See also: ABDUL LATIF BIN CHUCHU, HAJI.

BRUNEI OIL AND GAS AUTHORITY (BOGA): It was formed in early 1993, under the chairmanship of Prince Jefri Bolkiah (q.v.), who was also Brunei's Minister of Finance. The main aim of BOGA is to coordinate all aspects of planning within the oil and gas industry (q.v.), including the granting of exploration and extraction concessions. It is also to deal with questions relating to conservation and environmental impacts. It is located within the Petroleum Unit in the Prime Minister's Office. The formation of BOGA can be viewed as a move by the Brunei government to exert greater control over the industry, although at present the Brunei government retains a 50 per cent stake in Brunei Shell Petroleum (BSP) and its constituent companies. BOGA is expected to take over the responsibilities currently undertaken by the Petroleum Unit (q.v.). See also: BRUNEI SHELL PETROLEUM (BSP); PETROLEUM MINING ACT (LAWS OF BRUNEI, REVISIONS OF 1984); PETROLEUM UNIT.

BRUNEI SHELL PETROLEUM (BSP): It was formed and registered in Brunei in 1957 as a result of the implementation of the Brunei Companies Enactment on 1 January 1957. As such, on 15 March 1957, it took over the operations of its sister company, the British Malayan Petroleum Company (BMPC) (q.v.), which had been in operation in Brunei since 1922. The new name, BSP, was chosen in view of the expanding nature of oil (q.v.) development operations at that time, and especially on the continental shelf of Brunei. As such, it was felt that a new company should be formed under the new Enactment and that the name of the state where it was operating be identified with it. Sultan Omar Ali Saifuddien III (q.v.) graciously gave his permission for the use of the word "Brunei" in the name of the company. In addition, as the BSP had close connections with the Royal Dutch-Shell Group of Companies, it was also deemed necessary to include the word "Shell" so as to publically link the state and the company with the worldwide operations of the Royal Dutch-Shell.

When the BSP took over operations from the BMPC, its exploratory acreage extended from Seria to Labi and Tutong (q.v.) to Brunei Town (Bandar Seri Begawan) (q.v.). In 1963, the BSP obtained new concessions in exchange for older, less productive concessions. These new concessions included some 4,000 square kilometres on the continental shelf and a further 680 square kilometres in the Seria field. Again in 1968, the BSP obtained a further offshore concession of 3,735 square kilometres, with parts of it extending beyond the continental shelf, and in 1968 Shell got an additional 298 square kilometres near Labi. Shell further expanded her offshore concessions when in 1981 it was granted some 3,530 square kilometres. It is, at present, the largest concessionaire with some 10,107 square kilometres of territory, out of which some 73 per cent are offshore operations. At present, the five companies operating in Brunei are BSP; Jasra-ELF (formerly Jasra Jackson) (q.v.); Sunray Borneo Oil Company; Superior Oil and Clark Brunei Oil; and Woods Petroleum. Even so, the BSP still holds a virtual monopoly over exploration and production. In 1973, the Brunei government obtained a 25 per cent stake in the BSP, a move that reflected the former's desire to participate actively in the oil and gas industry. Further in 1985 the government's stake was increased to 50 per cent.

At present, the BSP operates as a group of five companies. The BSP is the main company in charge of exploration and production of oil and liquefied natural gas (LNG). The second company is the Brunei Shell Marketing, which was established in 1974 with the sole purpose of marketing oil and gas products within the state. It is jointly owned, on a 50 to 50 per cent basis, by the government and BSP. The other three companies, all formed to cater to the LNG trade with Japan (q.v.) are Brunei Liquefied Natural Gas (BLNG); Brunei Coldgas (BCG); and Brunei Shell Tankers. BLNG was formed in 1969 and is a joint venture between the government, BSP and the Mitsubishi Corporation where they hold a 50, 25 and 25 per cent interest respectively. Following this, in 1977, the BCG was established to market the LNG and like the BLNG, it is one-half owned by the Brunei government, while the BSP and Mitsubishi have one-third each. The final one is the Brunei Shell Tankers, which was formed in December 1986 and is responsible for transporting the LNG to Japan. The Brunei government and BSP have equal shares.

Like the BMPC earlier, the BSP continues to play a central role in the development of Brunei's economy. In addition to contributing to Brunei's revenue, Shell is also the second largest employer in Brunei, after the public sector. As such, Brunei at times is also referred to as a "Shell State" in view of its dominant role in the country's economy as well as the very close links between Shell and the state. See also: BRITISH MALAYAN PETROLEUM COMPANY (BMPC); JASRA JACKSON; PETROLEUM MINING ACT (LAWS OF BRUNEI, REVISIONS OF 1984).

BRUNEI TOWN: See BANDAR SERI BEGAWAN.

BRUNEI UNITED PARTY (BUP): This party was formed under royal patronage in December 1961 by Haji Hasbullah bin Haji Mohammad

Daud (q.v.). The BUP was formed with its main aim to oppose the growing strength of the Parti Rakyat Brunei (PRB) (q.v.). In the 1962 election, it fielded only one candidate, Hasbullah himself, who lost the Sumbiling seat in the Brunei-Muara District (q.v.) to Zaini Haji Ahmad (q.v.) from the PRB (q.v.). See also: BRUNEI ALLIANCE PARTY (BAP); HASBULLAH BIN HAJI MOHAMMED DAUD, HAJI.

BURUNENG: It is believed to be the ancient name of Brunei. A Javanese source of 1365, the *Nagarakertagama* the work of the famous court historian Prapanca, lists it as a vassal state of the Majapahit empire. With the decline of Majapahit around c.1400, Brunei began to emerge as an independent state. It was also during that time that Islam began to penetrate the region and was thus introduced to Brunei as well.

C

CABINET: Prime Minister and other ministers who are individually responsible for particular government activities (called portfolios) and collectively responsible for government policies. When Brunei achieved her independence in 1984, the ruling family adopted a ministerial style of government with the Sultan-in-Council having the ultimate responsibility for policy. Members of Brunei's present-day cabinet are drawn mainly from the ruling royal family and some senior civil servants closely linked to the ruling family. The present Sultan Hassanal Bolkiah (q.v.) himself is the Prime Minister as well as the Minister of Defence. His two brothers, Pengiran Muda Mohamed Bolkiah (q.v.) and Pengiran Muda Jefri Bolkiah (q.v.), are Minister of Foreign Affairs and Minister of Finance, respectively. Other important portfolios are closely guarded by the Sultan's relatives and persons close to the palace. See also: APPENDIX D.

CHETERIA: The word is presumably derived from that of the Hindu warrior caste *kshatriya*. In Brunei, these were traditional officials of the second order of officials in Brunei's traditional government and played an important role in the process of decision making in the state. They were recruited both from the core and common nobility unlike the *Wazir* which were chosen only from the core nobility. The highest-ranking official in this group was the *Pengiran Shahbandar*, or the minister of commerce.

CHINA: Brunei's relations with China go back as far as the 14th century when a Chinese source mentioned that the ruler of *Po-ni* in A.D.

1370 was "Ma-ha-mo-sa" (Muhammad Shah) (q.v.). Other than *Po-ni*, Chinese sources also called Brunei by other names such as *Bun-lai* and *Vijayapura*, a place in northwest Borneo. Further, another Chinese source stated that when Admiral Cheng Ho visited Brunei in 1405, it was already a Muslim state. As such, Brunei conducted a considerable amount of trade with China, which was one factor in the rise in eminence of this sultanate. In addition, as part of her strategy for survival, she also sought protection from China. As late as the 1770s, Brunei's trade with China still continued, namely in pepper, although the amount had very much declined due to the activities of Western powers who began to dominate the trade.

At present, Brunei has diplomatic relations with China (People's Republic of China/PRC), which were officially established in 1991. Since then, China has been slowly building up its interest in Brunei where in September 1994 some 200 Chinese workers arrived to work in a new cement factory at Muara. These men, consisting of engineers, technicians and workers were on contract from the Tian Jun Cement Design and Development Works of China. They are expected to complete the cement factory at Muara within a year and most of the machinery for the factory was also imported from China. In addition to this, a few Chinese trade delegations too visited Brunei in 1994, with a view to expand their business with Brunei, especially in the oil (q.v.) industry. It is also reported that China is planning to triple its oil imports from Brunei by the end of the decade. China's imports of Brunei's crude oil in 1991 was at B$6.1 million while in 1992, it was valued at B$7.5 million.

CHINESE: It is a predominant group amongst the foreigners resident in Brunei. The majority of them arrived in the 20th century, especially after the introduction of the Residential System (q.v.) in 1906, with large numbers coming not directly from China but Singapore (q.v.) and the Federated Malay States. The main dialect groups are the Hakka, Hokkien and Teochew. At present, the Chinese constitute some 18 per cent or 40,000, of Brunei's total population, which is about 256,500 (1990). The Chinese are not considered citizens and of the total Chinese population in Brunei, only ten per cent are considered permanent residents. This is mainly due to the Nationality Enactment of 1961 (q.v.), which laid down the rules for citizenship in Brunei. The indigenous groups were granted full citizenship, while members of the immigrant community were required to fulfill strict conditions, namely a period of residence of 20 out of the last 25 years and they were expected to pass a Malay-language test. For the Chinese, this virtually restricted them to gaining permanent residence only and not citizenship. In fact, some of the sections of the Malay-language test also included questions on flora and fauna, which even indigenous Bruneians were hard put to answer.

In the 1980s and as independence approached, the position of the Chinese in Brunei remained unclear for most of them were categorised as British Protected Persons. As less than 10 per cent were residents, there was the possiblity that they would lose the status of British Protected Persons. As such, an agreement was reached under the 1979 Treaty of Friendship and Cooperation, by which the Brunei government agreed that such persons who had permanent resident status in Brunei could remain and would be granted International Certificates of Identity for travel purposes, but would still be unable to own land and enjoy the benefits provided for citizens. Obviously, British attempts to have the requirements for citizenship relaxed failed and many Brunei Chinese did consider emigration. Thus far, the position of the Chinese in Brunei remains unclear, though the Chinese are the backbone of Brunei's commercial life. They are said to have kept to themselves, and they even educate their children in Chinese schools. Through their contacts in Brunei and Southeast Asia, they have managed to channel trade and business into their own hands. See also: NATIONALITY ENACTMENT.

COAL: It was considered an important economic activity before the emergence of the oil (q.v.) industry in 1932. The first concession to mine coal in Brunei was granted to William C. Cowie in 1882 by the Sultan of Brunei. In 1888, Cowie sold his concession in Muara Damit (Brooketon) to Rajah Charles Brooke (q.v.) for a sum of $25,000. Brooke bought the concession not due to its great economic potential but for political reasons. He turned Muara Damit into his base of operations with the hope of purchasing the whole of Brunei eventually. In addition to this concession in Muara Damit, Charles Brooke had another concession in Buang Tawar, not far away from the former. Both the mines were, in fact, running at a loss until their closure. The Buang Tawar mine ceased its operations in 1921, while the mine at Muara Damit was closed in November 1924. After its closure, the workers at Muara Damit moved to Miri and Sadong in Sarawak (q.v.). As for its contribution to Brunei's economy before the discovery of oil, coal alone, between 1916 and 1924, contributed some $2,088,560 (Straits dollars) in terms of Brunei's exports. The decline in production of the coal industry after 1924 was mainly due to the sharp decrease in output of the mines in Muara Damit and Buang Tawar and the emergence of the rubber industry. Since then, coal has not been mined for some decades now.

COMMONWEALTH: It is an international cooperative organisation of former British colonies that was established to foster close ties between Britain and her former colonies. Brunei joined this organisation in 1984, upon achieving her independence. For Brunei, membership in this organisation, in addition to her membership in ASEAN (q.v.) and the United Nations (q.v.), was viewed with great importance, especially to enable her to continue her special relationship with Britain as well as other member countries of the Commonwealth. In July 1986, Brunei together with many other Commonwealth countries boycotted the Commonwealth Games held in Edinburgh, because of her opposition to apartheid. A year later, in 1987, Sultan Hassanal accompanied by his second wife, Queen Mariam (q.v.), attended the Commonwealth Heads of Government Meeting (CHOGM), which was held in Vancouver, Canada. Brunei also sent a large delegation to attend the Commonwealth Conference held in Cyprus in October 1994. See also: FOREIGN POLICY.

CONSOLIDATED FUND: The 1959 Constitution (q.v.) provided for the setup of a Consolidated Fund into which all the revenues of the state would be paid. Each year the Sultan-in-Council was obliged to present to the Legislative Council (q.v.) the annual budget. Estimates of expenditures, which were to be met from the Consolidated Fund, were to be tabled in a bill called the Annual Supply Bill. There was also a provision for the tabling of a Supplementary Supply Bill if additional funds were needed. The Legislative Council was empowered to authorise expenditure according to these two enactments. There was total prohibition on the drawing of monies from the Consolidated Fund, except as provided for by law. Even the stipends and allowances of the Sultan and his consort were to be specified in Civil Lists passed as law by the Legislative Council. Provision was made for the appointment of a state auditor who was to have free access to all relevant records for the purpose of auditing the accounts of the state. These reports were to be submitted to the Sultan, who then presented them to the Legislative Council. Since independence in 1984, these procedures have not been complied with. In fact, there is no more Legislative Council. The demarcation between the Sultan's personal purse and the state's revenues seems to have disappeared as well.

CONSTITUTION OF 1959: It is the first modern written Constitution for Brunei, which was proclaimed on 29 September 1959. When Omar Ali Saifuddien III (q.v.) ascended the throne of Brunei in 1950, he had wished to terminate the Residential System (q.v.) so that the international status of Brunei would be enhanced and, more importantly, he himself would assume absolute powers in the state. The protecting power, Britain, was also keen to see more advancement in terms of political reforms. Therefore, as early as 1954, the Sultan announced that Brunei would get a constitution, and in the same year the Sarawak (q.v.) government seconded its legal expert, P. H. Hickling, to Brunei to produce a report for the proposed constitutional reform. After being in Brunei for about three months, Hickling submitted his report, in January 1955, to the Colonial Office. The report traced the development of the state's constitution before and after the 1906 Agreement. Following this, the Colonial Office sent another official to make further investigations with regard to the proposed changes in Brunei. After a series of negotiations, the Sultan promulgated the constitution in 1959. The immediate consequence of the promulgation was that the Residential System, introduced in 1906, came to an end and power in the state passed from the British Resident to the Sultan. Brunei still remained an ordinary British protectorate, but became self-governing. The important provisions of the 1959 Constitution were:

(a). By the Constitution of 1959, Islam of the sect of Shafeite was declared the official religion of the state, the Sultan being appointed as head of the faith. Freedom of profession and practice of other religions was allowed.

(b). Supreme executive authority in the state was vested in the Sultan. The monarch was empowered to appoint administrators and functionaries to help him administer the state, chief among whom in the executive branch were the *Menteri Besar* (Chief Minister) and a State Secretary, who by provision were to be of the Malay race professing the Shafeite faith.

(c). Three bodies representing the hierarchy of government were created. These were the Privy Council (Majlis Mesyuarat Negara) (q.v.), the Executive Council (Majlis Mesyuarat Kerajaan) (q.v.) and the Legislative Council (Majlis Mesyuarat Negeri) (q.v.).

(d). As far as the finances of the state were concerned, all revenues were to be paid into what was called the Consolidated Fund (q.v.).

(e). The public services were to be manned by a Public Service Commission whose members were to be appointed by the Sultan. The Sultan reserved the final power to appoint, transfer, promote or dismiss civil servants.

(f). The Sultan was also given other sweeping powers. These included the prerogative to declare a state of emergency. He was also empowered to revoke or amend any part of the constitution through a proclamation, which had been approved by the Legislative Council.

In a speech made, at Bandar Seri Begawan (q.v.), in conjunction with Brunei's tenth national day celebrations on 23 February 1995, Sultan Hassanal (q.v.) announced that the 1959 Constitution would be reviewed. Although much information was not disclosed, he also stated that a select committee of senior ministers and officials had been assigned the task. See also: CONSOLIDATED FUND; EXECUTIVE COUNCIL; LEGISLATIVE COUNCIL; PRIVY COUNCIL.

CURRENCY: Brunei issued its own currency on 12 June 1967, replacing the Malaya-British Borneo money, which it had previously shared with Singapore (q.v.) and Malaya. The currency consists of notes of $1, $5, $10, $100, $500 and $1,000; and coins of 1 cent, 5 cents, 10 cents, 20 cents and 50 cents. One Brunei dollar equals one hundred Brunei cents. The parity of the Brunei dollar is fixed at 0.290299 grammes of fine gold. Subject to fluctuation, US$1 is worth just over B$2 and £1 is about B$3. To ensure proper control over the circulation of currency and adequate asset levels in local banks, the Brunei government also estabished the Brunei Currency Board in 1967 (q.v.). In addition, also in June 1967, Brunei and Singapore signed an agreement whereby the two currencies of both countries are interchangeable at par and are accepted in either state. See also: BRUNEI CURRENCY BOARD.

CUTCH (or *Acacia Catechu*): It is obtained from the bark of the mangrove tree and is used as a tanning substance. Before the discovery of oil (q.v.), the cutch industry was the main revenue earner for the state, at least until the 1920s. It was, in fact, one of Brunei's pioneer industries which was operating even before the introduction of the Residential System (q.v.) in 1906. A beginning was made in 1901, when the Island Trading Company was given a concession by the Sultan to operate in Bandar Seri Begawan (q.v.). At that time, it employed some 100 Malays and was considered an important source of income by some of the people living in its vicinity. It soon became a major item for trade when between 1916 and 1924 alone, some $2,464,980 (in Straits dollars) worth of cutch was exported, mainly to England and the United States (q.v.). For the then impoverished economy of Brunei, the cutch industry was a major revenue earner obtained from the rental of the company's premises, payment for concessions of mangrove swamps leased out to the company and as export duty. At least until 1924, this industry was amongst the big three (in addition to coal and rubber) major exports of Brunei. However, the emergence of the rubber industry in the late 1920s soon undermined the prime position of the cutch industry, while with the development of the oil industry, cutch lost its significance.

D

DARUL HANA, ISTANA: The royal palace of Brunei, which was built in the mid-1950s, during the reign of Sultan Omar Ali Saifuddien III (q.v.). The royal family moved into this new palace from the old palace, Istana Darussalam, soon after its completion. Soon after the completion of the Nurul Iman (q.v.) in 1984, the Sultan and his family moved from Darul Hana to the new luxurious palace. In 1987, Prince Sufri (q.v.), a younger brother of Sultan Hassanal (q.v.), conducted his wedding at Darul Hana and decided to live in this old palace.

DATO DI GADONG: He was the principal chief who started a rebellion in Tutong (q.v.) in early 1901. He was said to have been aided by the Sarawak (q.v.) government, then under Rajah Charles Brooke (q.v.). The intention of the latter was to create instability in Brunei, which was to be used to annex the said district. However, Charles Brooke's plan failed to materialise for the British government warned the former not to interfere in Brunei's domestic squabbles. In late 1901, although the Brunei government offered amnesty to most of the rebels, Dato Di Gadong was however, excluded. He and another leading rebel, Dato Kalam of Limau Manis, took refuge in Limbang (q.v.), from where both were convicted of buffalo thieving. Also accused of multiple murder, Dato Di Gadong was killed by the order of Sultan Muhammad Jamalul Alam II in 1902 when he illegally crossed into Tutong.

DISTRICT ADVISORY COUNCILS (DACs): The DACs were set up in all four districts of Brunei in September 1954. They had 91 members, of which the Brunei-Muara District (q.v.) had 36, Belait (q.v.) 24, Tutong (q.v.) 19 and Temburong (q.v.) 12. Of the total, 33 (one-third) councillors were chosen by the people whilst the rest were appointed by the government. In addition, there were also ex officio members, namely District Officers and extra-government appointed members. The government appointees were mainly *penghulu* (village headmen) while the extra-government appointees were *menteri* or *wazir* (traditional ministers). To represent the Chinese community, there were also eight Chinese in the four DACs: three each in Brunei-Muara and Belait and one each in Tutong and Temburong. In addition, the Shell (q.v.) Company had three councillors in the Belait Advisory Council. The ratios of the representation were based on the percentage of the population in each district. The four DACs had to choose from among themselves seven councillors to sit on the State Council as observers. It was agreed that the DAC of Brunei-Muara would have three, Belait was given two, while Tutong and Temburong would each get one.

These observers were allowed to address the council on matters pertaining to the welfare of their own districts. See also: ELECTIONS.

DRUG ABUSE: It is currently becoming a serious problem in Brunei. Using data supplied by the Brunei government, the United Nations International Narcotics Control Board revealed in February 1993 that there was a 60 per cent rise in drug abuse since 1990, concentrated especially amongst the youth. In addition, Brunei's Ministry of Home Affairs also revealed that the number of drug-related arrests in 1993 was 681, compared with 595 in 1992. According to the Brunei Narcotics Control Board, the drugs were smuggled from abroad by individuals rather than syndicates. While opening a seminar on drug abuse in June 1993, the Minister of Education stressed the importance of parental control and example in helping to stamp out this problem. He also called for the Muslim youth organisations to play a more important role in educating the youth on matters concerning Islam (q.v.). In connection, a convention of village and community headmen was also organised in 1993 to draw attention to this growing problem. The Sultan (q.v.) too called for more serious efforts in combating this major menace.

E

ECONOMIC DEVELOPMENT BOARD (EDB): It was established during the Third National Development Plan (NDP 3, 1975–1979) (q.v.), under the supervision of the Ministry of Finance. Modelled after Singapore's (q.v.) Development Board, its primary concern is to elaborate and administer programmes to encourage private local and foreign investments in Brunei. As such, it is also empowered to provide tax relief for certain industries granted special status. It can also enter into joint venture agreements and is allowed to make loans available to Brunei citizens as a measure of encouraging local business expansion. The rate of interest is currently at 6 per cent, with loans payable over 10 or 12 years. Since its formation in the 1970s till 1989, the EDB had made loans totalling B$70 million to small- and medium-sized businesses. The EDB is also allowed to purchase, hold and lease land for industrial purposes. Apart from this, the board also monitors the insurance industry in the state as well as the activities of the recently created Tourism Promotion Committee. See also: THIRD NATIONAL DEVELOPMENT PLAN (NDP 3, 1975–1979).

ECONOMIC PLANNING UNIT (EPU): It was established in 1973 within the Ministry of Finance with the main aim to compile, coordinate and monitor development in the state. It has a statutory right to information from businesses established in Brunei and its statistical section compiles a range of information on business conditions in the state. As government revenues began to increase more than fivefold between 1973 and 1975, this necessitated the introduction of a new fiscal and economic context for development planning. Within this context, the EPU was formed and, till the present, has achieved significant success in coordinating and promoting planned development in Brunei. See also: ECONOMIC DEVELOPMENT BOARD (EDB); NATIONAL DEVELOPMENT PLANS (NDPs); THIRD NATIONAL DEVELOPMENT PLAN (NDP 3, 1975–1979).

EDUCATION: Being an Islamic state, Brunei had its own traditional system of religious education known as the *sekolah pondok* (village schools) where Muslim children were sent to acquire knowledge of Islam, in addition to learning some art or handicraft. Formal secular education was, however, introduced to Brunei only in the 20th century with the establishment of the British Residential System (q.v.). The Residential System encouraged the establishment of Malay vernacular schools, with the first being established in 1914 in Bandar Seri Begawan (q.v.). This was soon followed by the establishment of the first Chinese (q.v.) vernacular school in 1916, also in Bandar Seri Begawan, while English education was introduced only in 1931, when the British Malayan Petroleum Company (BMPC) (q.v.) set up a school in Kuala Belait. Following this, Brunei witnessed the growth of a vernacular system of education and until World War II there was not a single secondary school in Brunei.

The growth of Malay primary education was the effort of the government, while Chinese schools were established by Chinese communities, and English education was mainly the effort of the Christian missionaries (q.v.), although the latter categories did receive forms of government funding. Only after the war did the Brunei authorities work toward the establishment of secondary education by setting up a few government-sponsored secondary schools. By 1959, there were ten secondary schools in Brunei, only five of which were government sponsored while the other five were run solely by the Roman Catholic mission. In 1959, through a decision made by the State Council, all funding to schools sponsored by the Christian missionaries ceased as it was considered un-Islamic by the state to fund these schools.

At present, the government gives free education to all Brunei citizens from kindergarten upward, including at universities overseas. It also takes care of the schooling of its employees children who attend non-government schools. In 1988, there were 291 government educational institutions comprising one university, one Institute of Education, one Institute of Technology, two teacher-training colleges, five vocational/technical schools, 112 preschool classes, 153 primary schools and 18 secondary schools in Brunei. For the same year, there were some 44,000 students attending these institutions, which use Malay, English or Arabic as their mediums of instruction. In addition to government-sponsored education, there are also 69 nongovernment schools, including one artisans training school run by Brunei Shell and the rest being mission, Chinese or private schools. The mediums of instruction in these nongovernment institutions is either English or Chinese. In 1988, an estimated 18,000 students were attending such institutions. See also: MISSIONARIES, CHRISTIAN; UNIVERSITI BRUNEI DARUSSALAM (UBD).

ELECTIONS: Brunei's first elections, scheduled for August 1962, were to be held on a two-tier system. In the first stage, direct elections were to be held for 55 seats of the four District Councils. In the second stage, the elected district councillors would chose 16 from amongst themselves to sit in the 33 member Legislative Council. When the nomination date for the election closed, the Parti Rakyat Brunei (PRB) (q.v.) won 32 seats uncontested. The contest for the 23 remaining seats saw the PRB contesting all 23, the Brunei National Organisation (BNO) (q.v.) in six areas, namely in the Tutong District (q.v.), the Brunei United Party (BUP) (q.v.) contesting in one area with independent candidates contesting in 18 areas. The PRB won all but the Labu seat in the Temburong District (q.v.), which was won by Metudin bin Ali Bakar who ran on an independent ticket but later joined the PRB. The 23 contested seats witnessed a two-cornered fight between the PRB and candidates from either the BNO, BUP or independents. Only in five areas was there a three-cornered fight between the PRB, BNO and independents, and this was in Kupang-Birau, Tanjung Maya, Ukong and Rambai (all in the Tutong District) as well as Bukit Sawat (Belait District) (q.v.). One interesting feature of this election was the participation of one woman candidate, Dayang Nahriah binti Md. Daud, who contested the Pemancha-Sultan Lama seat in the Brunei-Muara District (q.v.) on an independent ticket but lost to Sulaiman bin Puteh from the PRB. In addition, there was also only one Chinese independent candidate, Lim Leong Kui, who ran for the Bukit Sawat seat, but lost to Arshad bin Abu Bakar from the PRB, in a three-cornered fight. Thus effectively, the PRB won all the 55 District Council seats. This would have meant that all the 16 members of the Legislative Council would be from the PRB. The government feared that if the Legislative Council was convened, the PRB would make a bid for political power. This reluctance of the government precipitated the outbreak of the PRB-led revolt of December 1962. Due to the outbreak of the PRB-led rebellion in 1962, the council was suspended. In March 1965, direct elections to the Legislative Council (q.v.) were held where some 36 candidates, mostly independents, contested for ten seats. Unlike the elections of August 1962, which saw active involvement of three political parties, namely the PRB, BNO and BUP, these elections in 1965 did not witness much activity from political parties. Some candidates did contest under the banner of the BNO, mainly in the Tutong District, while the BUP did not field any candidate. Three of the independents who won were, in fact, former members of the PRB. They were Muhammad Yusof Bin Pengiran Muda Haji Limbang, Abdul Wahab bin Orang Kaya Setia Negara Safar and Zainal Abidin bin Puteh. The 1965 elections also saw a decrease in voter turnout when only 80 per cent of the 19,144 registered voters went to the polls. On the other hand, the 1962 elections witnessed some 89 per cent of the total electorate, which was 17,316, going to the polls. Since 1965, no direct election has been held in Brunei.

EMERGENCY COUNCIL: Also known as the Majlis Darurat, it was formed by Sultan Omar Ali Saifuddien III (q.v.) on 20 December 1962, after the outbreak of the Parti Rakyat Brunei (PRB) (q.v.) revolt and the declaration of emergency on 12 December. This council comprised 14 members, namely four ex officio members, including the British High Commissioner, Sir Dennis Charles White, as well as ten members appointed by the latter himself. Most of its 14 members were, in fact, earlier members of the Majlis Mesyuarat Negeri (Legislative Council) with Sultan Omar Ali Saifuddien III as the chairperson of this council. It temporarily replaced the Majlis Mesyuarat Negeri and took upon itself the task of administration, especially in normalising the situation in Brunei.

EMERGENCY EXECUTIVE COMMITTEE: Known as the Jawatankuasa Kerja Darurat (JKD), it temporarily replaced the Majlis Mesyuarat Kerajaan (Executive Council) on 20 December 1962, after the Emergency Council (Majlis Darurat) (q.v.) had been established. This committee was formed as a result of the 1962 Parti Rakyat Brunei (PRB) (q.v.) led revolt and was empowered to assist in the administration of the country, which was interrupted by the rebellion. In doing so, an amount of $1 million was allocated for the JKD to provide housing and other facilities for the British army, which was brought in to suppress the rebellion. The JKD was chaired by Dato' Marsal bin Maun (q.v.), the *Menteri Besar* (Chief Minister). Other members were Sir Dennis Charles White, the British High Commissioner,

Cikgu Othman Bidin, Newn Ah Foot, Pengiran Abu Bakar bin Pengiran Omar Ali and W. I. Glass.

ENVIRONMENT POLICY: An attempt by the Brunei government to seriously address environmental issues was highlighted by several events in 1991. One such measure was the organising of a two-day seminar on "Current Practices on Environment in Brunei" in March 1991. In his opening speech at the seminar, the Minister of Development, Pengiran Dato Seri Paduka Dr. Haji Ismail bin Pengiran Haji Damit, stressed that an assessment on the impact on environment must be made in any development project so as to determine the viability of these projects as well as minimize any adverse effect to the environment. In fact, prior to this, the Ministry of Industry and Primary Resources through the Forestry Department implemented a policy to control logging and rehabilitate forests where for a start, the production of timber in the state was reduced by 50 per cent, or 100 thousand cubic metres from the beginning of 1990. This also included its efforts to promote ecotourism in Brunei.

Whilst announcing plans for a greener Brunei in 1991, the Sultan also called for a comprehensive forest conservation policy whereby long-term efforts included reafforestation projects involving 30,000 hectres and a plan to develop a national park in Temburong (q.v.). Apart from this, a Brunei Rainforest Field Centre was established at Sungai Belalang in the Temburong District, with the intention of becoming a centre of teaching, training and research. As of October 1991, the centre had undertaken nine long-term and 33 short-term projects.

On World Forestry Day in November 1992, Brunei launched a special forestry programme to plant 8,000 trees at Sungai Liang in the Belait District (q.v.). This was partly due to the damage done to forests as a result of the outbreak of fires in 1992, the worst ever in Brunei. In the first quarter of 1992 alone, more than 2,500 hectres of forests (including more than 400 houses) were destroyed by fires, the worst being in the Belait District. As most of Brunei's oil and gas (q.v.) extraction is carried out at sea, the government also began addressing the possibility of oil spills at sea in 1992. As such, in September 1992 the Brunei government also established a special body to deal with the matter. Although earlier National Development Plans (NDPs) (q.v.) have been more concerned with improving the infrastructure of the country, the Sixth National Development Plan (NDP 6, 1991–1995) (q.v.) however witnessed more serious efforts concerning the environment. Of the nine major overall objectives of this plan, one concerned the environment. Further, on 7 December 1995, Brunei and Malaysia (q.v.) signed a Memorandum of Understanding

(MoU) on Standard Operating Procedure (SOP) for joint measures in combatting oil spills in the South China Sea, including the Brunei Bay. The MoU signed in Kuala Lumpur, was between Malaysia's (q.v.) Director General of Environment, Tan Meng Leng and Brunei's Director of Marine, Othman Momin.

EXECUTIVE COUNCIL (MAJLIS MESYUARAT KERAJAAN): This body was created by the Constitution of 1959 (q.v.) to advise the Sultan in governing the state. It replaced the earlier State Council. In 1984, after Brunei achieved independence, the body was renamed Council of Ministers (Majlis Mesyuarat Menteri-Menteri).

Membership: By the provisions of the 1959 Constitution, the Executive Council was to consist of 14 members, nine of them ex officio and seven unofficial. The ex officio members included the two traditional ministers (*wazir*), the *Pengiran Bendahara* and the *Pengiran Pemanca*, and four senior officials who were the *Menteri Besar* (Chief Minister), the State Secretary, the Attorney General and the State Financial Officer. In addition, the Religious Adviser and the British High Commissioner were the other two members. Of the seven unofficial members, six were to be elected members from the Legislative Council (q.v.) and one nominated. With the exception of the ex officio members, all others held their office at the Sultan's pleasure. Though the normal run of the period of their office was three years, an unofficial member could be asked to vacate his seat anytime if the Sultan felt that such a person was incapable of discharging his duties or if he was absent from the state for a period of more than one month without prior permission from the Sultan. Since independence in 1984, the composition has changed somewhat as indicated by the new name, Council of Ministers.

Functions: The present Council of Ministers exists in a consultative capacity to the Sultan. The Sultan as Chief Executive, and in the exercise of his powers and duties in governing the state, consults with the Council of Ministers. The Sultan, however, is not required to consult the council on all matters and these may include:

(a) matters where the state may sustain material prejudice by such consultations;
(b) matters which are too unimportant for advice; and
(c) cases of exigency.

The Sultan, however, is required to inform the Council of Ministers of the measures taken and the justification for such a course. The Sultan may also act in opposition to the advice of the Council of

Ministers if he deems it necessary, provided he gives his reasons in writing.

F

FIFTH NATIONAL DEVELOPMENT PLAN (NPD 5, 1986–1990): It was the first full plan since independence and had broader objectives than the earlier plans (q.v.). Once again, economic diversification policies dominated this plan in addition to the upgrading of human resources as well as creating a generation of Bruneian entrepreneurs. The total budget for this plan was B$2,610,000, from which 10 per cent was allocated to industrial development, with the aim to increase non-oil based investment by around 10 per cent per year. To facilitate such development, a range of institutions and programmes were created, such as the Development Bank, a National Training Scheme, the expansion of the Institute of Technology and a National Pension Scheme. Some of the outcomes of NDP 5 were: a rise in private sector employment from 29,973 in 1986 to 53,613 in 1990, which suggests some success in reducing dependence on government employment; a rise in GDP from B$22,963 in 1986 to B$29,404 in 1990; the creation of two textile factories; the non-oil sector GDP fell from 66.4 per cent to 53.0 per cent from 1986–1990; and the National Pension Scheme as well as the Development Bank did not materialise. See also: FIRST FIVE-YEAR DEVELOPMENT PLAN (NDP 1, 1953–1958); FOURTH NATIONAL DEVELOPMENT PLAN (NDP 4, 1980–1984); NATIONAL DEVELOPMENT PLANS (NDPs); SECOND FIVE-YEAR DEVELOPMENT PLAN (NDP 2, 1962–1966); SIXTH NATIONAL DEVELOPMENT PLAN (NDP 6, 1991–1995); THIRD NATIONAL DEVELOPMENT PLAN (NDP 3, 1975–1979).

FIRST FIVE-YEAR DEVELOPMENT PLAN (NDP 1, 1953–1958): The focus of this first plan was twofold: infrastructural development and the expansion of social services. A total of B$100 million was allocated, and by the end of 1958 some 75 per cent had been spent. This plan was drawn up under the close scrutiny of the Colonial Office and 80 per cent of the total budget was channeled for infrastructure development, namely for the construction of roads (especially the Brunei Town-Seria link road) and public utilities. In addition, there were also plans for the resettlement of Kampong Ayer's (q.v.) inhabitants; irrigation projects; development of a nursery for rubber seedlings; improving the wharves at Kuala Belait (q.v.); the construction of road bridges over the Tutong (q.v.) and Telamba rivers; the institution of a pensions and disability allowance; and the construction of a new hospital as well as some 30 new schools. Under this plan, about 20 per cent of the development budget was allocated to health and educational provisions. As the plan was fairly vague with no clear proposals to monitor its progress, it was therefore difficult to evaluate its achievements. See also: FIFTH NATIONAL DEVELOP-MENT PLAN (NDP 5, 1986–1990); FOURTH NATIONAL DE-VELOPMENT PLAN (NDP 4, 1980–1984); NATIONAL DEVEL-OPMENT PLANS (NDPs); SECOND FIVE-YEAR DEVELOPMENT PLAN (NDP 2, 1962–1966); SIXTH NATIONAL DEVELOPMENT PLAN (NDP 6, 1991–1995); THIRD NATIONAL DEVELOPMENT PLAN (NDP 3, 1975–1979).

FOREIGN POLICY: Since achieving its independence in 1984, the thrust of Brunei's foreign policy has been toward establishing friendly relations with all the countries around the world so as to ensure her security and well-being. In doing so, the major focus of her foreign policy makers, on achieving independence, was to establish cordial relations with countries in the region especially through its membership in ASEAN (q.v.). In addition, through her membership in the United Nations (UN) (q.v.), Commonwealth (q.v.) and the Organization of Islamic Countries (OIC) (q.v.) as well as bilateral relations, Brunei has successfully increased her circle of friends around the world. Until 1992, Brunei had established 20 permanent missions abroad in addition to 16 nonresident ambassadors accredited. The process of foreign policy making in Brunei is the responsibility of the Ministry of Foreign Affairs with the Sultan having an important say as most decisions are only implemented after consultations with the Sultan. The Ministry of Foreign Affairs is headed by the ruling Sultan's brother, Pengiran Muda Mohamed Bolkiah (q.v.). See also: ASEAN; CHINA; COMMONWEALTH; INDONESIA; JAPAN; MALAYSIA; MOHAMED BOLKIAH, PENGIRAN MUDA; ORGANIZATION OF ISLAMIC COUNTRIES (OIC); PHILIPPINES; SINGAPORE; UNITED NATIONS (UN); UNITED STATES OF AMERICA (U.S.).

FOURTH NATIONAL DEVELOPMENT PLAN (NDP 4, 1980–1984): From the very start, the formulation of NDP 4 had taken into account both the strengths and weaknesses of earlier plans (q.v.) as well as a number of changes in the state. Therefore, NDP 4 had a range of fiscal as well as development policies, where two of the major fiscal policies were to secure an average annual growth rate of at least 6 per cent in GDP and an increase in per capita income levels of at least 4 per cent per year. A number of objectives outlined by NDP 4 were to: maintain a high level of employment; diversify through the development of agriculture and non-oil-based manufacturing industry; keep inflation at manageable levels; reduce income disparities; establish a system of orderly rural and urban planning; expand education at all levels; and construct a number of rural clinics. The total budget allocated for NDP 4 was at B$1,749,814, a total that had tripled when compared with NDP 3 (q.v.), but once again the allocation for industry, agriculture, forestry and fisheries declined. At the same time, allocations for education (q.v.), health and social services remained unchanged whilst public construction and security received large allocations, totaling more than 31 per cent of the total budget. Overall, NDP 4 was not successful in terms of GDP changes as the GDP declined more than 4 per cent in this period, mainly due to a decline in oil prices and production. On the other hand, employment grew by about 4.5 per cent, a figure well ahead of the planned estimates of around 3.5 per cent. See also: FIFTH NATIONAL DEVELOPMENT PLAN (NDP 5, 1986–1990); FIRST FIVE-YEAR DEVELOPMENT PLAN (NDP 1, 1953–1958); NATIONAL DEVELOPMENT PLANS (NDPs); SECOND FIVE-YEAR DEVELOPMENT PLAN (NDP 2, 1962–1966); SIXTH NATIONAL DEVELOPMENT PLAN (NDP 6, 1991–1995); THIRD NATIONAL DEVELOPMENT PLAN (NDP 3, 1975–1979); TABLE 6.

G

GURKHAS: It is the name of an ethnic group living in Nepal. During the colonial era, especially in the 19th century, the Gurkhas were recruited into the British army and later came to form the backbone of British forces in the latter's empire. They are well known for their bravery and fighting spirit. Gurkha regiments served in all parts of the British empire. When the 1962 rebellion (q.v.) broke out in Brunei, in addition to the Queen's Highlanders, the Gurkhas too played an important role in suppressing the uprising. Since then, one Gurkha battalion has always been stationed in Brunei, especially to protect the oil fields in Seria (q.v.). In 1979, the Brunei government recruited an additional 1,000 retired Gurkha soldiers to perform guard duties at important installations and the royal palaces. In 1983, as independence approached, there was some disagreement between the Brunei and the British governments over the status of the British Army Gurkhas, especially those stationed in Seria. Although all the related expenses were the responsibility of the Brunei government (it costs Brunei some B$6 million a year), the British indicated that they would withdraw the battalion upon Brunei achieving its independence whilst the Sultan requested their retention. The Sultan also insisted that the battalion be placed under his command, which the British could not agree to. The Sultan later withdrew that demand. However, after independence Brunei expanded its own Gurkha battalion (now called the Gurkha Reserve Unit/GRU), which currently has some 2,300 men, organised into two battalions and is under the command of the Sultan. This is in addition to the British Army Gurkha battalion, which is still under British command. There is also talk of forming a third Gurkha Reserve Unit, one that can be undertaken only after the British withdraw their Gurkha battalion from Brunei. In addition, there is also a possibility of an increase in the number of Gurkhas in Brunei when Hong Kong reverts back to China (q.v.) in 1997. This would mean an additional 4,000 Gurkhas serving Brunei after 1997. The possibility of their absorption by Brunei was raised by King Birendira of Nepal, when he visited Brunei in late 1985. See also: HINDU WELFARE BOARD; INDIANS; ROYAL BRUNEI ARMED FORCES (RBAF).

H

HASBULLAH BIN HAJI MOHAMMED DAUD, HAJI: He was educated at the Victoria Institution, Kuala Lumpur, and had worked under various British Residents after World War I. He also joined the Government Hospital in Bandar Seri Begawan (q.v.), but then resigned. He had travelled to various parts of Malaya, Singapore (q.v.) and Sarawak (q.v.). In the 1930s and 1940s, Hasbullah was also a prominent figure of the Sahabat Pena (q.v.) of Brunei. In December 1961, he formed and led the Brunei United Party (BUP) (q.v.). In the August 1962 District Councils elections (q.v.), Hasbullah contested for the Sumbiling seat in the Brunei-Muara District (q.v.) on the BUP ticket. However, he lost miserably to Zaini Haji Ahmad (q.v.) from the Parti Rakyat Brunei (PRB) (q.v.), when he managed to obtain only 25 votes. See also: BRUNEI UNITED PARTY (BUP).

HASSANAL BOLKIAH MU'IZZADDIN WADDAULAH IBNI AL-MARHUM SULTAN HAJI OMAR ALI SAIFUDDIEN KHAIRI WADDIEN, SULTAN (1946–): Born on 15 July 1946, he is the eldest of Sultan Omar Ali Saifuddien's (q.v.) four sons and six daughters. He attended the Sultan Muhammad Jamalul Alam Malay Primary School in Bandar Seri Begawan (q.v.) from 1955 to 1959, and was later sent to the Jalan Gurney School in Kuala Lumpur. He entered the Victoria Institution, Kuala Lumpur, in 1961, and was proclaimed Crown Prince at the age of 15, in a ceremony held in Brunei on 14 August 1961. In 1963, when tensions developed between Malaysia (q.v.) and Brunei over Brunei's refusal to join Malaysia, he was withdrawn from the Victoria Institution and entered Form IV at the Sultan Omar Ali Saifuddien College in Brunei Town. Following this, he attended the Royal Military College at Sandhurst. In July 1965, he married his cousin, Pengiran Anak Saleha (q.v.), eldest daughter of Pengiran Pemancha Haji Muhammad Alam, and later in 1981, secretly married Pengiran Isteri Hajjah Mariam binti Haji Abdul Aziz (q.v.). On 5 October 1967, he was installed as the 29th Sultan of Brunei when his father abdicated the throne. He is the present Head of State as well as Head of Government, being Brunei's first Prime Minister since independence on 1 January 1984. He is also Minister of Defence and in February 1997 took up the finance portfolio. Considered one of the richest men in the world today, his investments span from Asia to Europe. He has four sons and six daughters. See also: MARIAM BINTI HAJI ABDUL AZIZ, PENGIRAN ISTERI HAJJAH (QUEEN MARIAM); SALEHA BINTI AL-MARHUM PENGIRAN PEMANCHA PENGIRAN ANAK HAJI MUHAMMAD ALAM, PENGIRAN ISTERI HAJJAH ANAK (QUEEN SALEHA).

HASSIM, PENGIRAN RAJA MUDA: He was the *Bendahara* of Brunei (Chief Minister), but his appointment was resented by Pengiran Usop, the father-in-law of Sultan Omar Ali Saifuddin II's (q.v.) son, Pengiran Hashim. Due to the rise of factional politics at the palace, the former was sent away in 1835 to the Sarawak (q.v.) River to crush a rebellion led by the Malay aristocracy there as well as Land Dayaks. In fact, the decision by the Sultan to send Raja Muda Hassim away from the capital was basically taken because the Sultan (and Raja Muda Hassim too) knew that Hassim would never return, for the latter would be unable to suppress the uprising, which had been going on for some time. However, with the help of James Brooke (q.v.), Raja Muda Hassim succeeded in suppressing the rebellion, and upon completing his mission, returned to the capital in Brunei in 1844 only to find himself unwelcome. His return to Brunei aggravated factionalism at the capital that had existed even prior to his departure to Sarawak. As a result, in 1846 Hassim and his entire family were massacred by the Pengiran Usop's faction, under the Sultan's orders.

HINDU WELFARE BOARD, BRUNEI: Initially known as the Hindu Cremation Board, it was believed to have been formed in 1962. It was not until 1970, however, that this organisation was registered and renamed as the Hindu Welfare Board. Its basic purpose is to arrange funerals of Hindus in Brunei where it maintains a burial ground and crematorium at Seria (q.v.). This board admits members irrespective of their national identity where Brunei citizens and Indians (q.v.) from Malaysia (q.v.), Sri Lanka, Singapore (q.v.) and India are free to participate in this organisation. However, the board has been unable to obtain land to build a temple but has been allowed to use the Kali temple at the Gurkha (q.v.) cantonment in Seria (q.v.) for religious purposes. Currently, the board estimates that there are around 250 Hindus living in Brunei. See also: INDIAN ASSOCIATIONS; INDIANS.

I

INDIAN ASSOCIATIONS: The earliest attempt to organise Indians (q.v.) living in Brunei was made in the pre-World War II years when the Indian Association at Kuala Belait-Seria (q.v.) was formed. Some of its founding members were V. K. A. Pillai (a senior engineer with the Public Works Department), N. Subramaniam and M. Chidambaran. With V. K. A. Pillai as its first president, it was established to promote social, cultural and sports activities within the community. However, the association's premises were destroyed in an aerial bombing of Seria during World War II. After the war, an attempt was made to revive the association such that by 1951 a new building was created in Seria. Thus far, this association, though centered in Kuala Belait-Seria, has remained an active association among Brunei Indians. However, another attempt to organise Indians in Brunei was made in Bandar Seri Begawan (q.v.) in 1938, which was attended by Indians living in Brunei Town, Muara and Tutong (q.v.). The first meeting held at Muthian's shop in Brunei Town resulted in the election of a committee with A. Muthian as President, Nadaraja Ayer as Vice President as well as Secretary and A. M. Mohammed Ali Maricar (an Indian muslim) as Treasurer. In another meeting held in 1942, attended by some 30 members, Thandapani was elected President, Nadaraja Ayer retained as Vice President, V. A. George (an Indian Christian) as Secretary and Mohammed Ali Maricar was retained as Treasurer. In 1954, the Indian Association at Bandar Seri Begawan (q.v.) was reconstituted with about 20 members and a constitution. Following this, in 1964, the association was granted a piece of burial ground by the government to be used as an Indian cemetery and by 1971 the association was renamed Bandar Seri Begawan Indian Association. See also: HINDU WELFARE BOARD; INDIANS.

INDIAN CHAMBER OF COMMERCE, BRUNEI: Formed in April 1972 by a Brunei Indian lawyer, Bikram Jit, along with 25 other Indian businessmen, its main aim was to cater to all Indians (q.v.) living in the state of Brunei, unlike the Indian Association Kuala Belait-Seria and the Indian Association Brunei Town, which was established to cater to the needs of local Indians in the two geographical areas only. It makes representations whenever the need arises and participates in state-level trade missions. However, all its 45 members in 1984 were from Bandar Seri Begawan (q.v.), and currently its membership is predominantly Tamil Muslim, an indication of the widespread presence of the latter in the business sector of Brunei, namely Bandar Seri Begawan. See also: INDIAN ASSOCIATIONS; INDIANS.

INDIANS: The term Indian in 20th century Brunei has generally been used to describe all persons who originated from contemporary India, Pakistan, Bangladesh, Sri Lanka (Ceylon) and Nepal. The Indians are the second largest migrant community residing in Brunei. From a total of less than 66 persons in 1911, there were some 5,919 Indians living in Brunei in 1981. The Indians began to come into Brunei after 1906, when the Residential System (q.v.) was introduced and especially with the development of the rubber (q.v.) industry in the 1920s. In fact, some of the European estates operating in Brunei approached the government in 1920 with a view to import South Indian labour to Brunei. This was soon followed with the implementation of the Indian Immigration Enactment in 1924, with provisions to allow the entry of South Indian labour into Brunei from the Federated Malay States and Singapore (q.v.). However, the scheme fell short of succeeding as the industry was hit by the Great Depression of the late 1920s. After World War II, a small number of Indians continued to flow into Brunei either as security forces or teachers. Another major factor that encouraged the entry of Indians into Brunei was the influx of Nepalese into deluxe security forces since 1962. At present, the majority of the Indians in Brunei live in the Belait District (q.v.) and in Bandar Seri Begawan (q.v.). Like the Chinese (q.v.), the Indians are also treated as second-class citizens for most of them are categorised as permanent residents and only a very small number are citizens. Unlike the Chinese, who are perceived as a threat mainly due to their achievement in business in Brunei and above all the presence of a successful Chinese business community in the region, the Indians on the other hand are viewed with less suspicion. See also: HINDU WELFARE BOARD, BRUNEI; INDIAN ASSOCIATIONS; INDIAN CHAMBER OF COMMERCE, BRUNEI; NATIONALITY ENACTMENT.

INDONESIA: Brunei's relations with Indonesia go back a very long way to the 14th century, when Brunei was listed as amongst the vassal states of the Majapahit empire. In modern times, Indonesian-Brunei ties have not been cordial due to the confrontation of the mid-1960s and the extending of asylum to Parti Rakyat Brunei's (PRB) (q.v.) leader A. M. Azahari (q.v.) by Jakarta. This was during the presidency of Suharno when he announced his plans to build a greater Malay region through his "Melayu Raya" concept, which would eventually incorporate all the other Malay states then not under Indonesia. This meant the incorporation of Malaysia (q.v.) as well as Brunei. In addition, his strong support for the Tentera Nasional Kalimantan Utara (TNKU) (q.v.) and PRB's leaders also irritated Brunei. Until lately, Brunei has always viewed Indonesia with great suspicion. However, now relations between both parties have greatly improved, particularly with Brunei joining ASEAN (q.v.) in 1984. The ice in Indonesia-Brunei relations was broken when in 1980, President Suharto proposed that Brunei be made ASEAN's sixth member. Further, on a visit to Jakarta in September 1987, Sultan Hassanal Bolkiah (q.v.) extended to Indonesia a soft loan of US$100 million payble in 25 years. In mid-1995, the Brunei government entered into a joint venture with Butra Djajanti Cement Sendirian Berhad of Indonesia to set up a cement factory in Brunei. The project, with a capital of B$75 million, is said to have put Indonesia as the leading foreign investor in Brunei. Apart from this, Brunei also has some large investments in Indonesia. See also: ASEAN.

ISLAM, IN BRUNEI: It is believed that Islam was first introduced to Brunei during the reign of Alak Betatar (q.v.) (r.1363–1402), who is believed to be the first Sultan of Brunei to convert to Islam, using the name Sultan Muhammad. A recent discovery noted that Islam could have been introduced to Brunei somewhere around c.1370. This evidence is also supported by a Chinese record that states that the ruler of Brunei in 1370 was named "Mo-ha-mo-sha." Since its introduction, Islam spread from Brunei to southern parts of the Philippines (q.v.) and Kalimantan. In the 16th century, Muslim missionaries from Brunei took up the task of introducing this religion to Sulawesi, Tidore and Ternate in Indonesia (q.v.) as well as to Palawan, Sulu and Tawi-Tawi in the Philippines. During the reign of Sultan Saiful Rijal (r.1535–1581), he himself spread Islam from Brunei to other parts of the region, especially those in close proximity to Brunei. This venture brought Brunei into an open conflict with the Spaniards (q.v.) in the Philippines when in 1574, the former attempted an attack on the Spaniards. In return, on 14 April 1578, the Spaniards attacked Brunei in a war that lasted two years. Since its introduction to Brunei, Islam has played an important role in theological and political philosophy of the state. In fact, the Brunei government recently introduced the *Melayu Islam Beraja* (q.v.) (Malay, Islamic, Monarchy) concept

as the basis of the state's ideology. See also: MELAYU ISLAM
BERAJA/MIB.

J

JAPAN: The entry of Japanese business interests into Brunei began in
the 1960s, when firms from Japan were granted big construction con-
tracts in Brunei. Japan is also currently Brunei's largest trading partner as most of Brunei's oil and natural gas supplies (q.v.), estimated
at some 5 million tons of liquefied natural gas (LNG) annually, are
shipped to Japan. In fact, Japanese companies play an important role
in the development of the hydrocarbon industry in Brunei as well as
the banking sector.

In addition, between 1984 and 1986 most of Brunei's imports were
from Japan, when the latter was only second to Singapore (q.v.) in
terms of Brunei's imports. Before 1932, in addition to some western
companies prospecting for oil in Brunei, there was also one Japanese
company, Kuhara. In 1969, when Brunei formed Brunei Liquefied
Natural Gas (BLNG) to cater to the LNG trade with Japan, a joint
venture company was established between the Brunei government,
Brunei Shell Petroleum (q.v.) and Mitsubishi Corporation where
Shell and Mitsubishi each had 45 per cent of the shares. Further, the
construction of the Lumut LNG plant (at present the largest in the
world) in 1973 once again saw involvement of Japanese companies,
namely the Mitsubishi Corporation and Nipon LNG, as well as some
companies from the west.

In addition, of the four foreign consultant companies appointed to
advise the Brunei Investment Agency (BIA) (q.v.), two of them are
Japanese securities firms, the Daiwa and Nomura Securities. In 1985,
after the restructuring of Brunei's largest local bank, the Island Development Bank (IDB), Japan's Dai Ichi Kangyo Bank managed to secure a 20 per cent stake in that bank. Further, in April 1993 Brunei
signed a new 20-year gas contract with Japan whereby under the
terms of the contract, BSP will supply an average of 5.54 million
tonnes of LNG per annum over a 20 year period to three Japanese
power companies: Tokyo Electric Power, Tokyo Gas and Osaka Gas.

Prior to this, in January 1993, Japanese Prime Minister Miyazawa
visited Brunei, highlighting the increased economic links between
both countries as well as stressing Japan's keen interest in participating more actively in Brunei's economy. The visit was also, in part,
to finalise the details of the new LNG contract mentioned above. In
anticipation, it can be said Brunei-Japan relations will continue to
grow for the relationship is reciprocal. Whilst Japan needs Brunei's

petroleum and gas supplies, Brunei, on the other hand, is in dire need of Japanese technology and investments for its economic diversification policy to succeed. See also: JAPANESE OCCUPATION.

JAPANESE OCCUPATION: The Japanese invasion of Brunei began in the early morning of 16 December 1941, when some 10,000 men of the Japanese Kawaguchi Detachment landed at Kuala Belait (q.v.) and thereafter occupied the oil fields at Seria (q.v.). Six days later, on 22 December 1941, Japanese forces occupied Brunei Town (q.v.) and all the British government officials there were interned at the Batu Lintang camp in Kuching, Sarawak (q.v.). In fact, the Japanese forces were met with little resistance from the British forces because of the small number of British forces stationed in Brunei at the time of the invasion. The Japanese reorganised their conquests in Borneo into five prefectures and the Brunei prefecture also included Baram (q.v.), Labuan (q.v.), Lawas and Limbang (q.v.).

During this period of occupation by the Japanese, people living around Kuala Belait were driven to work in the oil fields at Seria, and throughout their occupation of Brunei for a period of three and a half years, the Japanese managed to extract some 1,594,000 tons of oil (q.v.). In addition, the Japanese also recruited some educated Malays to assist in the administration of the state and some of them were even sent abroad to undergo training in various fields. A. M. Azahari, for example, was sent to study veterinary science in Bogor, Indonesia (q.v.), while Muhammad Yusof Bin Pengiran Muda Haji Limbang (q.v.) was sent to Hiroshima University. Three others, Jamil Umar, H. B. Hidup and Jassin Affandy (q.v.) were sent for military training in Kuching, Miri and Labuan. It can be said that to a certain extent, the three and a half years of Japanese occupation did contribute to the emergence of nationalism in Brunei after the war. However, by 1944, the Allied Forces began daily air raids over Brunei, resulting in the destruction of major towns such as Brunei Town and Kuala Belait. Kampong Ayer (q.v.), however, escaped these daily bombing raids. On 10 June 1945, Allied forces (mainly Australians) landed at Muara and proceeded to Brunei Town while in the meantime, Japanese forces were busy destroying installations and setting fires to the oil fields at Seria. Soon after, the Japanese occupation of Brunei was ended when the remaining Japanese forces surrendered unconditionally. See also: JAPAN.

JASRA JACKSON: It was formed in 1982 to lessen dependence on Brunei Shell Petroleum (BSP) (q.v.) in matters relating to the exploration and drilling of oil in Brunei. It was a joint venture where Jackson Exploration Incorporated of Dallas held a 75 per cent stake, while the remaining 25 per cent was held by the royal family under a company named Jasra. It started off by obtaining an offshore concession area of about 1,220 square miles where it conducted exploratory drilling but was unsuccessful. Jasra Jackson eventually became fully owned by the royal family when the American partner, Jackson Exploration, withdrew from the joint venture. In 1986, Jasra Jackson joined with another European partner in France's state-owned oil company, ELF-Aquitaine which took a 72.5 per cent interest in the new joint venture. As such, the company came to be known as Jasra-ELF and began to prospect for oil in Jasra Jackson's concession area. Under this new arrangement, ELF-Aquitaine was to pay Jasra Jackson B$90,000 a month for support facilities while drilling exploratory wells, and in the event of a strike, between B$1 and B$5 million every month based on the level of production. Since then, Jasra-ELF has made a number of promising finds in the Maharaja Lela 2 field, which is likely to produce sizable quantities of hydorcarbons. Jasra-ELF also plans to use Brunei Shell's storage and processing facilities on a lease basis as the set-up costs of establishing its own infrastructure are at present not justifiable. See also: BRUNEI SHELL PETROLEUM (BSP).

JASSIN/JESSIN/YASSIN AFFANDY: He was Secretary-General of the Parti Rakyat Brunei (PRB) (q.v.) and Deputy Prime Minister designate as well as Commander in Chief of the Tentera Nasional Kaliman-tan Utara (TNKU) (q.v.). He was also leader of the Barisan Buruh Bersatu Brunei, or the Brunei United Labour Front (BULF) (q.v.). Prior to this, during the Japanese occupation (q.v.) of Brunei, Jassin was sent by the Japanese authorities to undergo military training in Kuching. Further, during the Brunei rebellion of 1962 (q.v.), as Com-mander in Chief of the TNKU, he with the aid of its Military Com-mander, Jais bin Haji Karim, established their headquarters at Bukti Salileh, near Brunei Town (q.v.). When this post was attacked by the Queen's Highlanders and Gurkha (q.v.) forces, he along with some 20 of his men took refuge in the mangrove swamps around the Brunei Bay. He and his men remained at large until 18 May 1963, when on that day a Gurkha patrol ambushed the former and his followers in a swamp near Kampong Serdang, a village situated four kilometers north of Brunei Town. Two of his men were killed and Jassin himself was seriously wounded. During the revolt, a reward of $15,000 was offered for information leading to his arrest, which eventually led to his detention at the Berakas Detention Centre under the Internal Se-curity Act. In July 1973, Jassin, along with Zaini Haji Ahmad (q.v.) and six others, managed to escape from the detention centre and fled into Limbang (q.v.) and then to Kuala Lumpur. It was in Kuala Lum-pur that the PRB formed its government in exile and conducted its activities. At least until the late 1970s, Jassin was still living in exile in Kuala Lumpur. See also: BARISAN BURUH BERSATU BRUNEI (BULF); PARTI RAKYAT BRUNEI (PRB); REBELLION OF 1962; TENTERA NASIONAL KALIMANTAN UTARA (TNKU).

JEFRI BOLKIAH, PENGIRAN MUDA (PRINCE): He is the third brother of Sultan Hassanal (q.v.) and was the Minister of Finance until he resigned in February 1997, due to some disagreements with Sultan Hassanal. Prior to this appointment, he was Minister of Law as well as Minister of Communications. He is also Chairman of the Brunei Investment Agency (BIA) (q.v.) and the recently created Brunei Oil and Gas Authority (BOGA) (q.v.). Prince Jefri is a polo enthusiast and was considered closer to the Sultan than Prince Mohammed Bolkiah (q.v.) for both the Sultan and Prince Jefri often traveled abroad together. He is also considered extremely shy, like the Sultan. He is married to Princess Noorhayati, who spends most of her time with their children in a large mansion in Hampstead Garden, London.

K

KAMPONG AYER: Literally translated as water village, this settlement, which comprises a cluster of villages, is a part of Bandar Seri Begawan (q.v.). This settlement, with houses built on stilts, has existed since time immemorial and has been the centre of political, economic and social activities for centuries for it was indeed Brunei's capital.

It is believed that the origins of Kampong Ayer go back to a time, some centuries ago, when a settlement was built in Kampong Sungai Lampai, situated a mile away from the present Kampong Ayer. The Sultan's palace, which was in Kota Batu, was moved to this place at a village known as Kampong Sultan Lama. When Antonio Pigafetta visited Brunei in 1521, he reported that some 25,000 families dwelt in this water village. In fact, some of the writers have even called Kampong Ayer "this greatest ever of Malay cities" (K. G. Tregonning, "The Partitioning of Brunei," *Journal of Tropical Geography*, Vol. 11, April 1958: 84), while another source described it as a settlement resembling Venice, for like the former, Kampong Ayer too had/ has many water lanes. One source of 1848 claimed that Kampong Ayer had a population of about 100,000 at that time while another source stated that its population was around 25,000.

When the Residential System (q.v.) was introduced in 1906, the first British Resident, Malcolm Stewart Hannibal McArthur (q.v.), estimated Kampong Ayer's population to be between 8,000 and 10,000. In addition, the British Resident also undertook a serious attempt to start a settlement on land, mainly due to hygiene considerations. To begin, McArthur built his Resident's office on land, though the Sultan's palace remained in Kampong Ayer. In addition, as an incentive to lure the inhabitants of Kampong Ayer to the new settlement on land, building materials were also given out free. However, his plans fell short of succeeding when only some Chinese (q.v.) settlers moved despite a strong ultimatum issued by McArthur in 1910, when he stated that the government would be forced to take punitive action should the inhabitants fail to move by the end of 1911. Though such action was never taken, the settlement on land began to slowly grow whilst majority of Kampong Ayer's inhabitants continued to live in their villages on water. In January 1922, the Sultan moved his palace to the settlement on land known as Brunei Town (q.v.). Despite continous efforts by later Residents, the majority of Kampong Ayer's inhabitants continued their old lifestyle. Seeing little progress was being made to attract the inhabitants of Kampong Ayer to move to the settlement on land, the government began extending some of its facilities, such as medical and postal, to the inhabitants of Kampong Ayer.

In 1960, a year after the Residential System was ended, it was reported that there were still some 36 villages in Kampong Ayer, while a later source (1988) stated that the number of villages was 28. Despite the rapid expansion of Brunei Town (Bandar Seri Begawan), this water city continues to grow with its own unique character as Brunei's Venice. See also: BRUNEI-MUARA DISTRICT; BRUNEI TOWN/BANDAR SERI BEGAWAN.

KEDAYANS: It is the second most populous indigenous group after the Brunei Malays. Like the latter, they are Muslims, speak similar dialects of the Malay language, share many similar customs and appear to be of similar physical stock. They have traditionally been rice (q.v.) farmers of the coastal plains and low hills. Demographically, they live in scattered villages around the Brunei-Muara District (q.v.) as well as in the Temburong District (q.v.), where they are the main ethnic group, accounting for about 40 per cent of the district's population. The Kedayan population in Brunei appears to be on the decline; in 1911, they constituted some 23 per cent of the total population, while a recent figure stated that they account for only 5 per cent of Brunei's total population. It is also possible that they have been assimilated as Brunei Malays through intermarriage.

KESATUAN KAUM IBU MELAYU PELITA BRUNEI: A women's organisation that was formed after World War II, in the 1940s, and was led by Dayang Rodatan Nasrah Udana Leila, a Brunei woman of Indonesian origin. Concentrating on social reforms, its aim was to struggle for the betterment of Brunei Malay women, and one of its first demands was that the government recruit Malay women into the teaching profession. As a result of this agitation, the Brunei government in 1948 sent the first Malay woman to undergo teacher training at the Durian Daun Malay Teachers Training College in Melaka. During its heyday, this organisation also attracted women from the upper classes of Brunei Malays.

KESATUAN MELAYU BRUNEI (KMB): Like the Sahabat Pena (q.v.), the KMB, or the Union of Brunei Malays, was another nonpolitical organisation that emerged in Brunei in the 1930s. It is possible that the formation of the KMB was to some extent stimulated by the Kesatuan Melayu Singapura (KMS) in the 1920s, as well as the Kesatuan Melayu Malaya (KMM) in the 1930s. However, aside from sharing an almost similar name, the KMB had no political relations with either of these organisations. Sultan Omar Ali Saifuddien III (q.v.) was at one time President while his deputy was Pengiran Temenggong Haji Mohamad, and Pengiran Haji Abu Bakar bin Omar served as Secretary. The activities of the KMB were mainly social and cultural. Although the KMB continued to exist after Japanese occupation (q.v.), its activities, however, began to seriously decline and finally led to its deregistration in 1957. This was probably due to two factors, namely: (a) the installation of Omar Ali Saifuddien III in 1950, where the KMB lost one of its main pre-war leaders and royal patronage; and (b) the emergence of the Parti Rakyat Brunei (q.v.) in 1956, which must have overshadowed the KMB.

KHASHOGGI, ADNAN: Originally from Saudi Arabia, he was, in the 1970s and early 1980s, considered to be one of the richest men in the world, who amassed his wealth through arms deals predominantly in the Middle East. He was also considered a very close friend of Sultan Hassanal Bolkiah (q.v.) and a frequent visitor to call upon the Sultan either when the Sultan was at home or abroad. His personal relationship with the Sultan enabled Khashoggi to make some major sales to the Sultan for the former also acted as a purchasing agent for the Sultan. One such example was the purchase of a Boeing 727 by the Sultan. In addition, Khashoggi also managed to obtain some favours from the Sultan, using his yacht, *Nabila*, as collateral when the Sultan stood as his guarantor for a US$50 million loan from a Swiss bank. The 282-foot-long luxurious yacht, built in 1980, by M. & B. Benetti and Canieri Navali Fratelli Benetti at Viareggio, Italy, included in its facilities a medical clinic, a hairdresser, a discotheque and a landing pad for helicopters. When Khashoggi went into default on the loan in

1985, the Sultan had to pay it off under the terms of guarantee and this effectively gave the Sultan ownership of the yacht (it was eventually sold to Donald Trump for US$30 million). As such, this incident damaged the relationship between Khashoggi and the Sultan and the former soon fell out of favour. See also: AL-FAYED, MOHAMED.

KHOO TECK PUAT: A Malaysian business tycoon, he is a hotelier-financier and was born in the mid-1920s, in Singapore (q.v.). He had his early education at the St. Joseph's Institution, Singapore, and in 1933 began working as a junior clerk for the Oversea-Chinese Banking Corporation (OCBC), where he rose to the position of deputy general manager. In 1959, he left the OCBC to set up a rival bank, the Malayan Banking Corporation, from where he made his fortune but eventually, in 1966, lost control of the bank for allegedly channeling the bank's money to his own companies. It was reported that Khoo had used funds from the bank to acquire large interests in real estate and hotels (for example, Goodwood Park Hotel in Singapore and Southern Pacific Hotel in Australia).

He was also once a close friend of Brunei's ruling family, especially the present Sultan's father, the late Sultan Omar Ali Saifuddien III (q.v.). Khoo was instrumental in the establishment of the National Bank of Brunei (NBB) in 1965, where his family had a 70 per cent stake, while the remaining 30 per cent was in the hands of the Brunei royal family. Under Khoo's presidency, the NBB grew to become Brunei's largest bank with 12 branches and some 30,000 depositors. However, relations between Khoo and Brunei's royal family turned sour in 1983, when he sold his Holiday Inn Hotel in Singapore for B$135 million, a price that Sultan Hassanal felt was very much inflated, for the hotel market slumped shortly thereafter.

With the collapse of the United National Finance in June 1985, Sultan Hassanal (q.v.) ordered a thorough investigation on all the financial institutions operating in Brunei, which led to the arrest of some senior bank officials, including Khoo's son, Khoo Ban Hock. The charges brought were of false accounting and conspiracy to defraud where it was alleged that Ban Hock was responsible for some B$650 million in NBB loans to "Khoo-related companies" without proper documentation or security. In fact, the Finance Ministry of Brunei claimed that up to 98 per cent of the bank's loans were said to have gone to "Khoo-related interests." Khoo, on the other hand, apologetically called it a business misunderstanding whilst the Brunei government demanded that Khoo pay the government some B$475 million for the release of his son. In February 1988, Ban Hock was sentenced to four years in prison by the Brunei High Court. In fact, at the same time, it was reported that Khoo's business empire was in serious trouble.

KUALA BALAI: A small fishing village all along, it was made the Belait District's (q.v.) headquarters in September 1907 and remained so until 1929. This was mainly due to the tremendous increase in the granting of oil- (q.v.) prospecting licences awarded by the Brunei government. Despite the oil prospecting activities, Kuala Balai remained unchanged and significant development did not take place here but rather in Kuala Belait, (q.v.). With the development of the oil industry in the 1930s, the headquarters of the Belait District was moved to Kuala Belait which was at that time also the headquarters of the British Malayan Petroleum Company (Shell) (q.v.).

KUALA BELAIT: Before 1909, Kuala Belait existed only as a little fishing hamlet. Although oil-(q.v.) prospecting activities in the Belait District (q.v.) had begun as early as 1911, and some quantities of oil were found in 1914 in Labi, this did not have much impact on the development of Kuala Belait. However, with oil found in Labi, prospectors were convinced of the possibility of finding more oil along the upper banks of the Belait River.

As such, the oil companies concentrated their activities along the said area, and as a result, by 1927 a village with a significant population had emerged in Kuala Belait. At that time it was used as a port to ferry machinery vital for oil-prospecting activities mainly by the British Malayan Petroleum Company (BMPC) (q.v.). Therefore, Kuala Belait became the entry point for the upper reaches of the Belait River. Hence, the government too soon followed when it was made the headquarters of the Belait District in 1927. In 1929, the BMPC too moved its headquarters to Kuala Belait and as such provided further stimulus for the development of Kuala Belait. When large reserves of oil were finally found in April 1929 in Seria (q.v.), some 16 kilometers from Kuala Belait, the importance of the latter was further enhanced.

The 1930s witnessed rapid development in Kuala Belait, mainly due to the efforts of the BMPC. In fact, not only was the first English school in the state established here in 1931, but Kuala Belait had the best hospital in Brunei in 1931. In the same year, a Sanitary Board was established giving Kuala Belait the status of a town of some significance. From a population of 1,193 in 1931, Kuala Belait had a population of 3,000, by 1935. Before World War II, Kuala Belait continued to witness rapid growth as a result of the development of the oil industry. However, much of the town was destroyed because of aerial bombing during World War II, so much so that after the war an entirely new town began to emerge. The 1950s and 1960s witnessed rapid development in Kuala Belait as income from the oil industry increased tremendously. At present, Kuala Belait is considered Brunei's second-largest town after Bandar Seri Begawan, and the former is sometimes called a "Shell town" for much of its postwar development was also due to efforts undertaken by Shell. See also: BELAIT DISTRICT; KUALA BALAI; SERIA.

L

LABUAN: It is an island situated off the Brunei Bay, which was once part of Brunei and was ceded to the British in 1847 by the Treaty of Friendship and Commerce signed between Brunei and Britain. By ceding Labuan, Brunei had hoped that the British presence in Labuan would in turn act as a check against the expansionist activities of the Sarawak (q.v.) government. This, however, Brunei failed to achieve for the annexation of Brunei's territories continued unchecked. In 1890, the administration of this island was handed over to the newly formed British North Borneo Company (BNBC) (q.v.) and two years later to the Straits Settlements. After World War II, Labuan was once again transferred to North Borneo. When Sabah/North Borneo joined Malaysia (q.v.) in 1963, Labuan was part of it. In 1984, it was transferred to the jurisdiction of the Malaysian federal government and became a federal territory.

LANGUAGE: The official language of Brunei is the Malay language (Bahasa Melayu Brunei). In addition to the Malay language, English, some Chinese (q.v.), and Indian (q.v.) dialects are also commonly used by the non-Malay populace. Although Malay is the official language in all government schools, English and Chinese are also used as mediums of instruction in private schools. In addition to Malay and English, which are taught in all government schools, Arabic is also commonly used, especially in government-funded religious school. The Malay language of Brunei is very similar to that of Malaysia (q.v.). As a measure to promote the development of the Malay language, literature and culture in Brunei, the Language and Literature Bureau was established under the Ministry of Culture, Youth and Sports. The bureau has undertaken various efforts to widen the scholastic use of the Malay language. In addition, degree-level courses in Malay literature are currently offered at the Universiti Brunei Darussalam (UBD) (q.v.), and Brunei too has hosted a number of important seminars on Malay language. The Dewan Bahasa dan Pustaka Brunei also plays an important role in promoting the use of *Bahasa Melayu Brunei*. With the current emphasis on the concept of *Melayu Islam Beraja* (Malay Muslim Monarchy) (q.v.), the Malay language has taken a central role as a medium of communication and as a uniting force.

LEGISLATIVE COUNCIL (MAJLIS MESYUARAT NEGERI): By the provisions of the 1959 Constitution (q.v.), the Legislative Council was to consist of 17 appointed members and 16 elected members. Elections to the Assembly were to be on a two-tier system. Direct elections (q.v.) were to be held to District Councils within two years of the promulgation of the Constitution. The District Councillors were then to choose from amongst themselves the 16 elected members of the Legislative Council.

Members of the body were free to introduce any bill for discussion, but debate was not allowed in the case of certain matters without prior approval from the Sultan. These included bills or motions pertaining to the finances of the state, debts due to the state or its financial obligations, assignment of taxes, matters relating to the management of the Consolidated Fund (q.v.), the issue of bank notes, intergovernment treaties, defence, public security and the management of the armed forces. Taking into consideration the Constitution as a whole and other proclamations, the Legislative Council could not also debate such issues as the position of the Sultan and succession. Decisions were to be based on majority vote, the Speaker being entitled to a casting vote. Seven members were required to form a quorum. No bill could become law unless it was assented to and signed by the Sultan. On the contrary, the Sultan could declare any bill introduced, but not passed by the Legislature, to be enforced as law if he deemed it expedient for the good government of the state.

Members were free to express their views and protected from prosecution in any court of law. So were the Council proceedings or anything published under its authority. The Council had a tenure of three years, but the Sultan could, by proclamation, dissolve it at any time. Historically, the Legislative Council functioned from 1963 until 13 February 1984. As the 1962 rebellion (q.v.) by the Parti Rakyat Brunei/PRB (q.v.) led to the declaration of an emergency and the suspension of further democratisation, the Legislative Council during its existence consisted of appointed members and not elected members. In 1984, when Brunei obtained independence, Sultan Hassanal (q.v.) dissolved the Legislative Council. The dissolution remains in force until today. See also: CONSTITUTION, 1959.

LIMBANG: A district situated in the present-day state of Sarawak (q.v.) in East Malaysia (q.v.). It was a part of the Brunei sultanate before it was annexed by Charles Brooke (q.v.) in 1890. Despite the Sultan of Brunei's furious protests to the British governmant, the latter sanctioned Brooke's annexation of the Limbang in return for annual payment. The Sultan never accepted the compensation but continued to, till his death, plead to the British for help to recover the Limbang. Till the 1950's the Brunei government still demanded from the Malaysian government, for the return of the district to her. In 1973, when Haji Zaini (q.v.) of the Parti Rakyat Brunei (PRB) (q.v.) along with seven other detainees escaped via Limbang and was given political asylum in Malaysia as well as allowed to open an office of the PRB, the Limbang question once again reemerged. The Brunei government retaliated by reviving its claim on the Limbang. In fact, Sultan Omar Ali Saifuddien III sailed in a launch up the Limbang River and managed to obtain petitions from people in the Lower Limbang on their desire to join Brunei. This episode did affect Brunei-Malaysia relations when the Sarawak (q.v.) government organised anti-Brunei demonstrations while Brunei banned the entry of Sarawak government vehicles and recalled all Brunei students studying in Malaysia. The Limbang issue came to the fore once again in May 1987, when some reports claimed that Brunei had discussed with the Malaysian Prime Minister, Dato' Seri Dr. Mahathir Mohamed, the possibility of buying back Limbang. Nevertheless, relations with Malaysia remain friendly, and thus far, the issue is confined to certain undemarcated areas along the boundary between Limbang and Brunei. See also: MALAYSIA; SARAWAK.

M

MAJLIS PERUNDINGAN MUKIM DAN KAMPONG (MPMK): Or the Consultative Council for *Mukim* (subdistrict) and *Kampong* (villages). As a measure to mobilise the grassroots leaders as well as make them represent their population effectively, this was implemented in March 1992. Under this scheme, a form of popular representation was initiated in the selection and appointment of *kampong* and *mukim* leaders. The candidates for *penghulu mukim* (*mukim* head) are chosen through a secret ballot by citizens and permanent residents above the age of 18 living in the various *kampong* within a *mukim*. The district officers then select qualified candidates, who are appointed. Some of the criteria that must be met by the nominees are: possess at least Form Three education or its equivalent; have a sound knowledge of Islam (q.v.); be at least 30 years of age (but not older than 65); not be involved in any political parties; have never been declared bankrupt and; have been resident in the *mukim* for at least three years. The process of selection for the *ketua kampong* (village head) is similar to the former.

This approach is aimed at introducing accountability to those who have been nominated and supported by residents of the *kampong* as well as to forge closer links between the people and government. Further, in September 1993, the Government also conducted a two-day *majlis muzakarah* (seminar cum meeting) for the *penghulu mukim, ketua kampong* and *ketua rumah panjang* (longhouse heads) where the government revealed its intention to introduce additional sweeping reforms in order to strengthen the effectiveness of the community leaders. It was also revealed that MPMK would be administered by the Ministry of Home Affairs through a Management Board, which would replace the Communications Committee formed in 1984. As such, a new set of regulations known as the "Peraturan Lembaga Pengelola dan Majlis Perunding Mukim dan Kampong" (Regulations Governing the Management Board and Consultative Councils for *Mukim* and *Kampong*) would also be drawn up. As for the members of the Management Board, the Sultan would appoint the Minister and Deputy Minister of Home Affairs who would become Chairman and Deputy Chairman of the Board, respectively. The Permanent Secretary of the Home Ministry would be appointed as Secretary of the Board. Other members of the Board would include several permanent secretaries of other ministries, all the four district officers as well as four others who would be appointed from among the advisers of the *mukim* councils. The Board is also empowered to refer any of the council matters, whether at the *kampong* or *mukim* level, to the relevant authorities or ministries for appropriate action. The Sultan can also appoint "titled persons," Cabinet ministers and deputy ministers as advisers to the *mukim* councils as stipulated by the MPMK regulations. The Chairman of the Management Board, on the other hand, will appoint the adviser to the *kampong* council and these persons should be *orang-orang kenamaan* (prominent figures). Advisers to the consultative councils are to play an active role in their respective councils where they not only advise their council(s) on *mukim-* or *kampong*-related matters but are also to hold consultations from time to time on matters that have been decided by the council(s).

The members to the Majlis Perundingan Kampong (Village Consultative Councils) will be selected through meetings of residents of the respective *kampong*, and some of the *Kampong* Council members will represent the *kampong* in the Majlis Perundingan Mukim (*Mukim* Consultative Council). Although membership to the *kampong* and *mukim* levels is open to all citizens above the age of 18, the *mukim* level however, will also have principal of schools and *imam* (leader of congregational prayer) of mosques within the specific *mukim* as members of the *Mukim* Consultative Council.

By early 1994, the scheme to have elected grassroots leaders was already operational whilst the elected councils were formed in mid-1994. At present, Brunei has four districts, 38 *mukim* and 410 *kampong*.

MALAYSIA: From 1948 till 1963, it was known as the Federation of Malaya (Persekutuan Tanah Melayu), consisting of only the Peninsular Malay States (except Singapore). On 16 September 1963, the Federation of Malaysia was inaugurated. Malaysia consists of the Peninsular Malay States of Perlis, Kedah, Kelantan, Terengganu, Pulau Pinang, Perak, Selangor, Pahang, Negeri Sembilan, Melaka and Johor; together with the Bornean States of Sabah and Sarawak (q.v.). Singapore (q.v.) was with the Federation from 1963 to 1965, when it was expelled, while Brunei, though keen to join Malaysia initially, finally declined. As such, relations between Malaysia and Brunei were strained and remained so at least until the late 1970s.

Brunei's refusal to join Malaysia was not the only factor contributing to the emergence of tensions in the relations between both countries. In fact, Malaysia aggravated the situation by providing political asylum to eight former members of the Parti Rakyat Brunei (PRB) (q.v.). In addition, Malaysia also granted permission and gave tacit support to the PRB to conduct its activities on Malaysian soil. As such, relations between Malaysia and Brunei remained on a low key in the 1960s and 1970s.

However, in 1977, the third Prime Minister of Malaysia, Tun Hussein Onn, decided to effect a reconciliation with Brunei and sent emissaries for the purpose. The severely strained relations between both were patched up to some extent, and this move brought about a new era of closer ties between Brunei and Malaysia. Two years later, Hussein Onn broke the ice by attending a royal wedding in Brunei and, a year later, in 1981, Sultan Hassanal (q.v.) made his first official visit to Malaysia, not to Kuala Lumpur but to Kota Kinabalu, Sabah. Prior to this, Sultan Hassanal had visited Malaysia on a number of unofficial visits to attend royal weddings or play polo. This was followed by an official visit by Malaysian Deputy Prime Minister Dato' Musa Hitam in 1982 and a year later by the Malaysian Prime Minister, Dato' Seri Dr. Mahathir Mohamad. In fact, by the early 1980s, Malaysia was providing training and education (q.v.) facilities for Bruneian students and administrators.

Brunei-Malaysia relations entered yet another phase in 1984, when Brunei was admitted into ASEAN (q.v.). Since then, both have maintained good relations. Although the Limbang issue remains the thorn

Figure 1. Istana Nurul Iman: Larger than the Vatican Palace in Rome, this world's largest residential palace is a symbol of Brunei's overflowing wealth.

Figure 2. Queen Mariam: A former stewardess who caught the fancy of Sultan Hassanal.

Figure 3. Prince Jefri Bolkiah: The flamboyant youngest brother of the reigning Sultan who controls the important finance portfolio.

Figure 4. Prince Sufri Bolkiah: The second brother of Sultan Hassanal who enjoys little political clout.

Figure 5. Sultan Hassanal Bolkiah: The richest man in the world, who has given up his flamboyant past to emerge as a popular ruler.

Figure 6. Sultan Omar Ali Saifuddien: The architect of absolute monarchism in Brunei.

Figure 7. Queen Saleha: Once the favorite queen of Sultan Hassanal, she is now on the sidelines.

Figure 8. Prince Mohamed Bolkiah: The more moderate and less ambitious brother of the Sultan.

Figure 9. Kuala Belait: Once a little-known fishing hamlet, it is today Brunei's second largest town and the headquarters of Brunei Shell.

Figure 10. Sultan Omar Ali Saifuddien Mosque: Built in 1959, it was once considered the largest and most beautiful mosque east of the Suez Canal.

Figure 11. Kampung Ayer: A reminder of the sultanate's glorious past.

Figure 12. Lumut LNG Plant: The largest LNG plant in the world, it is also the lifeline of Brunei's newfound wealth.

Figure 13. Lumut LNG Plant: Supplying industries around the world.

Figure 14. Bandar Seri Begawan: Stands in stark contrast to the traditional centre of power, Kampung Ayer (at the far end).

in the side of Brunei-Malaysia relations, both parties have, however, agreed to settle it amicably. Malaysia is also currently Brunei's second-largest trading partner from amongst the ASEAN members, being only second to Singapore. See also: ABDUL RAHMAN PUTERA AL-HAJ IBNI AL-MARHUM SULTAN ABDUL HAMID HALIM SHAH, TUNKU; ASEAN; FOREIGN POLICY; LIMBANG; SARAWAK.

MANOUKIAN, BOB: A refugee from Armenia, this multimillionaire was also once one of Sultan Hassanal's (q.v.) close friends, especially in the 1970s and 1980s. He was also known to have a lavish car collection of at least 30 cars, which included 11 Rolls-Royces and Bentleys, seven Mercedes and four Ferraris. However, his car collection was considered small when compared with Sultan Hassanal's fleet of some 350 cars. Like Khashoggi (q.v.), Manoukian too has made some expensive sales to the Sultan. One was the custom-fitted Boeing 727 where a great deal of gold and mink was put into the plane. In addition, Manoukian sold the Sultan some paintings, which included a collection of Impressionist paintings by Monet, Van Gogh, Pissarro, Sisley and Renoir. He also sold cloths under the brand name Vincci to the Sultan and used to stay at the best suite in the Sheraton-Utama Hotel in Brunei whenever he visited the Sultan.

MARIAM BINTI HAJI ABDUL AZIZ, PENGIRAN ISTERI HAJJAH (QUEEN MARIAM): Born around 1955 or 1956 in Brunei Town (q.v.), she was a stewardess in the Royal Brunei Airways (q.v.) and is currently Sultan Hassanal's (q.v.) second wife. They were secretly married on 28 October 1981. Her marriage to Sultan Hassanal was very much resented by the Sultan's father, Sultan Omar Ali Saifuddien III (q.v.), for not only was she a commoner but was also of mixed parentage and was not a pure Malay. It was not until March-April 1987 that Sultan Omar Ali reconciled and began accepting her as his daughter-in-law. Mariam's mother, Rashidah Saleh, was a Bruneian, while her father, Jimmy Bell, a government servant in Brunei, was born of a Scottish father and a Japanese mother. Upon his marriage to Rashidah Saleh, Jimmy Bell converted to Islam (q.v.) and took a Muslim name, Abdul Aziz. The fourth child in the family, Queen Mariam is half Bruneian, a quarter British and a quarter Japanese. Mariam attended the Omar Ali Saiffudien School at Brunei Town. While at school, she is said to have been a sympathizer of the then outlawed Parti Rakyat Brunei (PRB) (q.v.). She has borne the Sultan four children: two sons and two daughters. The sons are Abdul Azim and Abdul Mateen, while the daughters are Fadzilah Lubabul Bulqiah and Azemah Ni'matul Bolkiah. She resides in a palace specially built for her by the Sultan—the Istana Nurulizza, which cost US$120 million. Although Queen Mariam ranks second to Queen Saleha (q.v.), there are strong indications that the former is currently more important than the latter. This is because the Sultan spends most of his time with Queen Mariam at home and she always accompanies the Sultan on his official as well as unofficial trips abroad. In addition, it is said that she is using her position as the Sultan's favourite queen to promote the appointment of her son, Abdul Azim, as the heir apparent to the throne. See also: HASSANAL BOLKIAH MU'IZZADDIN WADDAULAH IBNI AL-MARHUM SULTAN HAJI OMAR ALI SAIFUDDIEN KHAIRI WADDIEN, SULTAN; SALEHA BINTI AL-MARHUM PENGIRAN PEMANCHA PENGIRAN ANAK HAJI MUHAMMAD ALAM, PENGIRAN RAJA ISTERI HAJJAH ANAK (QUEEN SALEHA).

MARSAL BIN MAUN, DATO SETIA HAJI: He was educated at the Sultan Idris Training College, Tanjung Malim, Malaya, from which he qualified as a teacher during the 1930s. He was also a founding member of the Persekutuan Guru-Guru Melayu Brunei (PGGMB) (q.v.), or the Federation of Brunei Malay Teachers in the pre-World War II years. In the 1960s, especially during the Parti Rakyat Brunei (PRB) (q.v.) led rebellion of 1962 (q.v.), he was *Menteri Besar* (Chief Minister) of Brunei. At least until June 1982, he was said to be residing at the capital in Brunei.

McARTHUR, MALCOLM STEWART HANNIBAL: He was appointed Brunei's first British Resident when the Residential System (q.v.) was introduced in 1906. Prior to his appointment as Resident of Brunei, he was also instrumental in the series of negotiations that led to the signing of the 1905 and 1906 Agreement between Britain and Brunei and the introduction of the Residential System. As Resident, he served for two terms from 1906 to 1907, and again in 1908. He is best remembered for his success in establishing a western form of administration and a revenue system in Brunei. He also embarked on plans to encourage Kampong Ayer's (q.v.) population to move to houses on land. In fact, he laid the very foundation for Brunei Town (Bandar Seri Begawan) (q.v.). See also: RESIDENTIAL SYSTEM.

MELAYU ISLAM BERAJA/MIB (MALAY MUSLIM MONARCHY): The concept of MIB was officially declared as the new state ideology in 1984 just after Brunei became a sovereign state. It has, however, been pursued with vigour only since 1990. The ideology stresses the character of Brunei as a traditional Malay state, which still inherits and cherishes three important elements. One is its "pure" Malay character, which has not been impaired by the growth of a large citizenry of "alien" ethnicity, such as the Chinese (q.v.) and Indians (q.v.), as in the case of the Peninsular Malay States. The Malay language, the Malay culture, Malay ethnicity and the Malay political system are the major components of the "Malayness" of Brunei. The second important element is that it is a Muslim state. As such, the state and society have been/must be run according to Islamic principles. The most important point that the government wants to instill in the people is the legitimacy of absolute monarchism. The first two points are supposed to logically lead to the third and its inevitability. The monarchical system is a product of the Malay historical tradition and in Islamic terms, the Sultan is the "shadow" and symbol of God (Allah) on earth. Absolute monarchism is, therefore, the only system sanctioned by God, and Brunei Malays being Muslims are duty bound to obey and respect the Sultan as long as he governs according to Islamic tenets. The MIB concept has been propagated mainly to safeguard absolute monarchism in Brunei from internal subversion. The 1962 rebellion (q.v.) and the failure of the second experiment in limited democracy from 1985 to 1988 has convinced the rulers of Brunei that there is no place for either political parties or democratic processes in Brunei. Since 1988, the government has also been worried about the possible danger to internal security posed by rising unemployment and related social problems. Many young Bruneians have become addicted to alcoholism and drugs. The MIB concept is also aimed at instilling a sense of purpose and identity among the younger Brunei generation.

MISSIONARIES, CHRISTIAN: The activities of Christian missionaries for the propagation of the gospel in Brunei began with the establishment of the Residential System (q.v.). Although it is difficult to ascertain the form of their activities, one area in which they made a significant contribution was education (q.v.), which was especially the effort of the Roman Catholic mission. The establishment of English primary and secondary schools in Brunei was mainly the effort of the missionaries. Out of a total of three English primary schools prior to World War II, two were run by the missionaries. After the war, there were seven schools out of a total number of ten schools, which were operated by the missionaries. In fact, by 1959, from a total number of ten secondary schools in Brunei, five were run by Christian missionaries who were Anglicans as well as Catholics. Until 1959, missionary-run English schools received a small grant from the government, but the decision was revoked in that year for the practise was considered un-Islamic by the State Council. Apart from the education field, their propagation activities were confined to non-Malay Muslim indigenes. See also: EDUCATION.

MOHAMED BOLKIAH, PENGIRAN MUDA (PRINCE): He is the second brother of Sultan Hassanal Bolkiah (q.v.) and is currently Brunei's Minister of Foreign Affairs as well as the *Perdana Wazir* (Prime Vizier). Prior to this, he was Minister of Culture, Youth and Sports as well as Deputy Minister of Finance. Like the Sultan, he too attended Sandhurst. Prince Mohamed also holds a high profile in the QAF Holdings (q.v.), the investment arm of the Brunei royal family. He was until 1984 President of the National Bank of Brunei (NBB). He is married to Pengiran Anak Zariah, Queen Saleha's (q.v.) sister. As such, his relationship with the Queen is much closer when compared with his other brothers. A devout Muslim, Prince Mohamed spends much of his time with his wife and children. In addition, being Brunei's Foreign Minister, Prince Mohamed also frequently visits other countries, making bilateral visits and attending international conferences.

MOSES, CHARLES LEE: He was appointed the first United States (q.v.) Consul to Brunei in July 1865. He was sent to Brunei after Joseph Balestier, the United States diplomatic agent, concluded a commercial treaty with Brunei, in 1850. Moses' appointment provided Sultan Abdul Mumin (q.v.) with the possibility of using the United States as a counterweight against the expansionist policies of Sarawak (q.v.). Anticipating that the United States would be able to guarantee Brunei's sovereignty in the near future should Moses be granted some land concessions that the latter would develop, Sultan Mumin approved a concession covering a large area in northern Borneo. In return, Moses was to pay the Sultan $4,200 a year, while Pengiran Temenggung Anak Hashim was to receive $4,000 annually. In addition to this concession, Moses also did request the Sultan to transfer to him mining rights at Muara, which the Sultan declined. However, Moses was not himself interested in developing the concession but rather had the intention of making a quick profit. He, therefore, in November 1865, sailed to Hong Kong and sold his concessions to an American merchant, Joseph W. Torrey.

MOSQUE, SULTAN OMAR ALI SAIFUDDIEN: Situated in the vicinity of Kampong Ayer (q.v.), this mosque was completed in 1959, costing some B$30 million. It has a 51-metre minaret, a gold dome covered with more than 3 million pieces of Venetian mosaic, Italian marble floors, Shanghai granite exterior walls and an escalator to take the royal family members up to their own private prayer room. It was once considered the most beautiful mosque east of the Suez Canal as well as the largest in Asia. Named after the then ruling Sultan, it is considered a source of great pride and an important symbol of the state. See also: BRUNEI TOWN/BANDAR SERI BEGAWAN.

MURUTS: The Muruts are one of the many non-Malay indigenous groups that inhabit the Bornean states of Sabah, Sarawak (q.v.), Brunei as well as Indonesian Kalimantan. Though found in large numbers in Sabah, there are only a few hundred of them in Brunei, mainly in the Temburong District (q.v.). In Brunei, they live in longhouses on the upper reaches of the Temburong River. Despite their insignificance now, they were in the past an important component of Brunei's empire, providing their military muscle for the Sultan. Most of them resided in Limbang (q.v.) and had a headhunting past. Today, they are mainly hill-rice farmers and are either animists, Muslims or Christians.

N

NATIONAL ANTHEM: The national anthem, adopted in 1958, was the work of Pengiran Yusof bin Pengiran Abdul Rahim and Awang Besar Sagap. Entitled "Ya Allah, Lanjutkan Lah Usia Duli Tuanku" ("Oh God, Long Live Our Majesty the Sultan"), it is very similar to the tune of Britain's national anthem "God Save the Queen." The words of Brunei's national anthem are:

Ya Allah Lanjut
Kanlah Usia
Kebawah Duli Yang Maha Mulia
Adil Berdaulat Menaungi Nusa
Memimpin Rakyat Kekal Bahagia
Hidup sentiasa Negara dan Sultan
Ilahi selamatkan Negara
Brunei Darussalam.

The following is a rough translation of Brunei's national anthem:

By the Grace of God
Long Live
Our Majesty the Sultan
Benevolently Sovereign
Protector of the Nation
Leading the People towards Perpetual Happiness

Forever Live our Nation and Sultan
God Save
The Nation of Brunei Darussalam.

NATIONAL DEVELOPMENT PLANS (NDPs): To ensure that development is properly coordinated and carefully implemented, Brunei's contemporary economic and social development policies are formulated within the framework of development planning. As such, development planning in Brunei, which has historically taken the form of five-year development plans, is macro, multi-sectoral and project-based. Between 1953 to 1995, the Brunei government launched six National Development Plans (NDPs) costing some B$10.9 billion. In connection, some governmental institutions, such as the Economic Planning Unit (EPU) (q.v.) and the Economic Development Board (EDB), were also set up to oversee the process of development. See also: FIFTH NATIONAL DEVELOPMENT PLAN (NDP 5, 1986–1990); FIRST FIVE-YEAR DEVELOPMENT PLAN (NDP 1, 1953–1958); FOURTH NATIONAL DEVELOPMENT PLAN (NDP 4, 1980–1984); SECOND FIVE-YEAR DEVELOPMENT PLAN (NDP 2, 1962–1966); SIXTH NATIONAL DEVELOPMENT PLAN (NDP 6, 1991–1995); THIRD NATIONAL DEVELOPMENT PLAN (NDP 3, 1975–1979).

NATIONAL FLAG: The present national flag of Brunei is yellow with a white and black stripe cutting across from left to right. In the centre is a crest comprising a *bendera* (flag) and *payong ubor-ubor* (royal umbrella), a pair of *sayap* (wing of four feathers), a pair of *tangan* or *kimhap* (hand) and a *bulan* (crescent). Beneath the crescent is a scroll that reads: "Brunei Darussalam" (Brunei: Abode of Peace). This flag, without the crest, first came into existence in 1906, when Brunei signed a treaty with Britain; until then she had no official flag. After the promulgation of the Constitution (q.v.) in 1959, the crest was added to the flag. The background yellow color with the two white and black stripes on the flag signify the royalty, while the *bendera* and *payong ubor-ubor* are ancient regalias of the sultanate. The *sayap* symbolises the protection of justice, tranquility, prosperity and peace. The *tangan* or *kimhap* signifies the government's pledge to promote welfare, peace and prosperity, while the *bulan* is the symbol of Islam (q.v.) with an inscription on it that reads "Always in service with God's guidance."

NATIONALITY ENACTMENT: This enactment was implemented after the Brunei government declared, in September 1961, that an election (q.v.) would be held and began to prepare a register of voters.

This necessitated a Nationality Enactment to determine who would be qualified to vote. In October 1981, the proposals were made public by which all members of a recognised indigenous race who were born within Brunei would be deemed subjects of the Sultan. Others could qualify for citizenship if they had been resident for 20 years out of the previous 25 years and passed a Malay-language (q.v.) test, which also included questions on flora and fauna. See also: CHINESE.

NURUL IMAN, ISTANA: It is the name of Brunei's new palace, which was completed in February 1984, in time for Brunei's independence celebrations. The palace was designed by a leading Filipino architect, Leandro V. Locsin, who remains a first-class exponent of uncompromisingly modern architecture. It is considered the world's largest residential palace currently in occupation and according to the *Guinness Book of World Records* it has the most number of rooms, totaling 1,788 (or 388 more than the Vatican Palace in Rome, the previous world record holder) with more than 1,000 closets, 257 toilets, 18 lifts and 44 staircases. The palace's throne room, which has four thrones, is said to be as spacious as a circus tent and behind every throne is a sixty-foot-high Islamic-style arch with two more arches within them, all covered with 22-carat gold tiles. It is lighted by the 12 biggest chandeliers in the world, each crystal colossus weighing to nearly 4,500 lbs. There are, in total, about 564 chandeliers in the palace in addition to 51,490 light bulbs. The royal banquet hall seats 4,000. Other impressive features are the gold fittings in the royal bathrooms, more than 2,000 telephones, close to two miles of air-conditioned, underground passages, an air-conditioned car park with 300 spaces and a polo practice field with air-conditioned stables. Materials for the construction of this palace were imported from some 31 countries where Brazil and the Philippines (q.v.) supplied most of the wood while Italy provided most of its marble, which covers 600,597 square feet (or equivalent to 14 acres/5.6 hectares). The palace is also equipped with a sports complex, which has a swimming pool, tennis, squash and badminton courts as well as a polo practice ground. Situated atop a man-made hill on a 300-acre site in clear view of Kampong Ayer (q.v.), it is one-third of a mile long with 2 million square feet of floor space (or 50 acres/20.5 hectares). The total cost of the palace was estimated at US$350 million and ever since it was built, the palace has been in a constant state of redesign and rebuilding. The Prime Minister's office is located in this palace. See also: BRUNEI TOWN/BANDAR SERI BEGAWAN.

O

OIL AND HYDROCARBON INDUSTRY: Oil and gas have made Brunei one of the richest states in the world. In 1993, hydrocarbons still accounted for 95 per cent of the exports revenue, which stood at B$3.68 billion while imports were at B$2.01 billion. Brunei's foreign reserves are at present more than US$30 billion. With the discovery of the first major oil field at Seria (q.v.) in 1929, the fortunes of Brunei changed drastically. Nevertheless, it was not fantastically rich even until about 1970. It was only in the 1970s and 1980s that Brunei struck it really rich. This was because of three major developments, namely: (a) the extraordinary rise in world oil prices. From a level of US$1.21 per barrel in 1970, the price jumped to US$36.01 per barrel in 1980; (b) the production of natural gas became a major source of export for Brunei; (c) and there was a tremendous increase in the production of both oil and gas in Brunei. The hydrocarbon-based income of Brunei rocketed as shown in the value of its exports for the following years:

1970	B$277 million
1980	B$9.71 billion
1993	B$3.68 billion

Since 1909, the Shell Group of Companies have dominated the search and exploitation of Brunei's hydorcarbon resources. Today the hydrocarbon industry is controlled by three major companies where the state holds a 50 per cent stake in each. Brunei Shell Petroleum (BSP) (q.v.) dominates and is responsible for exploration, production and refining. The second biggest company is Brunei LNG, which is a three-way partnership between the government, BSP and Mitsubishi Corporation. This company buys gas from the BSP and liquefies it at the LNG plant in Lumut, Brunei, one of the biggest of its kind in the world. The company then sells the gas to Brunei Coldgas (BC), which then takes care of sales and transportation to Japan (q.v.). See also: BRITISH MALAYAN PETROLEUM COMPANY (BMPC); BRUNEI OIL AND GAS AUTHORITY (BOGA); PETROLEUM UNIT.

OMAR ALI SAIFUDDIEN SA'ADUL KHAIRI WADDIEN III, SULTAN SIR HAJI (1914–1986): He was born on 23 September 1914 at Istana Kota, Kampong Sultan Lama, Brunei Town (q.v.) and was the second son of Sultan Muhammad Jamalul Alam II. He received his education at the Malay College of Kuala Kangsar, Malaya, and upon completing his education in 1936, he was posted as Cadet Officer in the Brunei Forestry Department. At the end of 1937, he was transfered to the legal department and in 1938 became Administrative Officer. During the period of Japanese occupation (q.v.) of Brunei, he worked under Awang Ibrahim bin Muhammad Jahfar (q.v.), the State Secretary. It was here that he acquired knowledge of administrative procedures and land administration. In July 1947, he was installed *Bendahara* and travelled widely in the country's districts. He ascended the throne on 6 June 1950, with the sudden death of his brother, Sultan Sir Ahmad Tajuddin in Singapore (q.v.) on 4 June 1950. He was crowned on 31 May 1951 and knighted by the British Sovereign in 1953. He abdicated on 4 October 1967, in favour of his eldest son, Hassanal Bolkiah (q.v.), and died on 7 September 1986 at the age of 72. He was also referred to as Sultan Seri Begawan or "the retired Sultan" and is considered the father of modern Brunei as well as the architect of absolute monarchism in the state. He ruled Brunei for 17 years from 1950 to 1967.

OMAR ALI SAIFUDDIN II, SULTAN (r.1828–1852): He was installed as the 23rd Sultan of Brunei in 1828. When his grandfather Sultan Muhammad Tajuddin died in 1807, Omar Ali was still an infant. The throne was usurped by his maternal grandfather Muhammad Kanzu but Omar Ali's mother succeeded in preventing her father from being appointed *Yang Di Pertuan*. On Muhammad Zul Alam's death, his son (and Omar Ali's uncle) Raja Api (Pengiran Muda Muhammad Alam) conducted a bitter struggle against his sister, which evetually culminated in his elimination and the appointment of Omar Ali. However, the resentment and hatred between the two families persisted and finally led to the massacre of the entire family of Raja Muda Hassim (q.v.) (a brother of Raja Api) in 1846. In addition to factionalism at the capital, it was also during his reign that Brunei's hegemony over its dependencies in Borneo began slowly decaying with a series of revolts especially in Sarawak (q.v.).

ORGANIZATION OF ISLAMIC CONFERENCE (OIC): Being herself an Islamic state, Brunei joined this organisation on 16 January 1984, after receiving her independence. Earlier, in 1984, the Sultan Hassahal Bolkiah (q.v.) had attended the OIC summit in Casablanca, Morocco, and later in the same year, Yassir Arafat, leader of the Palestine Liberation Organization (PLO), received a warm welcome in Brunei. Brunei's main links with the Muslim world are, however, with the monarchical Arab kingdoms, namely Oman, Jordan, Saudi Arabia and the United Arab Emirates, all of which are Sunni Muslim states with economies and sociopolitical systems similar to that of Brunei's. Apart from enhancing its relations with other Islamic countries vis-à-vis the OIC, Brunei has also joined the OIC members in condeming the injustices inflicted against Muslim minorities in Myanmar (Burma) and Bosnia Herzegovina. At the OIC conference held in Jeddah in December 1992, Brunei together with the other members of the OIC decided to put pressure on the United Nations (UN) (q.v.) to end the plight of the Bosnian Muslims by effective military intervention against the Serbs. In fact, in early 1994, Brunei was also visited by President Alija Izethbegovic of Bosnia-Herzegovina and in the same year too Brunei channeled some 3.75 million Saudi *riyals* through the OIC, in support of the Bosnian cause. Apart from being a member of the OIC, Brunei is also a member of the Islamic Education, Scientific and Cultural Organization (ISESCO) and the Islamic Development Bank (IDB). See also: FOREIGN POLICY.

P

PARTI BARISAN KEMERDEKAAN RAKYAT (PBKR): The Brunei Peoples Independence Party was formed in August 1966 as a result of a merger of a few political parties. It was led by H. A. Hapidz Laksamana (q.v.), a former active member of the outlawed Parti Rakyat Brunei (PRB) (q.v.). This party criticised Britain for not granting independence to Brunei and sent a memorandum to the British government demanding that the latter expedite the process for achieving independence. The British government, in turn, replied that it was keen to grant independence as soon as possible, but the delay was mainly due to Sultan Omar Ali Saifuddien (q.v.), thereby putting the burden on the Sultan. In March 1967, the PBKR demanded that the Sultan state his stand, but the latter declined and when the party sent a delegation to see the Sultan, he refused to meet them. Instead, the British High Commissioner, Arthur Robin Adair, received them, further making the Sultan look the odd man. The Sultan angrily flew to London but the British stayed firm on their stand. On 4 October 1967, Sultan Omar Ali abdicated the throne in favour of his son, Hassanal (q.v.). The activities of this party were not much heard of after the episode. See also: HAPIDZ LAKSAMANA, H. A.

PARTI KEMAJUAN RAKYAT (PAKAR): The Peoples Progressive Party was formed about the same time as the Barisan Rakyat Brunei (BARA), or the Brunei People's Front (q.v.). It was also registered in February 1966, and was led by Pengiran Dato Haji Ali bin Pengiran Haji Daud. Prior to this, Pengiran Dato Haji Ali was Deputy *Menteri Besar* (Chief Minister), and he resigned his post in order to participate actively in politics. Unlike the BARA, the PAKAR's membership was exclusively for the Malays and other indigenous people. Pengiran Dato Haji Ali demanded amendment to the 1959 Constitution (q.v.), which he felt was inappropriate for the introduction of an effective parliamentary government in Brunei. His main aim was to unite Brunei's nationalists into a single united front for achieving constitutional reform in Brunei. Therefore, in 1966, he proposed the setting up of a new party. The response was encouraging and at a meeting held at Brunei Town in August 1966, the Parti Barisan Kemerdekaan Rakyat (PBKR), or the Brunei Peoples Independence Party (q.v.), was formed.

PARTI RAKYAT BRUNEI (PRB): The Brunei Peoples Party was the first modern political party in the Borneo region. It was formed on 22 January 1956 at a gathering of some 150 people held in the house of Cikgu Saleh Masri (H. M. Salleh) (q.v.), who was then President of the banned Barisan Pemuda Brunei/BARIP (Brunei Youth Front) (q.v.). Though formed in January, it was only in August that the PRB was allowed registration. The executive committee of the PRB consisted of the following: A. M. Azahari (q.v.) as President; H. M. Salleh (q.v.) as Vice President; Jassin Affandy (q.v.) as Secretary; H. B. Hidup as Assistant Secretary; and Hapidz Laksamana (q.v.) as Treasurer. Other committee members were Pengiran Damit bin Pengiran Sungguh, Awang Yakub bin Zainal, Zaini Haji Ahmad, Awang Suleiman Putih, Jais bin Haji Karim, Kadir Jaluddin, Cigku Manan bin Muhammad and Zaini Haji Ahmad (q.v.).

The formation of the PRB was inspired by the Parti Rakyat Malaya (PRM), or the Malayan Peoples Party, which was formed two months prior to the establishment of the PRB. The PRB was immensely popular with the masses such that by 1957, it boasted a membership of 16,000. Although initially the PRB included as one of its aims the desire to revive the sovereignty of Brunei over North Borneo (Sabah) and Sarawak (q.v.), Sultan Omar Ali Saifuddien III (q.v.), however, took objection to this. Eventually the party amended its declared aims and the party's manifesto included opposition to all forms of colonialism, support for the monarchy and the attainment of self-government. Due to its immense popularity, the PRB soon became radical and overtly critical of the monarchy, and demanded immediate elections (q.v.). Not totally giving up its earlier aim to revive the sovereignty of Brunei over Sabah and Sarawak, the PRB now demanded a federation of British Borneo territories as well as *merdeka* (independence). It also began to agitate for speedy constitutional changes and even went as far as to send a delegation to London. The Sultan, on the other hand, began to drag his feet on the issue, thereby making the PRB even more frustrated.

Though the constitutional reforms eventually took place in 1959, the PRB was even more disillusioned, only to find that the monarchy was not willing to share power with it. To step up its agitation, the PRB in 1960 formed the Barisan Buruh Bersatu Brunei, or the Brunei United Labour Front (BULF) (q.v.). When the elections to the District

Councils were eventually held on 30 and 31 August 1962, the PRB won 54 out of the 55 seats. Fearing that his powers would pass into the hands of the PRB, the Sultan once again began to delay the convening of the Legislative Council (q.v.). Tired of using constitutional means, the PRB launched an armed uprising on 8 December 1962, supported by the Tentera Nasional Kalimantan Utara/TNKU (the National Army of North Kalimantan) (q.v.), its underground military arm. Sultan Omar Ali Saifuddien III declared an emergency and outlawed the PRB. Most of its leaders were arrested but Azahari managed to obtain political asylum in Indonesia. See also: BARISAN BURUH BERSATU BRUNEI (BULF); REBELLION OF 1962; TENTERA NASIONAL KALIMANTAN UTARA.

PENANS: A non-Malay indigenous group commonly found in Sarawak (q.v.), Malaysia (q.v.), and in a very small number in Brunei as well. In the past, they followed a nomadic lifestyle, living deep in the interior and collecting jungle produce. In 1963, a band of 21 Penans decided to try settled life at Sukang, far up the Belait (q.v.) River. They were later joined by another 15 Penans, and 20 years later, there were some 45 of them living in the area. At present, they are agriculturalists, growing both wet and hill rice (q.v.). The men still set off to hunt for days at a time. The integration of the Sukang Penans into Brunei's indigenous society has been extremely slow for until 1983, there had been only two intermarriages, to Bisayas (q.v.), and both ended in divorce. In addition, only one young man has ventured to the coast in search of wage-paying work.

PENGIRAN BENDAHARA: He was one of the most important officials of the state and normally chosen from the core nobility. He is also one of the four Ministers, or *Wazir* (Vizier), in the Brunei traditional government. He was the Chief Minister, the deputy to the Sultan and was in charge of land defence. He was considered the highest official administering the power or authority of the Sultan as well as the highest official in matters of law and the Islamic religion.

MUHAMMAD YUSOF BIN PENGIRAN MUDA HAJI LIMBANG, PENGIRAN SETIA NEGARA, PENGIRAN DATO HAJI: He was born in May 1923, in Tutong (q.v.). In 1939, he entered the Sultan Idris Training College (SITC), Tanjung Malim, Malaysia, but had to abandon his teacher training programme in 1941, when war broke out. He returned to Brunei in late 1941, and due to his linguistic talent in learning Japanese, he was sent to Hiroshima University. When the Americans dropped the first atomic bomb over Hiroshima in August 1945, he was going to enter a lecture room. Miraculously, he survived and vividly remembers this tragic incident. He was then sent back to Brunei after the war and was kept under surveillance by the British Military Administration (BMA) (q.v.). Wing Commander Keay met him several times in order to get information on how and why he was sent to Japan (q.v.). The BMA suspended Pengiran Yusof and many others, including Marsal bin Maun (q.v.), from public service. In 1946, he was one of the founding members of the Barisan Pemuda (BARIP) (q.v.). He was also an active member of the Parti Rakyat Brunei (PRB) (q.v.) and in the August 1962 election to the District Councils, he contested and won the Padang seat in the Brunei-Muara District (q.v.) on the PRB ticket. Again, in the March 1965 election to the Legislative Council (q.v.), he contested as an independent and won and was appointed to the Legislative Council. At least until 1982, he was still living at the capital in Brunei.

PERSATUAN BURUH CETIK: An association formed in the 1950s in Seria (q.v.), which consists mainly of migrant workers from Indonesia (q.v.). These men had earlier been brought to Brunei by the Japanese during the war to rebuild the Seria oil fields, which had been badly destroyed. Although this association was formed mainly to protect the rights of Indonesian migrant workers in Brunei, it also supported the Indonesian nationalists in their struggle to end Dutch rule over Indonesia. As a result of this, one of its members, Sukiman, was deported back to Indonesia by the British Malayan Petroleum Company (BMPC) (q.v.) for his alleged political activities.

PERSATUAN KERABAT DI RAJA MELAYU BRUNEI: The Brunei Royal Family Association was formed in the 1950s by the son of a *pengiran*. This association was basically formed to oppose the installation of Omar Ali Saifuddien III (q.v.) upon the death of Sultan Ahmad Tajuddin on 4 June 1950. It was estimated that this association had some 600 members. In addition, the association also opposed the practice of nepotism by Sultan Omar Ali Saifuddien, especially in the appointment of government officials, which according to this association should be based on meritocracy.

PERSATUAN MURID TUA (MUTU): The Old Pupils Association was formed in the late 1940s and was led by Pengiran Anak Saifuddin, a son of a *wazir*. It was formed to organise the Brunei youth as well as encourage discussions on political issues. Most of its founding members who were teachers were either graduates from the Sultan Idris Training College, Tanjung Malim, Malaysia or the Batu Lintang Teachers Training College at Kuching, Sarawak (q.v.).

PERSATUAN SULAM EMAS: An association formed in the 1950s in Seria (q.v.) by mainly migrant workers from Sarawak (q.v.). Some of its founding members, namely Nor Tahir, Haji Shahari and Haji Paun, were also involved in the Anti-Cession Movement in Sarawak in the second half of the 1940s.

PERSEKUTUAN GURU-GURU MELAYU BRUNEI (PGGMB): The Association of Brunei Malay Teachers was formed in the mid-1930s. It was formed with the aim of improving the lot of Brunei Malay teachers. It became an important platform for these teachers to exercise and cultivate leadership as well as to encourage more Malays to obtain higher education (q.v.). Amongst its founding members were Marsal bin Maun (q.v.), Basir bin Taha, Othman bin Bidin, Pengiran Ahmad bin Pengiran Shahbandar Hashim, Nordin bin Latif, P. M. Yusuf, Jamil Umar, Ali Tamin, Ibrahim Said and Salleh bin Masri (H. M. Salleh) (q.v.), who were themselves teachers who had graduated from the Sultan Idris Training College (SITC) in Tanjung Malim, Malaysia. They maintained close links with Malay teachers in Malaya through a magazine called the *Majalah Guru*, which was started in 1938. After World War II, when the organisational structure of PGGMB was revamped, it became even more important in its struggle to improve the standard of living of Malay teachers in Brunei when a cooperative society known as the Iktisad Guru-Guru Melayu Brunei (IGGMB) was formed to encourage the participation of Malays in business. By then the PGGMB had its own office premises located in Brunei Town (q.v.). This organisation was also instrumental in the formation of the Barisan Pemuda Brunei/BARIP, or the Brunei Youth Front (q.v.). which is considered the first organisation of Brunei nationalists.

PETROLEUM MINING ACT (LAWS OF BRUNEI, REVISIONS OF 1984): It is the main legislation governing the operations of the oil and gas industry (q.v.) in both onshore and offshore areas in Brunei. A number of conditions are laid down by the Act for the granting of concession areas and their operation. Some of these include clauses relating to the time period of the concession agreement, surrender conditions, fixed payments and royalty and taxation conditions. Concessions are normally granted for a period of 30 years, with the possibility of a renewal for a further 30 year extension. Relinquishing of concessions are also mentioned in the Act whereby 50 per cent of the concession is to be relinquished after eight years for onshore and ten years for offshore concessions. After 15 years for onshore and 17 years for offshore concessions, an additional 25 per cent has to be relinquished. As for work expenditure obligations, a minimum expenditure of a specified amount is required based on acreage of concession during the first three years for onshore and five years for offshore areas.

The payment of royalties differ from onshore and offshore concessions where for onshore concessions a flat royalty (in cash or kind) of 12.5 per cent is payable. Royalty payments for offshore fields are based on its location. Fields located between three and ten nautical miles pay ten per cent while fields beyond ten nautical miles pay eight per cent. The same conditions are also applied to natural gas production. Prior to 1982, royalties were not regarded as a cost for tax purposes but were credited against company taxes payable. However, since the amendments to the Petroleum Mining Act in 1982, royalties are treated as a cost when assessing taxable income, which is not offset against tax payable. As such, this brought about an increase in the amount paid as tax to the government by about 50 per cent of royalty levels. The legislation also specifies the government's right to participate in the company as well as its right to purchase a 50 per cent stake in the company in the event of new oil and gas discoveries. The Act also has clauses regarding the abandonment of wells, waste disposal and restoration of mined land.

PETROLEUM UNIT: It was established in 1982 as a unit that safeguards and develops Brunei's oil and gas industries (q.v.) and is currently under the direct control of the Prime Minister's Office. It is responsible for the government's relationship with existing concessionaires, namely the Brunei Shell Petroleum (BSP) (q.v.), as well as prospective concessionaires. To ensure that Brunei's concession terms are in line with industry practice worldwide, the Unit also monitors developments in the international oil and gas industries, particularly price movements. In addition, it also administers the awarding of new concessions (which includes the terms and bidding procedures), awards licences and negotiates agreements. Current legislation gives the Brunei government an option to participate, up to a level of 50 per cent, in the development of any commercial fields. The level of royalty, which varies between 8 and 12 per cent, is based on the location of a particular concession while tax levied on petroleum revenue is at a rate of 55 per cent. Apart from this, the Petroleum Unit also monitors the budgets and work programmes of concessionaires in connection with exploration, development and production activities. This is to ensure that the concessionaires conform to the existing agreements and that the most cost-effective production methods are used. The Unit also acts as an advisory body to the goverment in connection with the appointment of board members of BSP companies. As such, the Petroleum Unit is the custodian of the country's oil and gas reserves. Lastly, the Unit is also given the responsibility for coal (q.v.) development in the state. It is anticipated that the recently (1993) formed Brunei Oil and Gas Authority (BOGA) will soon assume the responsibilities currently undertaken by the Petroleum Unit. See also: BRUNEI OIL AND GAS AUTHORITY (BOGA); PETROLEUM MINING ACT (LAWS OF BRUNEI, REVISIONS OF 1984).

PHILIPPINES (FILIPINA): Contact between the Philippines and Brunei began even before the coming of the Spaniards (q.v.) to colonise the former. Southern parts of the Philippines, namely the Muslim area of Sulu, conducted active trade with Brunei. When the Spanish extended its control over the Philippines, Brunei's trade with the said area was greatly reduced.

In the 20th century, the Parti Rakyat Brunei's (PRB) (q.v.) leadership maintained close contacts with some sectors in Manila, namely the Kiran Corporation, a Filipino company, which was alleged to have thrown its support behind A. M. Azahari's (q.v.) proposal for the resurrection of Brunei's empire in the form of a Unitary State of Kalimantan. Intergovernmental relations however, were not affected. On the contrary, Brunei decided to recruit government officers from the Philippines when the Malaysian (q.v.) government decided to call back all its officers serving in Brunei upon the latter's refusal to join the Malaysian Federation in 1963.

During the celebrations held in February 1984 on achieving its independence, Brunei invited many foreign leaders amongst whom was Ferdinand Marcos, then President of the Philippines, who was accompied by a 120-strong entourage. In fact, one of the major contractors for the construction of the new *istana* (palace) Nurul Iman (q.v.) was Enrique Zobel (q.v.), a leading Filipino businessman, who owns the Ayala Corporation. At present, Brunei and the Philippines maintain cordial relations partly because both are members of ASEAN (q.v.), and partly because a significant portion of Brunei's foreign manual labour is from the Philippines. In fact, for the construction of the new palace, some 5,000 Filipino workers were imported by Brunei. This is in addition to the thousands of manual Filipino labourers and maids present in Brunei. The Philippines on the other hand, imports crude oil from Brunei, in 1993 alone it imported crude oil valued at B$81.6 million. Further, in March 1994, four of the ASEAN member states— Brunei, Indonesia (q.v.), Malaysia (q.v.) and the Philippines (BIMP)—formed the East Asian Growth Area (BIMP-EAGA) to enhance economic cooperation between the four states through joint business ventures. The Secretariat for the BIMP-EAGA is currently located at Bandar Seri Begawan (q.v.). See also: ASEAN; SPANIARDS.

PORTS: Having a 161-kilometre-long coastline along the South China Sea, sea transportation is an important form of communication in Brunei. In addition to having a long-standing maritime tradition, the present oil industry too has made sea transportation indispensible. As such, Muara, located some 28 kilometres northeast of Bandar Seri Begawan, is currently Brunei's major port. It was opened in 1973, with a wharf length of 428 metres, which was extended a further 183 metres in 1985. Additional improvements to the wharf and dredging of the harbour has reduced waiting time for ships to an average of three hours. Also, some 12,542 square metres of warehousing has been constructed. This port handles regular freight shipments to and from all ASEAN (q.v.) countries, Hong Kong, Japan (q.v.), Taiwan, Australia and the United States (q.v.). Cargo tonnage at the Muara Port in 1987 was at 827,000 freight tonnes with 683 ships calling at that harbour.

In May 1994, a section of the Muara Port was declared an Exporting Zone, providing incentives such as a 40 per cent discount on monthly rent of port warehouse, 50 per cent discount on port charges as well as free transportation of export goods within the port. This decision is not only in line with Brunei's policy to make the Muara a major port within the ASEAN region, but also is a step to overcome common complaints from foreign investors with regards to the high operational cost in Brunei.

In addition to the Muara Port, the Kuala Belait (q.v.) Wharf, on the other hand, serves the oil (q.v.) fields in the Belait District (q.v.). When compared with Muara, the Kuala Belait Wharf is a much smaller port with a length of 91 metres situated on the Belait River. Apart from this, there are also smaller jetties in Bandar Seri Begawan and in the Temburong District (q.v.). The administration of all ports in Brunei is the responsibility of the Ministry of Communications and the assistance from the Port Authority of Singapore is frequently sought.

PORTUGUESE: After capturing Melaka (Malacca) in 1511, the Portuguese concentrated their efforts on establishing their control as well as trade monopoly over the Spice Islands, or Maluku (Moluccas). Despite their policy of subjugation and control over the Maluku, with Brunei the Portuguese followed a more amicable policy with an aim of fostering friendly relations and obtaining trading facilities. Therefore, the Portuguese made several attempts to open official relations with Brunei. One such attempt was undertaken in 1524, when Jorge d'Albuquerque (q.v.), then Captain of Melaka, sent a mission under Antonio de Pinta. Following this, many prominent Portuguese officials, mostly captain-designates of Maluku, visited Brunei. In 1530,

Goncalo Pereira, the Captain-designate of the Maluku visited Brunei to convey the following message: that the King of Portugal, learning of the greatness of the Sultan, wanted to establish friendly relations with him; the Portuguese offered Brunei merchants free trade in Portuguese possessions; and that the Sultan grant permission for the Portuguese to trade in his territory on the assurance that they would pay all reasonable dues and observe the same regulations as his subjects. The Sultan, Abdul Kahar (r.1524–1535), welcomed these missions and agreed to establish friendly relations with the Portuguese. Brunei-Portuguese relations remained cordial, conducted on the principle of equality and reciprocal advantages and the Portuguese accepted the viability of Brunei laws and customs, without attempting to ask for extraterritorial rights. After the capture of Melaka by the Dutch in 1641, the Portuguese retreated to Macao, from where they continued to trade with Brunei. See also: ALBUQUERQUE, JORGE D'.

PRIVY COUNCIL (MAJLIS MESYUARAT NEGARA): It was established after the promulgation of the 1959 Constitution (q.v.). The members of the Privy Council are known as Privy Councillors and consist of Regents, if a Council of Regency is appointed, and six ex officio members and appointed members. They hold office at the pleasure of His Majesty the Sultan and *Yang Di Pertuan* and are subject to the conditions specified in the appointment. Before any member holds office he must subscribe to an oath or a declaration. The Attorney General, although not a member of this council, has the right of audience before it in certain cases. The function of the Privy Council is to advise the Sultan in the exercise of the prerogative of mercy, matters relating to the amendment of the Constitution, including revocation of any of its provisions, conferment of Malay customary honors on persons, and to perform such other functions as may be prescribed by law or conferred upon it by the Sultan. The Privy Council is a body that cannot be summoned except by authority of the Sultan, or in his absence, by the Senior Regent. No meeting may be held if there are less than one-third of the members of the Privy Council present and an objection has been made. See also: CONSTITUTION OF 1959.

Q

QAF HOLDINGS: It is the name of the company owned by Brunei's royal family and also frequently referred to as "Royal Family, Inc." Formed in 1982, the QAF became a public company in 1984. It was formed to bring under one umbrella close to 20 royal family wholly owned or joint-venture companies involved in shipping, newspaper publishing, food manufacturing and retailing, automotive sales and Brunei's oil industry. The QAF is said to have stakes in some of the following companies: Brunei Oxygen (manufacture and sale of industrial gases); Q-Carrier (sale and manufacturing of air-conditioners); QAF-Solus (Offshore) (supporting services for offshore rigs); QAF-Reading and Bates (offshore drilling contractor); QAF Jack Tighe (offshore contractor); QAF-Ben and Company (a subsidiary of Straits Steamship); Dairy Farm (Brunei) (catering services); Singapore Emporium Holdings (supermarkets and department stores); Fitzpatrick's (Brunei) (food wholesaler and retailer); and Boustead (auto and consumer dealer); Spices of the Orient (Soto) Australia (food); Hemphill's Herbs and Spices Pvt. Ltd. (food). QAF's partners in these businesses are leading multinationals such as Carrier and British Oxygen and in most cases, the QAF has a 50 per cent stake. The company is currently listed on the Singapore Stock Exchange and has begun expanding into China (q.v.) and Myanmar (Burma). It is also the third largest employer in Brunei after the public sector and Brunei Shell (q.v.). Pengiran Muda Mohamed Bolkiah (q.v.), the Sultan's brother, currently owns some 65 per cent of the QAF. See also: BRUNEI INVESTMENT AGENCY (BIA).

R

REBELLLION OF 1962: This Parti Rakyat Brunei- (PRB) (q.v.) sponsored uprising started at 2.00 A.M. on 8 December 1962 and was mainly undertaken by the Tentera Nasional Kalimantan Utara/TNKU (q.v.), the underground military arm of the PRB. By 3.00 A.M. the TNKU had captured the Seria (q.v.) Police Station and the airport at Anduki, Seria. It then proceeded to take the Panaga Police Station, some four kilometres away from Seria. In Brunei Town (q.v.), the TNKU's attempt to capture the headquarters of the Royal Brunei Police (q.v.) and the Istana Darul Hana (q.v.), however, failed. The main targets of the TNKU were police stations and important government buildings such as the headquarters of the Radio Station and the Telecommunications Station. After capturing a few telecommunications substations, the TNKU also tried to contact the Indonesian (q.v.) and the Philippines (q.v.) governments but was unsuccessful in making contact. In addition to these places, the TNKU also succeeded in taking a few small towns in Brunei. As soon as the Brunei government declared a state of emergency, Brunei's Commissioner of Police, A. N. Autram, also declared a curfew in the whole state with effect from 6 P.M. to 6 A.M. The police also began to fortify some important places such as the palace as well as its headquarters. By the evening of 8 December 1962, the Brunei government's request for help from the British government began to arrive in Brunei. These additional forces were mainly the Sabah Police, the Gurkha (q.v.) Rifles, the King Edward I Battalion and the Queen's Highlanders. Immediately, these forces began recapturing TNKU-held areas. Within less than two weeks, the situation in Brunei had been normalized but mopping up operations against the rebels who remained at large took longer. On 17 April 1963, the leader of the TNKU, Brigadier General Sheikh Othman (Azahari's brother) was killed in an ambush at Kampong Bunut, some four kilometres from Kampong Kilanas in the Tutong District (q.v.), and on 17 May 1962, Jassin Affandy (q.v.) was also arrested. In fact, most of the TNKU and PRB members either surrendered or were captured. See also: PARTI RAKYAT BRUNEI (PRB); TENTERA NASIONAL KALIMANTAN UTARA (TNKU).

RESIDENTIAL SYSTEM, BRITISH: This system of appointing a British officer-styled Resident was established in Brunei in 1906, when the latter signed the Supplementary Agreement of 1905 and 1906 with the British government. By the agreement, Brunei received a British Resident who was to advise the Sultan on all matters pertaining to the administration of the state, except those affecting Islam (q.v.). In fact, such a system had already been established in the Malaysian states of Perak, Selangor, Negeri Sembilan and Pahang beginning in 1874. However, in the case of the Malaysian states, the Resident was to advise the Sultan of the state on all matters relating to the administration of state, except those affecting Islam and Malay custom. The Resident in Brunei, in fact, had wider powers when compared with those of the Malaysian states. The Residential System continued till 1959, when it was replaced by the appointment of a British High Commissioner. With the end of the Residential System in Brunei in 1959, the Sultan and three newly created bodies, namely the Privy Council (q.v.), the Executive Council (q.v.) and the Legislative Council (q.v.) assumed a wider role in the administration of the state. In other words, Brunei regained its internal independence with the ending of this system, though matters relating to foreign affairs and defence remained a British concern until 1983. Under the Residential System of administration, some 22 British Residents served in Brunei between 1906 and 1959, the last being Sir Dennis Charles White, who was appointed Brunei's first British High Commissioner from 1959 to 1963. See also: McARTHUR, MALCOLM STEWART HANNIBAL.

RICE (PADDY/PADI): Rice cultivation and especially dry or hill rice cultivation is the oldest agricultural activity in the country. During the Residential (q.v.) period, an attempt was made to encourage wet rice cultivation not only to reduce the government's burden of importing large amounts of rice but also to stop the practice of hill rice cultivation, which was mainly undertaken by non-Malay indigenes. These people were shifting cultivators and their slash-and-burn method was considered hazardous to forests. Therefore, in 1909, the government brought in wet rice seeds from Krian in Malaya and a year later, some 500 families were brought in from Banjarmasin in Dutch Kalimantan for the sole purpose of cultivating wet rice in Brunei. However, most of these efforts failed to produce the desired results due to either droughts or heavy rains. Only in 1920 did Brunei enjoy a good harvest. From then onward, wet rice cultivation began to expand and in 1931, a total of 7,400 acres were under rice cultivation.

Before the pre-World War II years, Brunei was already producing some one-third of its annual rice consumption and the major rice-growing areas were in Kilanas, Sengkurong and Lumapas. As an incentive to encourage wet padi cultivation, cultivators were exempted from land tax for the first five years and as a measure to discourage hill padi cultivation, cultivators were levied 50 cents for every acre.

However, with the discovery of oil (q.v.) and the immense increase in revenues it contributed, the government's attention shifted away from encouraging rice cultivation. In fact, Brunei was a consistent importer of rice and has retained that characteristic to the present. Brunei's rice imports almost quadrupled from about B\$3 million in 1963, to B\$17.6 million in 1986. In view of such heavy reliance on rice imports, the Brunei government in the 1970s embarked on a plan to encourage rice cultivation with the objective of attaining 30 per cent self-sufficiency in rice production. Therefore, between 1978 and 1979 alone, the government approved B\$9.7 million of capital expenditure to develop about 1,000 acres of land at Mulaut and about 5,000 acres in Rambai for rice cultivation. In addition, the government also imposed higher prices for locally grown rice as an incentive to local producers. However, these efforts have failed to encourage rice production for the area and production of rice still remains low. In fact, the area under rice cultivation even declined from 2,833 hectares in 1962 to only 930 hectares in 1989. In connection, rice production too has decreased from 5,100 tons in 1962 to only 1,6000 tons in 1989. It is also said that the loss of Limbang (q.v.) in 1890 has denied this state of an important rice-growing region.

ROYAL BRUNEI AIRLINES (RBA): It is the national government-owned carrier, which was established in 1974 after the completion of the Brunei International Airport in 1972, located in Berakas, near Bandar Seri Begawan (q.v.). The airport, furnished with the most modern facilties, has a 12,000-foot runway, capable of handling the biggest aircraft in current production and handles no less than 400,000 incoming and outgoing passengers. Today, the RBA provides services to 26 major destinations in Europe, Middle East, East and Southeast Asia and Australia. In 1994, the RBA had three Boeing 757s and seven Boeing 767-300s. One distinguishing characteristic of this airline is the gold-plated fittings in the first-class sections (including its bathrooms) as well as its fully reclining leather seats. In addition to the RBA, the Royal Brunei Executive, a company run separately from the RBA, serves the VIP charter market with its executive Boeing 727–100.

ROYAL BRUNEI ARMED FORCES (RBAF): An attempt to recruit the indigenes into Brunei's security forces was undertaken on 31 May 1961, when Sultan Omar Ali Saifuddien III (q.v.) founded the Brunei Malay Regiment (BMR) under the command of Lieutenant Colonel D. M. Fletcher. At its fifth anniversary, its name was changed to Royal Brunei Malay Regiment (RBMR) and in 1971, Sultan Hassanal (q.v.) awarded the Sultan's colours to the RBMR. Further, as Brunei approached independence, the name of the RBMR was changed to Royal Brunei Armed Forces (RBAF) in 1983. To mark its 27th anniversary in 1988, the Sultan presented new colours to the First and Second Battalions of the RBAF. In addition, in 1981, the Women's Company of the RBMR was formed with Pengiran Isteri Hajjah Mariam (q.v.) as the Colonel Commandant of the Women's Company. From its formation in 1961 until 1986, the RBMR/RBAF was under the command of British officers. On 1 January 1986, 25 years after its formation, Brigadier General Pehin Dato Haji Mohammed bin Haji Daud took over the command of the RBAF from Dato Paduka Seri John Freidberger, who had commanded the RBAF for three and a half years. Whilst Mohammed was the first Bruneian to hold the appointment, the outgoing Freidberger was the seventh Briton to command Brunei's security forces.

The delay in recruiting the local populace into the armed forces was mainly due to the presence of British security forces in Brunei as well as, according to some analysts, the Sultan's distrust of his own people. Although recruitment in the RBAF is open to all indigenous people, the Malays, however, form the bulk of the RBAF.

At present, the total strength of Brunei's armed forces is 4,400 (including 250 women). The army is organised into three infantry battalions with some 3,400 officers; the navy comprises 700 officers, while the air force has 300. Apart from this, in 1988, Brunei established the Royal Brunei Malay Reserve Regiment (RBMRR), which is made up of two elements, namely compulsory and voluntary members. All ex-servicemen who had completed five years service with the RBAF are obliged to join this regiment. The volunteer service comprises former soldiers who have completed ten years of service with the RBAF as well as other citizens between 18 and 45 years. Each reservist is required to undergo military training of up to 30 days annually.

As for Brunei's defence budget, in 1988 alone it allocated some 24 per cent of the year's B$930 million national budget to defence expenditure. Further, in October 1990 Brunei concluded its largest ever arms deal, valued at US$400 million, with British Aerospace. The contract for Brunei was undertaken by the Royal Brunei Technical Service Sendirian Berhad, established in May 1988, for the sole purpose of purchasing military armaments for Brunei. This company is the only agency permitted to conduct armament purchasing with foreign countries and was granted a monopolizing licence under the state's Monopoly Act. See also: GURKHAS; ROYAL BRUNEI POLICE FORCE.

ROYAL BRUNEI POLICE FORCE (RBPF): The establishment of the police force in Brunei can be traced to the introduction of the Residential System (q.v.) in 1906. Further, in 1920, steps were taken for the formation of an independent police force in Brunei when legislation was passed to terminate the services of the Straits Settlements Police. As such, on 1 January 1921, the Brunei Police Force was formed. Following this, in 1965 Sultan Omar Ali Saiffudien III (q.v.) conferred the Royal title on the Brunei Police Force and in 1971 Sultan Hassanal (q.v.) consented to become the Inspector General of Police. In 1974, Brunei's police force also embarked on a programme to recruit women and in 1988, they represented some 12 per cent of the total force. After achieving independence in 1984, Brunei joined the ASEANAPOL and in 1986, hosted the sixth ASEAN (q.v.) Chiefs of Police Conference, which was held in Bandar Seri Begawan (q.v.). The association is designed, amongst other things, to promote regional cooperation in combatting crime and to allow wider access to training facilities in ASEAN countries. In addition, the RBPF is also a member of the Interpol. The RBPF is at present under the jurisdiction of the Prime Minister's Department. There are some 2,300 officers attached with the RBPF as well as the Marine Police and the entire force is run along British lines. In addition, there is also a Police Training Centre, which was established in 1970. See also: GURKHAS; ROYAL BRUNEI ARMED FORCES.

ROYAL COMMISSION: It was formed by Sultan Omar Ali Saifuddien III (q.v.) in connection with the idea for the formation of Malaysia (q.v.). Its chairman was the *Menteri Besar* (Chief Minister) of Brunei, Marsal bin Maun (q.v.) with various community representatives such as A. M. Azahari (q.v.) representing the Malays, as well as the Parti Rakyat Brunei (PRB) (q.v.), Orang Kaya Gimang Anak Perait representing the Ibans, Orang Kaya Pekerma Dewa Lukan bin Uking representing the Dusuns and Pehin Bendahari China Hong Kok Tien, who was representative of the Chinese (q.v.) community. In addition, Hashim Tahir was appointed as Secretary of this commission. The commission was given the task to survey public opinion with regard to the formation of Malaysia and especially the reaction of the Bruneians toward joining the Malaysian Federation.

RUBBER (*Hevea Brasilinsis*): It was first introduced to Brunei in 1908 when a Malay, Haji Mohammed Daud, started a plantation in Berakas. Following this and due to the tremendous success of this industry in Southeast Asia, the British Resident (q.v.) in Brunei began promoting its cultivation. Attractive prices immediately encouraged many landowners and especially Malays to cultivate this crop. In addition to local participation, there was also some foreign investments especially of European origin. In fact, by 1911 there were already five European-owned rubber estates operating in Brunei. Of the 2,200 acres under rubber cultivation in 1914, some 1,245 acres were European-owned estates. Rubber, totalling some 7,054 lbs., was exported for the first time in 1914, and a year later, rubber exports had increased tremendously to some 50,063 lbs.

Due to the rapid growth of this industry, in 1920 some of the European-owned estates approached the Government with a view to import south Indian (q.v.) labour. A year later, this scheme fell short of succeeding due to a slump in international rubber prices. As a result, the government in 1922 introduced a Rubber Restriction Scheme, and a year later rubber prices began to improve. In 1925 alone, rubber exports were contributing some 71 per cent (or $1,318,218 Straits dollars) of Brunei's total exports valued at $1,859,736. Though the total acreage under rubber cultivation in Brunei had increased to some 8,500 acres by 1928, its contribution to Brunei's total exports had sharply decreased to a level of $581,265. This was mainly due to the Great Depression, which saw yet another slump in rubber prices.

During the Great Depression years, the industry was badly hit and never recovered because although rubber prices did improve in the mid-1930s, the discovery of large reserves of oil at Seria (q.v.) began to undermine the position of this industry. Although the total acreage under rubber cultivation in Brunei in 1938 had increased to 14,747, its ouput on the other hand had sharply decreased. Attracted by the higher wages offered by the oil (q.v.) industry, many rubber smallholders began to abandon their estates to move to this more lucrative industry. The government's attention also shifted to the oil industry and rubber began to receive less attention. By 1984, there were only 10,728 acres under rubber cultivation as compared with 1958, when there were some 33,600 acres.

S

SAHABAT PENA, BRUNEI: Literally translated as Pen Friends. Before the emergence of the Parti Rakyat Brunei (PRB), there were a few nonpolitical organisations in Brunei, especially during the pre-World War II years. The Sahabat Pena, which was formed in July 1936, was one such example. It was headed by Pengiran Pemancha (later Bendahara) Pengiran Haji Mohamad Yasin while its Secretary was Mohamad Zain (the latter was originally from Labuan and at that time was working at the Government Hospital in Brunei Town). Other active members of this organisation were Marsal bin Maun (q.v.), Pengiran Di Gadong Pengiran Haji Mohamad Salleh, Haji Hasbollah bin Haji Daud and Haji Basir bin Taha. In addition to the branch in Brunei Town (q.v.), there was also another branch in Kuala Belait (q.v.), established in 1937, under the leadership of Inche Ludin, a Malay from Negeri Sembilan (Malaya), who was a seconded officer from Malaya serving Brunei's Forestry Department. When Ludin left, his post was taken over by Sergeant-Major Pengiran Nasaruddin bin Pengiran Omar Ali, who was with the Brunei Police Force (q.v.). Like the Sahabat Pena in Malaya, which existed around the same time, the main objective of the Sahabat Pena in Brunei was to enhance social contact amongst the educated Malays of Brunei so as to allow the exchange of ideas amongst themselves. As such, they frequently contributed articles to Malayan newspapers, namely *Saudara* and *Utusan Melayu*. In Brunei Town, the residence of Pengiran Yasin was used temporarily as the headquarters of this society. However, in 1941, as a result of Japanese invasion (q.v.), the society ceased to exist. It can be said that the Sahabat Pena, though nonpolitical in its objectives, was the first attempt to organise educated Malays in Brunei.

SALEHA BINTI AL-MARHUM PENGIRAN PEMANCHA PENG-IRAN ANAK HAJI MUHAMMAD ALAM, PENGIRAN RAJA ISTERI HAJJAH ANAK (QUEEN SALEHA): She is the first wife of Sultan Hassanal Bolkiah (q.v.), whom she married at the age of 16, in July 1965. Born of royal birth, she is also a cousin of Sultan Hassanal. She has borne the Sultan six children: two sons and four daughters. The sons are Al-Muhtadee Billah and Abdul Malik. The daughters are named Rashidah Sa'adutul, Muta-Wakkilah Hayatul, Majeedah Nuurul and Nafizah Sururul. She lives with her children at the Istana Nurul Iman (q.v.). Since the Sultan's second marriage to Queen Mariam (q.v.), Queen Saleha has been forced to take a backseat. For during most official functions and trips abroad, Queen Mariam accompanies the Sultan. In addition, although her son, Al-Muhtadee Billah being Sultan Hassanal's first male heir, should be proclaimed as Regent, this has not been done thus far. As such, it is possible that in the event of the death of the present Sultan, there could emerge a conflict within the royal family on the question of succession. See also: HASSANAL BOLKIAH MU'IZZADDIN WADDAULAH IBNI AL-MARHUM SULTAN HAJI OMAR ALI SAIFUDDIEN KHAIRI WADDIEN, SULTAN; MARIAM BINTI HAJI ABDUL AZIZ, PENGIRAN ISTERI HAJJAH (QUEEN MARIAM).

SALLEH MASRI (H. M. SALLEH): A veteran politician and a former graduate of the Sultan Idris Training College (SITC), Tanjung Malim, Malaysia, Salleh together with Pengiran Yusof (q.v.) and Jamil Umar, formed the Barisan Pemuda (BARIP) (q.v.), or the Youth Front, in 1938. Salleh was appointed President of the BARIP. During the Japanese occupation (q.v.) of Brunei, Salleh was appointed an officer with the Japanese propaganda unit in Brunei, for which he was sentenced to six months imprisonment by the British authorities in 1946, for collaborating with the Japanese. After the period of Japanese occupation (q.v.), the BARIP was once again revived, and in 1947 it submitted a memorandum to Malcolm MacDonald, the Governor General in Singapore (q.v.), urging progress toward independence with some form of representative government. Following this, in August 1956, Salleh was also one of the founding members of the Parti Rakyat Brunei (PRB) (q.v.) where he was appointed Vice President. In 1958, Salleh, A. M. Azahari (q.v.) and several other leaders of the PRB were fined between $10 and $20 for failing to submit the PRB's annual financial accounts to the Registrar of Societies. In mid-1958, Salleh was once again jailed for a few months, on a charge of being under the influence of alcohol at a social gathering at Brunei Hotel in the capital. After being released from prison in September 1958, Salleh tendered his resignation from the PRB. His activities were not much heard of after he left the PRB. When the Brunei National Solidarity Party (BNSP) (q.v.) was formed in 1986, H. M. Salleh was said to have entered politics once again. In April 1996, Haji Latif bin Haji Chuchu (q.v.) resigned from his post as President of the BNSP and H. M. Salleh, who was then Vice President, was appointed as the acting President of the BNSP.

SARAWAK: Located on the Island of Borneo, it is at present one of Malaysia's (q.v.) 13 states. The nucleus of modern Sarawak is located around the Sarawak River (also known as Old Sarawak), which was then a province of the Brunei sultanate. In 1841, an English adventurer, James Brooke (q.v.), was granted the governorship of Old Sarawak when he successfully aided Pengiran Raja Muda Hassim (q.v.) to crush an uprising there. Following the assassination of Raja Muda Hassim in Brunei, in 1846 James Brooke openly declared his intentions to expand Old Sarawak by annexing Brunei's *jajahans* (dependencies). By the time of James Brooke's death in 1868, Sarawak extended from Tanjung Dato to Tanjung Kidurong consisting of some major rivers, namely the Sarawak, Samarahan, Batang Lupar, Skrang, Sadong, Saribas, Rejang, Oya, Kakus, Mukah and Bintulu. James Brooke was succeeded by his nephew, Charles Brooke, who further expanded Sarawak to include the Baram (1882) (q.v.), Trusan (1884) (q.v.), Limbang (1890) (q.v.) and Lawas (1905). As such, modern Sarawak had already been formed by 1905, through the expansionist policies of the white Rajahs. In 1941, Sarawak, like other states of the region, witnessed the harsh period of Japanese occupation (q.v.). When the war ended, the third and last white Rajah of Sarawak, Charles Vyner Brooke (q.v.), made a decision to surrender Sarawak to the British, thus making Sarawak a British colony and ending about 100 years of white Rajah rule over the state. From 1946 till 1963, Sarawak was administered by British Governors, and in 1963 it joined the Federation of Malaysia (q.v.).

Before 1963, most of the officers serving in Brunei were either from Malaya or Sarawak. In fact, some of Brunei's teachers too were trained at the Batu Lintang Training College in Kuching. However, as Brunei decided not to join Malaysia in 1963, relations between Brunei and Sarawak turned sour. This was further aggravated by the fact that in 1973, when Zaini Haji Ahmad (q.v.) and seven other detainees of the outlawed Parti Rakyat Brunei (PRB) (q.v.) fled the Berakas Detention Centre, they were smuggled into Malaysia via Limbang. Relations between the Malaysian federal government and Brunei were further strained when Zaini was allowed to reactivate the PRB in Malaysia.

However, since independence in 1984, and the reforging of relations between Malaysia and Brunei, Sarawak is currently becoming more important in terms of trade to Brunei. Most of Brunei's food supplies are imported from Sarawak, and by 1987 most of the roads linking Sarawak to Brunei, which have been neglected all these years, had been resurfaced (especially the 24-kilometre route between Belait and Baram). Cross border travel between Brunei and Sarawak has increased because of improvements in air, land and sea transportation.

In fact, as a long-term strategy to promote tourism in Brunei, Brunei is also planning to become a gateway to Sarawak, Sabah, Kalimantan, Sulawesi and the southern Philippines (q.v.). Sarawak's exports to Brunei in 1983 were valued at RM22.5 million (in Malaysian *ringgit*) and by 1992, it had increased to RM112.7 million. In another direction, Sarawak's imports from Brunei in 1983 stood at RM1.65 million and by 1993, it was at RM2.9 million. Further, on 27 and 28 March 1995, Sarawak sent a trade mission to Brunei. The mission was led by Sarawak's Industrial Development Minister Datuk Abang Haji Johari Tun Openg. As a result, Sarawak and Brunei agreed to embark on a joint-venture project to set up a livestock farm and venture into food processing. See also: ABDUL RAHMAN PUTERA AL-HAJ IBNI AL-MARHUM SULTAN ABDUL HAMID HALIM SHAH, TUNKU; ASEAN; LIMBANG; MALAYSIA.

SECOND FIVE-YEAR DEVELOPMENT PLAN (NDP 2, 1962–1966): This plan was launched some four years after the first plan, where a Planning Committee from different ministries was given the task to frame their respective programmes. This was in addition to eight advisory groups also involved in the drafting of the plan. The key economic objectives of NDP 2 was diversification and reduction of disparities in regional growth, where a high priority was given to securing a sustained increase in per capita GDP. In addition, the other key aims were to achieve a greater equity in income distribution; the creation of a comprehensive system of education (q.v.); and the creation of a national health service. As such, the focus of the plan was on the provision of necessary economic and social infrastructure in the state. The plan also identified a few areas for attention, namely to increase the agriculture output where a few pilot projects for new crops (coffee, groundnuts, maize) and existing crops were proposed, in addition to improvement in fishery and forest production. Like NDP 1, some 54 per cent of the total budget for NDP 2 was also allocated to transport, communications and infrastructure, where housing and education were the largest recipients of that fund. The total budget for NDP 2 was B$492 million, but as the case with NDP 1, budget control was weak. As such, there were major expansions of expenditure namely in education, which increased eightfold in the period from 1966 to 1968. NDP 2 lasted far longer than was originally anticipated and some of the specific activities continued through late 1972. See also: FIFTH NATIONAL DEVELOPMENT PLAN (NDP 5,1986–1990); FIRST FIVE-YEAR DEVELOPMENT PLAN (NDP 1, 1953–1958); FOURTH NATIONAL DEVELOPMENT PLAN (NDP 4, 1980–1984); NATIONAL DEVELOPMENT PLANS (NDPs); SIXTH NATIONAL DEVELOPMENT PLAN (NDP 6,

1991–1995); THIRD NATIONAL DEVELOPMENT PLAN (NDP 3, 1975–1979);

SERIA: It is a coastal town situated in the Belait District (q.v.). Once described as a small and insignificant fishing village known as Padang Berawa (Wild Pigeon's Field), it is now considered one of the most important towns in Brunei. This was mainly due to the discovery of large reserves of oil (q.v.) in the vicinity of this place in 1929, which immediately changed the fortunes of Seria. By 1935, there were 36 productive oil wells in Seria, and a year later the number had increased to 53. Though Seria's oil industry became the most important revenue earner for the state, progress in this place, however, was quite slow. This was mainly due to Kuala Belait (q.v.) being the headquarters of the British Malayan Petroleum Company (BMPC) (q.v.), where most of its staff members resided as well. It was not until the late 1930s that a small town slowly began to take shape there. However, due to heavy bombing during the Pacific War nothing of this town remained by 1946. After the war, a fresh attempt was made to rebuild Seria when a new town began to take shape. By the early 1950s, a new feature was added to this town when the "nodding donkey" oil pumps were introduced. Today her oil fields are guarded by a Gurkha (q.v.) battalion, which has been placed there since 1964, after the outbreak of the 1962 rebellion led by the Parti Rakyat Brunei (q.v.). See also: BELAIT DISTRICT; KUALA BELAIT.

SINGAPORE: Situated in a strategic position south of the Malaysian Peninsula, it was in ancient times known as Temasik. In 1819, Sir Thomas Stamford Raffles established a post on this island, on behalf of the English East India Company (EIC). This marked the emergence of Singapore as an important trading centre and entrepôt. From 1826 to 1941, Singapore along with Melaka and Pulau Pinang (Penang) were administered as the Straits Settlements, headed by a Governor. From 1946 to 1963, Singapore was administered as a separate entity when Melaka and Pulau Pinang were amalgamated into the administration of the Malayan Union in 1946 and the Federation of Malaya in 1948. In 1963, Singapore joined Malaysia (q.v.) but, two years later in 1965, was expelled from the federation. As such, since 1965 Singapore has been an independent republic with a flourishing economy. Being herself a ministate (city-state) like Brunei, Singapore has fostered close relations with the latter. It is also probable that Singapore's expulsion from Malaysia and Brunei's decision not to join Malaysia was an important factor that consolidated relations between both these states, as both had a sour relationship with Malaysia. In fact, former Premier of Singapore, Lee Kuan Yew was a long-time friend of Sultan Omar Ali Saifuddien III (q.v.) and still maintains such a relationship with Sultan Hassanal (q.v.). As independence approached and when Indonesia suggested in 1980 that Brunei be admitted as ASEAN's (q.v.) sixth member, it was Lee who strongly forwarded the proposal to Sultan Hassanal.

Since Brunei's independence in 1984, Singapore has continued to assist Brunei in various economic and administrative matters. Some of Brunei's governmental institutions are modelled on those of Singapore and to name a few: the Economic Planning Unit (EPU) (q.v.); Economic Development Board (EDB) (q.v.); Brunei Currency Board (q.v.); Brunei Investment Agency (BIA) (q.v.); and the Brunei Port Authority. In fact, much of Brunei's capital resources are channeled through Singapore, and Singapore supplies Brunei with most of its demand for manufactured goods. Singapore ranks fourth, after Japan (q.v.), South Korea and Thailand, as the principal buyer of Brunei's crude petroleum. Not only do leaders of both countries frequently visit each other, even some of Singapore's military exercises are conducted in Brunei. Some of Sultan Hassanal's prime investments are located in Singapore, namely in the hotel industry. The QAF Holdings (q.v.), though owned by Brunei's royal family, is actually based in Singapore.

On 23 January 1995, Brunei joined Singapore in a regional infrastructure fund, which is aimed at investing in projects in China (q.v.), ASEAN, Vietnam and India. The fund, Asian Infrastructure Fund, is promoted by an American consortium led by American International Group (AIG). Whilst Singapore has a US$250 million stake in the fund, Brunei contributed by channeling US$100 million. In short, it can be said that Brunei's relations with Singapore are close when compared with the former's relations with other ASEAN member states.

SIXTH NATIONAL DEVELOPMENT PLAN (NDP 6, 1991–1995): For the purpose of establishing a sustainable and diverse economic base, some B$5.5 billion was allocated under this plan. As such, it embarked on some 2,000 projects, with job creation as the central objective, whereby the projects in the manufacturing, financial and service sector will lead to 40,000 job opportunities.

As with the earlier plans (q.v.), once again the focus is to reduce dependence on the government sector and encourage the development of the non-oil sector. The plan also includes the building of some 11,000 housing units, enhancement of telecommunication services, as well as the upgrading of electricity generation and water supply. In addition, a number of organisational changes have been introduced, and one example is the establishment of a Trade and Industry Council in January 1992 with the aim of securing greater investment in the industrial sector. In 1992, Brunei was also visited by trade delegations from Japan (q.v.) and Taiwan, which came to investigate investment opportunities in Brunei.

In another direction, Brunei too sent a trade delegation to Hanoi to discuss bilateral economic cooperation, namely in the expanding offshore petroleum sector in Vietnam, in which Brunei is keen to invest. See also: FIFTH NATIONAL DEVELOPMENT PLAN (NDP 5, 1986–1990); FIRST FIVE-YEAR DEVELOPMENT PLAN (NDP 1, 1953–1958); FOURTH NATIONAL DEVELOPMENT PLAN (NDP 4, 1980–1984); NATIONAL DEVELOPMENT PLANS (NDPs); SECOND FIVE-YEAR DEVELOPMENT PLAN (NDP 2, 1962–1966); THIRD NATIONAL DEVELOPMENT PLAN (NDP 4, 1975–1979).

SPAIN: Brunei's contact with the Spaniards began in the second half of the 16th century, when the latter were attempting to consolidate their position in the East, namely in the Philippines (q.v.). Although Brunei remained relatively strong throughout the 16th and the first half of the 17th centuries, its capital was, however, captured by the Spaniards in 1578. The Spaniards were keen to destroy the wide influence of the sultanate, which was not merely confined to Borneo but also extended to the Sulu Archipelago. Despite the attack and brief seizure of Brunei's capital, the Spaniards were, however, unable to control Brunei for long.

SRIBUZA: This name appeared in a work called *Ajaib al-Hind* (*Wonders of the Indies*), which was written by an Arab sea captain around A.D. 950. It is believed that it refers to a place located on the Brunei Bay, which probably points to ancient Brunei. It was ruled by members of the royal family of Funan (in the area of present-day Cambodia), who were driven away from the mainland by the Khmers during the seventh century. Like the Bruneians, the Funanese as well were seafarers. In fact, other Arab sources too have made mention of a trading centre around this region about the same time as Sribuza. See also: VIJAYAPURA.

SUCCESSION AND REGENCY PROCLAMATION, 1959: In addition to the main body of the Constitution of 1959 (q.v.), a separate proclamation called the Succession and Regency Proclamation was also promulgated by Sultan Omar Ali Saifuddien III (q.v.) in 1959. This proclamation was to deal with matters and regulations concerning succession and the institution of a regency when the need arose. Succession to the throne was to take place only upon the death of the reigning Sultan, or the "occurence of any other event by reason of which the reigning Sultan, shall cease to occupy the throne of Brunei." The latter included abdication, or confirmation by at least eight traditional nobles that the Sultan was mentally or physically incapable of ruling. The succession was to go to the eldest male issue of the reigning Sultan, provided he was a Malay, a Muslim, and of full royal blood. A potential candidate would be disqualified if he had been convicted for certain offences under the Penal Code. A Council of Succession was to determine the ultimate heir in accordance with the rules spelled out in this proclamation. No person could succeed to the throne without the approval of this council. The Sultan could declare his successor during his lifetime, but only after obtaining approval of the council. There was also provision for the proclamation of a regency and the establishment of a Council of Regency. These applied especially if the Sultan at his accession was under the age of 18 years.

SUFRI BOLKIAH, PENGIRAN MUDA (PRINCE): Styled the *Pengiran Di Gadong,* he is the youngest brother of Sultan Hassanal (q.v.) and is said to be suffering from skin cancer. He has been married three times, the latest to a 22-year-old Malaysian pop singer known as Mazuin Hamzah, whom he met in July 1987. The wedding is said to have cost some B$1.5 million. He is also said to be close to Prince Jefri and was appointed acting Sultan in 1987, when all his brothers together with their families went to Mecca to perform the hajj. Due to his health, he does not hold any portfolio in Brunei's Cabinet (q.v.).

T

TABUNG AMANAH ISLAM BRUNEI (TAIB): The Brunei Islamic Trust Fund was launched personally by Sultan Hassanal (q.v.) in September 1991. It was formed to manage a fund and eventually sponsor investment and trade, including investments in the stock and financial markets as well as participate in industrial and economic development in the state. The fund operates through a financial savings system whereby investments are made and dividends paid on a profit basis after the deducting payment for the *zakat* (tithe) as well as the cost of management. The TAIB also offers special loans for mortgage purposes and also insurance cover. It was also disclosed by the Sultan that the International Bank of Brunei (IBB) would become the nucleus for the first Islamic bank in the state. In fact, this was done in 1993 when the IBB was restructured and began operating in accordance with the Islamic principle of avoiding interest (*riba*). In August of that year, 14 million shares were offered for Muslims only, with the Sultan taking the bulk of it.

TEMBURONG DISTRICT: It is one of the four districts of Brunei today and is separated from Brunei proper by the district of Limbang (q.v.), Sarawak (q.v.). In addition, in the north it shares a common border with the district of Trusan (q.v.), Sarawak. It is 1,304 square kilometres in size and has a population of 8,500 (1986). Due to its isolated location from Brunei proper and sparse population, it is considered the most backward district in Brunei. It is populated mainly by Malays and non-Malay indigenes such as the Kedayans (q.v.), Muruts (q.v.) and Ibans, who still practice shifting cultivation. The major town in this district is Bangar. Currently, the interior of this district also serves as a training area for the Royal Brunei Armed Forces (q.v.) and war games are also frequently conducted between Brunei's and Singapore's (q.v.) military forces here.

TENTERA NASIONAL KALIMANTAN UTARA (TNKU): The National Army of North Kalimantan was formed in August 1960 at the house of A. M. Azahari's (q.v.) father in Kampong Padang near Brunei Town (q.v.). It was an underground military arm of the Parti Rakyat Brunei (PRB) (q.v.). Its formation was attended by all the PRB's leaders, and Sheikh Othman, Azahari's brother, was appointed Brigadier General of the TNKU. In connection, a war committee was also formed in March 1962, with the aim of recruiting members and preparing for military training. The members of the War Committee were Sheikh Othman, Jais Haji Kiram, Mesir Keruddin, Jassin Affandy (q.v.), Abdullah Jahfar, Mayor Mumin Ahmad and Haji Yusuf Tamit. One of its earliest training grounds was located at Kampong Kilanas in the Tutong District (q.v.) where recruits were given military training by Pudin Ladi, Abdullah Jahfar and Jais Haji Kiram. Following this, the first batch of recruits, totaling 40 men, were sent for further training at Merapok (located at the border of Sabah and east Kalimantan) under the charge of the Tentera Nasional Indonesia (Indonesian National Army). Before the outbreak of the 1962 Brunei rebellion (q.v.), Azahari did boast of having some 30,000 members in the TNKU, though the exact figure was never revealed. However, in the aftermath of the revolt, only some 2,063 members of the TNKU were arrested. In a meeting held at Kampung Padang, Brunei Town (q.v.), in early December 1962, the TNKU decided to launch an armed struggle and the decision was sanctioned by Azahari on 5 December 1962. Two major factors that led to this decision were: that the TNKU's recruits were getting restless and impatient; and a few of the TNKU recruits had been arrested in Sundar, Sarawak (q.v.) in early

November 1962, where during the interrogation they had informed the Sarawak authorities about the activities of the TNKU. Thus at 2.00 A.M. on 8 December 1962, the TNKU started the rebellion, and a state of emergency was immediately declared by the government. The government also requested assistance from the British where troops from Singapore (q.v.) were brought in. Hardly two weeks later, most of the TNKU members had been arrested and thus the rebellion was crushed. See also: PARTI RAKYAT BRUNEI (PRB); REBELLION OF 1962.

THIRD NATIONAL DEVELOPMENT PLAN (NDP 3, 1975–1979): This plan was formulated at a time when government revenues increased more than fivefold between 1973 and 1975. As such, the Economic Planning Unit (q.v.) was established in 1973, with the aim to specifically coordinate and monitor the development plans as well as create measures for strong budgetary control. As a solution to reduce structural imbalance in the economy, which was identified as a critical problem, the aim of diversification became the thrust of this plan. As such, developments in agriculture, forestry, fishing and manufacturing were seen vital to the long-term sustainability of the economy. It sought to achieve a 6 per cent annual growth in GDP as well as create 10,000 new jobs over the period of the plan. Also under NDP 3, the Economic Development Board (q.v.), modelled on the Singapore board, was established with the aim to attract inward and domestic investment in industrial ventures mainly through the provision of tax privileges and other incentives. Despite the stated aim to diversify Brunei's economy, very little allocation, in fact, was channeled to agriculture, fisheries, forestry and industrial projects. Much of it was still used to upgrade infrastructure such as roads, telecommunications, water supply, education and health. This resulted in the non-oil GDP remaining unchanged at around 20 per cent, and the GDP contribution from agriculture and non-oil manufacturing sector declined. Also unsuccessful were attempts to establish some major industrial projects, namely a pulp mill, an ammonia-urea plant and a glass-manufacturing industry. The total allocation for NDP 3 was at B$533,554,000. See also: FIFTH NATIONAL DEVELOPMENT PLAN, (NDP 5, 1986–1990); FIRST FIVE-YEAR DEVELOPMENT PLAN (NDP 1, 1953–1958); FOURTH NATIONAL DEVELOPMENT PLAN (NDP 4, 1980–1984); NATIONAL DEVELOPMENT PLANS (NDPs); SECOND FIVE-YEAR DEVELOPMENT PLAN (NDP 2, 1962–1966); SIXTH NATIONAL DEVELOPMENT PLAN (NDP 6, 1991–1995).

TORREY, JOSEPH W.: A Hong Kong merchant who bought from Charles Lee Moses (q.v.) a concession covering large territories in

North Borneo. Torrey together with his associates formed the American Trading Company of Borneo for the purpose of developing the territories. Not long after, Torrey arrived in Brunei to negotiate afresh with the Sultan, who appointed him Supreme Ruler and Governor with the title of Raja of Ambong and Marudu with "all other powers and rights usually exercised by, and belonging to Sovereign Rulers." This manoeuvre by the Sultan created a stir and the British government queried the United States (q.v.) about its aims in Borneo. However, Torrey not only failed to establish a settlement in North Borneo but his efforts to obtain United States' (q.v.) support were futile. Therefore in 1875, he sold his concessions to the Austrian Consul General in Hong Kong, Baron von Overbeck. See also: BRITISH NORTH BORNEO COMPANY (BNBC).

TREATY OF PROTECTION, 1888: When Brunei lost further territory with the cessions of the Trusan (q.v.) in 1884 and the Padas in 1887, Charles Brooke (q.v.) had ambitions of annexing the Limbang (q.v.) while Peter Leys, the British Consul General in Labuan (q.v.), had plans of partitioning Brunei. Had that been allowed, the Sultan would be left only with his capital and Muara. Therefore, Sultan Hashim Jalilul Alam Aqamaddin appealed to Queen Victoria to halt the activities of Charles Brooke and stop Leys's plan from being implemented. The Queen, in turn, directed the Foreign Office not to implement Leys's plan and appointed a commission under Sir Frederick Weld to investigate the situation in Brunei. As a result of the findings of the Weld Commission, Brunei entered into this treaty with the British on 17 September 1888, with the sole purpose of ensuring the survival of what was left of Brunei. Thus, by this treaty Brunei became a British protectorate, handing over her foreign relations to Britain. In addition, a similar treaty was extended to Sarawak (q.v.) and North Borneo. However, the treaty failed to ensure Brunei's survival, for in 1890 Charles Brooke seized Limbang and the British government, instead of assisting the Sultan to recover it, sanctioned the annexation.

TRUSAN: It was formerly a part of Brunei's "southern rivers" and is at present situated in the State of Sarawak (q.v.). It was ceded to Sarawak in 1884 by Hashim Jalilul Alam, then the *Temenggong* of Brunei, without the prior approval or seal of the Sultan and was therefore considered as an illegal transaction by the latter. When Hashim was appointed Sultan to succeed Sultan Abdul Mumin (q.v.) in 1885, the former tried all means to recover the Trusan from the Sarawak (q.v.) government. His attempts to recover Trusan were not successful for under preasure by Peter Leys, then British Consul General in Labuan (q.v.), Hashim finally, in 1885, approved the cession of Trusan. See also: BROOKE, CHARLES.

TUTONG DISTRICT: Sandwiched between the Brunei-Muara (q.v.) and Belait (q.v.) districts, Tutong is 1,166 square kilometres in size and is also Brunei's third largest district. Its population in 1986 was at 136,100, making it Brunei's second most populated district. The majority of its populace are Malays and non-Malay indigenes with a relatively large number of Chinese (q.v.) as well. Its very strategic location situated in-between the Brunei-Muara and Belait districts gives Tutong a more advantageous position when compared with Temburong (q.v.), which is isolated from Brunei proper. This is because although its economic potential is low as in the case of Temburong, its location gives the district a better lead in terms of development as all the major roads and highways connecting the Brunei-Muara District or the administrative centre of the state, with the Belait District as the hub of Brunei's economy, pass through the Tutong District as well. Most of Tutong's population live in the coastal areas of this dictrict for much of its interior is still covered with thick forest where some of the non-Malay indigenes dwell. The major economic activities of this district are rice (q.v.) and rubber (q.v.) cultivation, logging and fisheries whilst the non-Malay indigenes practice shifting cultivation. It is also used occasionally for military training by the Royal Brunei Armed Forces (q.v.). The major town of this district is Tutong.

U

UNITED NATIONS (UN): An international organisation that was formed on 26 June 1945 in San Francisco, to replace the defunct League of Nations. All independent states are members of this organisation. Brunei became its 159th member on 21 September 1984, and currently contributes 0.03 per cent of the UN's regular budget. The ceremony in New York in 1984 was attended by Sultan Hassanal (q.v.) and in his acceptance speech to the UN General Assembly, the Sultan condemned Israel for its prosecution of Palestinians and supported the latter in their struggle for a homeland. While in New York, the Sultan also donated US$1 million to the United Nations Childrens Fund (UNICEF). Further, at the 42nd session of the UN General Assembly in New York on 2 October 1986, Brunei's representative to the UN, Pengiran Bahrin, who was also the Law Minister, adopted a strong stand against apartheid. Brunei's firm stand was, however, marred, by reports later in the year that oil shipments from

Brunei were finding their way to South Africa in defiance of a Brunei government ban. It was reported that embargoed oil worth at least US$700 million, which had disappeared with 30 tankers after loading at Seria (q.v.), had reached South Africa through intermediaries and that most of it was sold to the Shell refinery in Durban. Responding to the claims, Brunei Shell Petroleum (BSP) (q.v.) undertook to vet all its customers to find out how the oil had leaked to South Africa.

Thus far, Brunei has also done her part toward the maintenance of international peace and security by participating in the UN's peacekeeping efforts. In November 1992, it despatched a group of 12 personnel from the Royal Brunei Police Force (RBPF) and three observers from the Royal Brunei Armed Forces (RBAF) to participate in the peacekeeping process in Cambodia under the supervision of the United Nations Transitional Authority in Cambodia (UNTAC).

In October 1994, Sultan Hassanal delivered his second address to the UN General Assembly where he reaffirmed the cooperation between ASEAN and the UN. Brunei is also a member of the World Health Organization (WHO), International Maritime Organization (IMO), United Nations Conference on Trade and Development (UNCTAD), Universal Postal Union (UPU), International Civil Aviation Organization (ICAO), World Meteorological Organization (WMO) as well as the Economic and Social Commission for Asia and Pacific (ESCAP). See also: FOREIGN POLICY.

UNITED STATES OF AMERICA (U.S.): The first contact between Brunei and the U.S. took place in 1845, when the U.S. ship *Constitution* arrived in Brunei to offer immediate protection and obtain a trade treaty in return for the exclusive right to work all coal (q.v.) deposits in the sultanate. The protection was offered in view of Sarawak's (q.v.) expansionist policy, which was usurping Brunei's territory. The Bruneians, however, rejected the offer for they were already negotiating with the British on the same matter and were awaiting news from that quarter. By 1850, when the British had failed to stop Sarawak's expansionist policy, the Bruneians once again took steps to reactivate relations with the U.S. The latter sent Joseph Balestier as their agent and negotiations were held, by which both parties entered into a Treaty of Friendship and Commerce in 1850. This treaty, however, remained ineffective for 15 years, and only in 1865 did the U.S. send their first Consul, Charles Lee Moses (q.v.), to Brunei. The Sultan sought to utilize this renewed American interest for his own purposes by which he willingly gave Moses a large concession covering territories in North Borneo for a period of ten years. Shortly after, Moses sold all his concessions to Joseph W. Torrey (q.v.), who formed the American Trading Company of Borneo. Alarmed by this development, the British government queried the U.S. and the latter denied having any political aims in Borneo. Between 1850 and 1895, when the Sarawak (q.v.) government renewed its schemes to seize the remaining territories of Brunei, relations between the U.S. and Brunei remained very low. Alarmed by Sarawak's revived strategy, the Bruneians once again appealed to the U.S. for protection, only to be warned by the British authorities not to enter into communications with other powers.

At present, Brunei maintains cordial relations with the U.S. as a strategy by a small state to ensure its survival by diversifying its foreign relations with major powers. About a year after achieving independence in 1984, Brunei established its official relations with the U.S. when it opened its embassy in Washington, D.C.. Earlier, in September 1984, Sultan Hassanal (q.v.) made his first postindependence visit to the U.S., when Brunei was admitted to the United Nations (q.v.). While in New York, the Sultan donated US$500,000 to feed the needy of New York. Following this, in mid-1986, the U.S. Secretary of State, George Schultz, while en route to Manila, was granted a three-hour audience with the Sultan. In fact, Shultz's Bechtel Corporation of which he was Vice President between 1974 and 1981, was the principal consultant for the construction of the Istana Nurul Iman (q.v.). In the same year, Admiral James Lyon Jr., Commander in Chief of the U.S. Pacific Fleet paid a goodwill visit to Brunei. Further, in July 1993 Prince Mohamed (q.v.), Brunei's Foreign Minister met Warren Christopher, U.S. State Secretary, in Singapore (q.v.), where both discussed a Memorandum of Understanding regarding U.S. Navy visits to Brunei. In addition, there were also plans to waive visa requirements between the U.S. and Brunei.

The present Sultan too has a number of major investments in the United States, namely the Beverly Hills Hotel (or the "Pink Palace") in Los Angeles, which was purchased in 1987 for some US$200 million. In early 1988, the Sultan bought three of the finest residences in Beverly Hills for a total of US$15 million. Apart from this, two major American companies were appointed as investment consultants to the Brunei Investment Agency (q.v.), which was formed in 1983. They are Morgan Guarantee Trust and Citibank.

UNIVERSITI BRUNEI DARUSSALAM (UBD): It is Brunei's only university, which was officially established on 28 October 1985. Plans to establish tertiary education in Brunei were announced as early as 14 August 1976, in a speech made by Sultan Hassanal (q.v.) at the Qu'ran Reading Competition held at the Omar Ali Saifuddien Mosque (q.v.). Following this, a committee was set up by the Education Ministry to study the feasibility of having tertiary education in

Brunei. This was soon followed by a series of consultants coming to Brunei, mainly from the British Council in London and some British universities. As a result, the first Bachelor of Education degree programme was inaugurated at the Sultan Hassanal Bolkiah Teachers College (SHBTC) in 1984, when the latter was upgraded to become the Institute Pendidikan Sultan Hassanal Bolkiah (IPSHB) or the the Sultan Hassanal Bolkiah Institute of Education. It successfully opened with 32 students, and by 23 April 1985, it was also announced that the UBD would be established.

The final preparations to set up the university began in June 1985, and the Ministry of Education forged formal links with the University of Wales College of Cardiff and the University of Leeds to assist in the formulation of various English-medium courses. In addition, to overcome the shortage of teaching staff a number of lecturers were recruited from overseas primarily from Malaysia (q.v.), Singapore (q.v.), Indonesia (q.v.) and Britain. The university finally began operating on 28 October 1985, when it opened with its first batch of 176 students enrolled for a four-year degree programme. It was temporarily housed in a renovated primary school near the Sultan Hassanal Bolkiah Institute of Education in Bandar Seri Begawan. In 1988, the Sultan Hassanal Bolkiah Institute of Education was amalgamated with the UBD. The UBD is at present situated in Gadong and currently offers 11 first-degree programmes, three Master's degree programmes, a postgraduate Certificate in Education, a Certificate in Education and two other certificate-level programmes. The Chancellor of the UBD is Sultan Hassanal Bolkiah, while the Vice-Chancellor is Dato Seri Laila Jasa Awang Haji Abu Bakar bin Haji Apong. See also: EDUCATION.

V

VIJAYAPURA: It was cited by Chinese (q.v.) sources from the sixth to the ninth centuries and is believed to be a kingdom located in the northwestern part of Borneo, which existed some 1,400 years ago. According to these Chinese sources, Vijayapura was highly developed socioeconomically. Some historians believe that it is the ancient kingdom of Brunei for it existed around the same time as "Sribuza" (q.v.) mentioned in the *Ajaib al-Hind* (*Wonders of the Indies*). See also: SRIBUZA.

W

WALKER, SIR WALTER: He was Commander of the 17th Gurkha (q.v.) Division in Nepal when the Brunei rebellion (q.v.) broke out on 8 December 1962. From Nepal, he was despatched to Brunei where he arrived on 19 December 1962 to take over as Commander of British Forces in Borneo (COMBRITOR). He was the military genius behind the success of the British forces in suppressing the Brunei uprising.

WAZIR: Literally translated as vizier, this group of officials are considered the most important of all other officials in the traditional government of Brunei. The four officials (*wazir*), according to their respective ranking, are the *Pengiran Bendahara, Pengiran Di-Gadong, Pengiran Pemancha* and *Pengiran Temenggong*. The *Pengiran Bendahara* was the Chief Minister, the deputy of the Sultan and in charge of land defence while the *Pengiran Di-Gadong*, the next most important *wazir* was the "lord of the treasury" and in charge of palace affairs. Next in rank was the *Pengiran Pemancha*, best described as "home minister," and the fourth *wazir* was the *Pengiran Temenggong*, or the "lord of the sea" and in charge of naval defence.

WELFARE STATE: Endowed with its riches from its oil and gas (q.v.) revenues, Brunei currently enjoys one of the highest GNP per capita incomes in the world, which is at an average of US$25,000 a year. As such, it is run like a welfare state where the citizens enjoy benefits and facilities that are not available to most people in Asia. In fact, Brunei has a highly developed welfare state and its administration is the responsibility of the Ministry of Culture, Youth and Sports.

There is no personal income tax in this oil-rich sultanate and duties on imports are the lowest overall in the region. In addition, free education (q.v.) is provided to all citizens from kindergarten upward. This also includes further education in universities. The government also takes care of the schooling of its employees' children who go to nongovernmental schools. In addition to this, government employees are also provided interest-free car and housing loans, which adds up to three times their annual salaries. With 153,351 vehicles registered in 1993, Brunei has the distinction of having ratios of 1:1.8 persons per vehicle and 1:2 per private car.

In 1955, a national noncontributory pensions scheme was introduced and it provides monthly pensions to ex-government employees above the age of 60. Financial aid is also provided to other categories, namely the blind, disabled and mentally retarded. In 1987 alone, some B$10 million was paid out to pensioners and their dependents. Apart from education, medical and health care services are also provided free by the government.

The Resettlement Department, which comes under the Ministry of Development provides land and houses for citizens with 20-year interest-free mortgages. To provide proper housing, more than 500 to 600 houses are built annually and are of high quality by Asian standards. The government also subsidises annual pilgrimages to Mecca, with about 3,000 Bruneians making the journey each year on chartered jets. In terms of health, education, welfare and spending power, the Bruneians are much better off when compared with any other Asians, except the Japanese.

Z

ZAINI HAJI AHMAD, HAJI: Born on 21 January 1935 at Kampong Sumbiling, he was considered the right-hand man of Parti Rakyat Brunei's (PRB) (q.v.) leader, A. M. Azahari (q.v.). Zaini's father, Pehin Orang Kaya Syahbandar Dato Setia Haji Ahmad, was a key figure in Brunei for he was not only special adviser to the Sultan but also the latter's Legal Adviser. In fact, Haji Ahmad was one of the Sultan's advisers for the promulgation of the 1959 Constitution (q.v.). He was also appointed to the Privy Council (q.v.). Zaini's father did attempt to discourage him from becoming active in the PRB, but was unsuccessful.

Prior to joining the PRB, Zaini was a civil servant and some of his appointments were: as a clerk at the Brunei Immigration Department between 1954 and 1955; as Administrative Officer at the Economic Development Unit of the State Government Secretariat; and at the Labour Office in Kuala Belait between 1960 and 1961. When the 1962 rebellion (q.v.) broke out, Zaini together with Azahari were in Manila. After the abortive coup, Zaini renounced his allegiance to his ambitious leader, Azahari, and sought political asylum with the British authorities in Hong Kong. The British, in turn, handed him over to the Brunei government, which placed Zaini under detention at the Berakas Detention Centre. In 1966, Amnesty International took up his cause by calling upon the Sultan of Brunei, the Commonwealth Relations Office in London and the United Nations Commission on Human Rights to obtain his release. However, all these efforts proved futile. Thus, Zaini made a new bid for his freedom by announcing that he was ready to renounce his Brunei citizenship in return for exile, which was turned down by the Brunei government.

Following this, in 1973, Zaini along with seven other detainees broke out from the detention camp and fled to Limbang (q.v.), where he was granted political asylum by the Malaysian authorities. While living in exile in Malaysia, Zaini, together with some other members of the PRB who fled with him, revived the PRB and continued their political activities by demanding independence for Brunei as well as appealing to some international organisations and countries. Some of these appeals were: to the United Nations (q.v.) (March 1975, July 1975, November 1975 and October 1977); to the Non-Aligned Summit Conference (July 1976); to the Commonwealth (q.v.) (March 1975); and to the Muslim Foreign Ministers' Conference in Kuala Lumpur (1974).

At least until 1992, Zaini was living in Kuala Lumpur and submitted his doctoral dissertation to the University of Malaya in the same year. When he returned to Brunei to appeal for pardon from the present Sultan (q.v.) in late 1992, he was detained. It is believed that he was released in 1996 and remains in Brunei. See also: PARTI RAKYAT BRUNEI (PRB); REBELLION OF 1962.

ZOBEL, ENRIQUE: He is a leading "Mestizo" Filipino businessman who is a member of the Zobel de Ayala family, which is of Spanish origin. The family is related to the Roxases and Sorianos, and has been rich and well known since Spanish times. Its family founder, Jacobo, married Trinidad Ayala and inherited Ayala y Cia, the predecessor of the present Ayala Corporation. It was founded in 1834 and was engaged primarly in estate agriculture. Zobel's entry into modern business began in 1910, when the family established the Insular Life Insurance, which is at present known as the FGU Insurance Corporation, a member of the Ayala group. In 1969, the Ayala Corporation bought a controlling interest in the Bank of the Philippines Island. Zobel's firm the Ayala Corporation was awarded the tender to build the Istana Nurul Imam (q.v.). He was also a polo-playing buddy of Sultan Hassanal (q.v.) and was the main force behind the establishment of the Island Development Bank (IDB) in 1980, a fifty-fifty joint venture between him and Brunei's royal family. Zobel's Ayala had a 25 per cent stake in the IDB, while the Bank of the Philippine Islands, of which Zobel was then the Director, held another 25 per cent. A restructuring of the IDB in 1985 left Zobel with a 20 per cent stake while the royal family had increased its share to 60 per cent and another 20 per cent was owned by Japan's largest bank, Dai Ichi Kangyo Bank. On 19 August 1986, Zobel, who was until then Chairman and Chief Executive of the IDB, quit all his posts in the IDB for reasons unknown.

Bibliography

This bibliography includes selected major and important works on Brunei. Priority is given to writings readily available in English or in English translations. The bibliography is divided into two basic parts. Part 1 provides the general bibliographies, general studies and indexes, directories, professional periodicals and newspapers. Part 2 is divided into seven main subject headings, which are further subdivided with each main subject heading or subdivision. The selected books, articles and manuscripts aim at a representative treatment of the historical development of Brunei: culture, economy, politics, sciences and society. Entries are arranged alphabetically by authors.

Unlike most other countries, sources on Brunei's past are extremely limited. Though Brunei became a strong power in the Borneo region prior to the 19th century, it remained relatively isolated from mainstream Southeast Asian writings. The scanty material during this period can be located from Chinese, Portuguese and Spanish sources. Some good sources for the 16th and 17th centuries are: E. H. Blair and J. A. Robertson, *The Philippines Islands*; M. Teixeira, "Early Portuguese and Spanish Contacts with Borneo," *Da Sociedade De Geografia De Lisboa* (July-December 1964); Robert Nicholl, *European Sources for the History of the Sultanate of Brunei in the Sixteenth Century*.

In the nineteenth century, Brunei's vast empire began to dwindle. Two new states, Sarawak and North Borneo (Sabah), were carved out from its territories. Sarawak especially which was created by a dynasty of white Rajahs —the Brookes —caught the fancy and imagination of most western writers. Brunei, the sick man of Borneo, was almost totally neglected. It is therefore inevitable and imperative for a researcher to actually use writings on Sarawak to reconstruct the history of Brunei in the nineteenth century. In this respect, a great deal of information on the social, economic and political conditions of Brunei in the early part of the nineteenth century, is contained in the journals of Sir James Brooke, the first Rajah of Sarawak. These journals have been partially reproduced in such works as: G. L. Jacob, *The Raja of Sarawak: An Account of Sir James Brooke*; Henry Keppel, *The Expedition to Borneo of H.M.S. Dido for the Suppression of Piracy; with extracts from the*

Journal of James Brooke of Sarawak; Rodney Mundy, *Narrative of Events in Borneo and Celebes, Down to the Occupation of Labuan: from the Journal of James Brooke, Esq., Raja of Sarawak and Governor of Labuan together with Narrative of the Operations of H.M.S. Iris.* Official primary records on Brunei, North Borneo and Sarawak are now mainly deposited in the Public Records Office, London; Rhodes House Library, Oxford; Brunei Museum, Bandar Seri Begawan; Sabah State Archives, Kota Kinabalu; and Sarawak Museum, Kuching. Two works that have extensively used the sources for the reconstruction of Brunei's history in the nineteenth century are: Nicholas Tarling, *Britain, the Brookes and Brunei*; and Graham Irwin, *Nineteenth Century Borneo: A Study in Diplomatic Rivalry.* In the 20th century, especially from 1906 to 1959, Brunei's history was mainly the history of the Residential System. This has been well covered in the work of A. V. M. Horton, *The British Residency in Brunei, 1906–1959.* After World War II and until the present, the major themes that dominate the writings of Brunei's story are: the struggle between the monarchy and Parti Rakyat Brunei (PRB) in their quest for independence and national identity; various plans to integrate Brunei into larger political units; the economic riches of the country; and postindependence developments. Some of the major works pertaining to these themes are: Zaini Haji Ahmad, *Pertumbuhan Nasionalisme di Brunei, 1939–1962* (The Growth of Nationalism in Brunei, 1939–1962); Mohamed Noordin Sopiee, *From Malayan Union to Singapore Separation, Political Unification in the Malaysian Region, 1945–1965*; B. A. Hamzah, *The Oil Sultanate: Political History of Oil in Brunei Darussalam* and *Oil and Economic Development Issues in Brunei*; Mark Cleary and Shuang Yann Wong, *Oil, Economic Development and Diversification in Brunei Darussalam*; James Bartholomew, *The Richest Man in the World, The Sultan of Brunei*; and David Leake, *Brunei, The Modern Southeast Asian Islamic Sultanate.* Apart from this, a comprehensive work on Brunei's social history is Donald E. Brown, *Brunei, The Structure and History of a Bornean Malay Sultanate.*

In addition to the sources mentioned above, the *Sarawak Museum Journal* provides the most extensive and authoritative literature on Borneo, including Brunei. In this respect, it might be worth the while of a researcher to look at Tom Harrisson's article, "Brunei in the Sarawak Museum Journal," *Brunei Museum Journal* (Vol. 1, No. 1, 1969: 180–189). This is an annotated list of 40 articles about Brunei published in the *Sarawak Museum Journal* from 1949 to 1969. Of course, with the establishment of the Brunei Museum in 1965, more information on Brunei began to appear in the *Brunei Museum Journal*, which has been published since 1969. Another three great compendiums of information on contemporary Brunei are: *Southeast Asian Affairs, Asian Survey*, and *Asia Yearbook.*

Last but not least, no researcher can go without referring to the most comprehensive annotated bibliography on Brunei by Sylvia C. Engelen Krausse and Gerald H. Krausse, *Brunei*.

Bibliographies, General Studies and Indexes

Ave, Jan B., Victor T. King and Joke GW de Wit. *West Kalimantan: A Bibliography*. Dordrecht, The Netherlands: Foris Publications Holland, 1983.

Bastin, John. *Western Language Historical Sources in the British Borneo Territories*. Kuala Lumpur: University of Malaya, Department of History, 1962.

Bernado, Gabriel Adriano. *A Critical Annotated Bibliography of Philippine, Indonesian and other Malayan Folk-lore*. Radaza, Francisco Demetrio Y. (ed.), Cagayan de Oro City, Philippines: Xavier University, 1972.

Bibliografi mengenai Brunei. (Bibliography concerning Brunei). Bandar Seri Begawan: Dewan Bahasa & Pustaka, [n.d.].

Chua Sui Gim. "Guide to Modern Archives and Manuscripts found in the United Kingdom relating to Brunei, Sabah and Sarawak," *Brunei Museum Journal*, Vol. 5, No. 1, 1981: 56–77.

Collins, James T. "Dialek Melayu Brunei: Catatan Bibliography" (Brunei Malay Dialect: A Bibliography), *Dewan Bahasa*, Vol. 28, June 1984: 390–411.

Cotter, Conrad Patrick and Shiro Saito. *Reading List of English Language Materials in the Social Sciences on Borneo (With Critical Annotation)*. Honolulu: University of Hawaii, 1960.

———. *Bibliography of English Language Sources on Human Ecology: Eastern Malaysia and Brunei*. Honolulu: University of Hawaii, Department of Asian Studies, 1965, 2 vols.

Cotter, Conrad Patrick, William G. Solheim and T. R. Williams. *North Borneo, Brunei and Sarawak: A Bibliography of English Language Historical, Administrative and Ethnographic Sources*. Hilo: University of Hawaii Peace Corps Training Center, 1963 (Mimeograph).

Crisswell, Colin N. "A Select Bibliography of Published Works with Relevance to Bornean History," *Borneo Research Bulletin* (Michigan), Vol. 4, 1972: 1–22.

Harrisson, Thomas H. "Brunei in the *Sarawak Museum Journal*," *Brunei Museum Journal*, Vol. 1, No. 1, 1969: 180–189.

Hellman, Florence C. *British Malaya and British Borneo: A Selected List of References*. Washington, D.C.: Library of Congress, 1943.

Hill, Lewis. *A Checklist of English Fiction Relating to Malaysia, Singapore and Brunei*. Hull: University of Hull, Centre for Southeast Asian Studies, 1986.

Hill, Winifred. *The Overseas Empire in Fiction: An Annotated Bibliography*. London: Oxford University Press, 1930.

Hughes, Roger. *Southeast Asia, Malaysia, Singapore and including Hong Kong.* London: Commonwealth Institute, 1973.

Human Relations Area Files, British Borneo Research Project. *Bibliography of British Borneo.* New Haven: HRAF British Borneo Research Project at the University of Chicago, 1956.

Krausse, Sylvia C. Engelen and Gerald H. Krausse. *Brunei.* Santa Barbara, Calif.: Clio Press, 1988 (World Bibliographical Series, Vol. 12).

Kuak Sim Joo, Monica and Puteh Ismail. *Prehistory and Archaeology of Malaysia and Brunei: A Bibliography.* Kuala Lumpur: Perpustakaan Universiti Malaya, 1982.

Leigh, Michael B. and John Echolas. *Checklist of Holdings on Borneo in the Cornell University Libraries.* New York: Cornell University, Department of Asian Studies, Southeast Asia Program, 1966.

Lent, John A. and Kent Mulliner (eds.). *Malaysian Studies: Archaeology, Historiography, Geography and Bibliography.* Occasional Paper No. 11, DeKalb, Ill.: Northern Illinois University, Center for Southeast Asian Studies, 1986.

Lim Huck Tee and D. E. K. Wijasuriya. *Index Malaysiana: An Index to the Journal of the Straits Branch, Royal Asiatic Society and the Journal of the Malaysian Branch, Royal Asiatic Society, 1878–1963.* Kuala Lumpur: Malaysian Branch Royal Asiatic Society, 1970.

Lim Pui Huen, Patricia. *The Malay World of Southeast Asia: A Select Cultural Bibliography.* Singapore: Institute of Southeast Asian Studies, 1986.

Loh Chee Yin. "A New Borneo Bibliography: II," *Sarawak Museum Journal,* Vol. 14, 1966: 350–375.

Pelzer, Karl Josef. *Selected Bibliography of the Geography of South East Asia.* New Haven: Southeast Asia Studies, Yale University Human Relations Area Files, 1949–1956, Vols. 1–3.

Roff, Margaret. *Official Publications of Malaysia, Singapore, and Brunei in New York Libraries.* Occasional Bibliographical Papers No. 1, New York: Southern Asian Institute, Columbia University, 1970.

Roff, William R. *Southeast Asian Research Tools: Malaysia, Singapore, Brunei.* Southeast Asia Paper No. 16, Pt. 4, Honolulu: Southeast Asian Program, University of Hawaii, 1979.

Rousseau, Jerome. "A Bibliography of Borneo Bibliographies," *Borneo Research Bulletin,* Vol. 2, 1970: 35–36.

———. *Central Borneo: A Bibliography.* Special Monograph No. 5, Kuching: The Sarawak Museum Journal, Vol. 28, No. 59 (New Series), December 1988.

Sardesai, D. R. and Bhanu D. Sardesai. *Thesis and Dissertations on Southeast Asia, An International Bibliography in Social Sciences, Education and Fine Arts.* Switzerland: Inter-Documentation Library Ag. Zug., 1970.

Saw Swee Hock and Cheng Siok-Hwa. *A Bibliography of the Demography of Malaysia and Brunei.* Singapore: University Education Press, 1975.

U.S. Library of Congress, Orientalia Division. *Southeast Asia Subject Catalogue.* Boston: G. K. Hall, 1972 (6 Vols).

Wijasuriya, D. E. K. and Lim Huck Tee. *Index Malaysiana, Supplement No. 2, 1974–1983.* Petaling Jaya, Malaysia: Malaysian Branch Royal Asiatic Society, 1985.

————. *Index Malaysiana, Supplement I, An Index to the Journal of the Malaysian Branch of the Royal Asiatic Society and the JMBRAS Monographs, 1964–1973.* Kuala Lumpur: Malaysian Branch Royal Asiatic Society, 1974.

Directories

Buku Panduan Badan-badan Perusahaan Perniagaan Negara Brunei Darussalam. (Directory on Business Undertakings, Brunei Darussalam). Bandar Seri Begawan: Unit Perancangan Ekonomi Kementerian Kewangan (Economic Planning Unit, Ministry of Finance), 1985.

Paxton, John (ed.). *The Stateman's Year-Book: Statistical and Historical Annual of the State of the World for the year 1987–1988.* New York: St. Martin's Press, 1987.

Professional Periodicals

Asian Survey. Berkeley: University of California Press, 1961- Monthly.

Asiaweek. Hong Kong: Asiaweek Ltd., 1975–Weekly.

Asia Yearbook. Hong Kong: Far Eastern Economic Review, 1947–Annual.

Berita, Malaysia-Singapore-Brunei Studies Group, Southeast Asia Council. Philadelphia: Temple University, Journalism Department, 1975–Triannual.

Borneo Research Bulletin. Williamsburg, Va.: Borneo Research Council, 1969– Semiannual.

Brunei Museum Journal. Bandar Seri Begawan: Brunei Museum, 1969–Annual.

Contemporary Southeast Asia. Singapore: Institute of Southeast Asian Studies, 1979–Quarterly.

CORMOSEA Bulletin. (Committee on Research Materials on Southeast Asia). Ann Arbor, Mich.: Association for Asian Studies, 1975/76–Irregular.

Economist Country Survey/Report/Profile, Malaysia and Brunei. London: Economist Intelligence Unit, Quarterly and Annual.

Far Eastern Economic Review. Hong Kong: Far Eastern Economic Review, 1946–Weekly.

Journal of Asian Studies. Ann Arbor, Mich.: Association for Asian Studies, 1956–Quarterly.

Journal of Contemporary Asia. Stockholm: Journal of Contemporary Asia, 1970–Quarterly.

Journal of Southeast Asian History (JSEAH). Singapore: Department of History, University of Singapore, 1960–1969–Semiannual.

Journal of Southeast Asian Studies (JSEAS). Singapore: McGraw-Hill Far Eastern Publishers (1970–1977); Singapore: University of Singapore Press (1978), 1970–Semiannual.

Journal of the Malayan/Malaysian Branch of the Royal Asiatic Society (JM-BRAS). Kuala Lumpur: Malayan/Malaysian Branch, Royal Asiatic Society, 1923–Semiannual.

Journal of the Straits Branch of the Royal Asiatic Society (JSBRAS). Singapore: Straits Branch, Royal Asiatic Society, 1878–1992–Semiannual.

Journal of Tropical Geography. Kuala Lumpur and Singapore: Department of Geography, The University of Malaya and The University of Singapore, 1953–Semiannual. (Split into *Malaysian Journal of Tropical Geography* and *Singapore Journal of Tropical Geography* in 1980.)

Modern Asian Studies. Cambridge: Cambridge University Press, 1967– Quarterly.

Pacific Affairs. Vancouver: University of British Columbia, 1928–Quarterly.

Sarawak Museum Journal. Kuching: The Museum, 1911–1937; 1949–Annual.

Southeast Asia Business. Ann Arbor, Mich.: University of Michigan, Center for South and Southeast Asian Studies, 1984–Quarterly.

Southeast Asian Affairs. Singapore: Institute of Southeast Asian Studies, 1974– Annual.

Southeast Asian Journal of Social Sciences. Singapore: Institute of Southeast Asian Studies and Department of Sociology, National University of Singapore, 1973–Semiannual.

Sudost Asien Aktuel. (Southeast Asia Today). Hamburg: Institut fur Asienkunde, 1982–Six times a year.

Major Newspapers

ENGLISH LANGUAGE

Borneo Bulletin
MALAY LANGUAGE

Pelita Brunei
Salam

General Works

Travel Accounts and Travel Guides

Beccari, Odoardo. *Wanderings in the Great Forests of Borneo.* Introduction by Earl of Cranbrook; Enrico H. Giglioli (trans.); rev. ed. F. H. H. Guillemard (ed.). Singapore: Oxford University Press, 1986. (Originally 1904).

Bock, Carl Alfred. *The Headhunters of Borneo: A Narrative of Travel up the Mahakkan and Down the Barito.* London: Marston, Searle & Rivington, 1881.

Fodor's Southeast Asia. London: Hodder & Stoughton, 1984.

Harrisson, Barbara. *Orang-Utan.* London: Collins, 1962.

Harrisson, Tom. *World Within: A Borneo Story.* Kuala Lumpur: Oxford University Press, 1984.

Map Collections

Atlas of Southeast Asia. With an introduction by D. G. E. Hall. London: Macmillan, 1964.

Blakiston, N. "Maps, Plans and Charts of Southeast Asia in the Public Record Office," *Southeast Asian Archives* (The Journal of the Southeast Asian Regional Branch, International Council on Archives), Vol. 2, July 1969: 21–64.

Broek, Jan O. M. "Borneo on Maps of the 16th and 17th Centuries," *Sarawak Museum Journal*, Vol. 11, 1964: 649–654.

Brown, D. E. "Maps and the History of Brunei," *Sarawak Museum Journal*, Vol. 3, No. 1, 1973: 88–90.

Fell, R. T. *Early Maps of South-East Asia.* Singapore: Oxford University Press, 1987.

Philip's Regional Wall Map of Northern Borneo: Sabah Sarawak and Brunei. London: London Geographical Institute, 1968.

Statistical Abstracts

Ajia Keizai Kenkyu Jo. *Bibliography of the Statistical Materials on Southeast Asia.* Tokyo: Institute of Asian Economic Affairs, 1960.

Book of Vital World Statistics, A Complete Guide to the World in Figures. (Introduction by Sir Claus Moser), London: The Economist Books Ltd., 1992.

Brunei Darussalam: Facts and Figures. Bandar Seri Begawan: Prime Minister's Office, 1986.

Brunei Statistical Yearbook. Bandar Seri Begawan: Economic Planning Unit, Statistics Section, Ministry of Finance, 1965/66–annual.

Jones, Laurence Walter. *Brunei: Report on the Housing Census held in Four Towns, May-August 1960.* Kuching, Sarawak: Government Printing Office, 1961.

Lee Kok Cho, Thomas. *Report on the Buffalo Census and Survey in Brunei 1980/81.* Tutong, Brunei: Sinaut Agricultural Centre, 1982.

Report on the Census of Population 1971. Bandar Seri Begawan: Star Press, 1973.

Statistics of External Trade. Economic Planning Unit, Statistics Section, Bandar Seri Begawan: Brunei State Secretariat, [n.d.], annual.

Culture

Archaeology and Prehistory

Bellwood, Peter. *Prehistory of the Indo-Malayan Archipelago*. Sydney: Academic Press, 1985.

Franke, Wolfgang and Ch'en T'ieh-fan. "A Chinese Tomb Inscription of AD 1264, Discovered Recently in Brunei," *Brunei Museum Journal*, Vol. 3, No. 1, 1973: 91–99.

Harrisson, Barbara V. "A Classification of Archaeological Trade Ceramics from Kota Batu," *Brunei Museum Journal*, Vol. 2, No. 1, 1970: 114–188.

———. "Brown Spouted Jars, A Facet of Ceramic History in Brunei View," *Brunei Museum Journal*, Vol. 3, No. 3, 1975: 186–200.

———. "European Trade Ceramics in the Brunei Museum," *Brunei Museum Journal*, Vol. 3, No. 1, 1973: 66–87.

———. "Pusaka, Heirloom Jars of Borneo," Ph.D. Thesis, Ithaca, N.Y.: Cornell University, 1984.

———. *Pusaka, Heirloom Jars of Borneo*. Singapore: Oxford University Press, 1986.

——— and P. M. Shariffuddin. "Sungei Lumut: A 15th Century Burial Ground," *Brunei Museum Journal*, Vol. 1, No. 1, 1969: 24–56.

Harrisson, Tom. "Ancient Glass Beads from Brunei and Sarawak Excavations (compared)," *Sarawak Museum Journal*, Vol. 3, No. 1, 1973: 118–126.

———. "Deep Level Carbon Dates from Kota Batu, Brunei (95 BC to 1300 AD)," *Brunei Museum Journal*, Vol. 2, No. 3, 1971: 96–107.

———. "First Radio-Carbon Dates from Kota Batu, Brunei and Associated Dating Problems in Borneo," *Brunei Museum Journal*, Vol. 2, No. 1, 1970: 188–197.

———. "Kota Batu in Brunei," *Sarawak Museum Journal*, Vol. 7, No. 8, December 1956: 283–319.

———. "Palaeolithic (Stone Age) Studies in Borneo and Adjacent Islands," *Brunei Museum Journal*, Vol. 3, No. 2, 1974: 235–252.

———. "Prehistoric Glass Analyses for Brunei," *Brunei Museum Journal*, Vol. 3, No. 2, 1974: 232–234.

———. "Recent Archaeological Discoveries in East Malaysia and Brunei," *JMBRAS*, Vol. 40, No. 1, July 1967: 14–148.

———. "Recent Archaeological Discoveries in Malaysia 1962–1963: Borneo," *JMBRAS*, Vol. 37, No. 2, November 1964: 192–200.

———. "Recent Archaeological Discoveries in Malaysia 1964: Borneo," *JMBRAS*, Vol. 38, No. 1, July 1965: 244–247.

———. "Recent Archaeological Discoveries in Malaysia 1965: East Malaysia and Brunei," *JMBRAS*, Vol. 39, No. 1, July 1966: 191–197.

———. "Recent Archaeological Discoveries in Malaysia 1967: East Malaysia and Brunei," *JMBRAS*, Vol. 41, No. 1, July 1968: 180–182.

———. "The Brunei Museum," *JMBRAS*, Vol. 45, No. 1, 1972: 119–120.

———. "The Ming Gap and Kota Batu, Brunei (with an appeal for help)," *Sarawak Museum Journal*, Vol. 8, No. 11, 1958: 273–277.

———. *The Minutti Collection of Bronzes in Brunei*. Bandar Seri Begawan: Muzium Brunei, 1973.

———. "The Prehistory of Brunei," *Asian Perspectives*, Vol. 13, 1970: 17–45.

Matussin bin Omar. *Archaeological Excavations in Protohistoric Brunei*. Brunei Museum, Special Publication No. 15, Bandar Seri Begawan: Muzium Brunei, 1981.

Metussin Omar. "A Note on the Stone Wall and Earthen Causeway at Kota Batu," *Brunei Museum Journal*, Vol. 5, No. 3, 1983: 27–50.

———. "A Preliminary Account of Surface Finds from Tanjong Batu beach, Muara," *Brunei Museum Journal*, Vol. 3, No. 3, 1975: 158–174.

———. "The Stone Age in Brunei," *Brunei Museum Journal*, Vol. 3, No. 4, 1976: 127–141.

——— and P. M. Shariffuddin. "Distributions of Chinese and Siamese Ceramics in Brunei," *Brunei Museum Journal*, Vol. 4, No. 2, 1978: 59–66.

Nicholl, Robert. "A Note on P'o-ni and Its Location," *Brunei Museum Journal*, Vol. 5, No. 4, 1984: 4–5.

———. "The Tomb of Maharaja Karna of Brunei at Nanking," *Brunei Museum Journal*, Vol. 5, No. 4, 1984: 35–45.

Pope, John. "Marks on Chinese Ceramics Excavated in Brunei and Sarawak," *Sarawak Museum Journal* (New Series), Vol. 8, No. 11, 1958: 267–272.

Sharma, A. "The Interpretation of a Sanskrit inscription in the ancient Brunei script," *JMBRAS*, Vol. 52, No. 1, June 1979: 99–101.

Solheim, William G., II. "Borneo," *Asian Perspectives*, Vol. 1, Nos. 1–2, Summer 1957: 93–100.

———. "Batu Tarsilah: A Short Comment," *JMBRAS*, Vol. 47, No. 2, July 1974: 151–152.

Tate, R. B. "Radio Carbon Ages from Quaternary Terraces- Prehistory in Brunei," *Brunei Museum Journal*, Vol. 2, No. 3, 1971: 108–123.

Arts

Abdul Latif bin Haji Ibrahim. "Dusun Tribal Dances," *Brunei Museum Journal*, Vol. 1, No. 1, 1969: 10–14.

Furness, William Henry. *Folklore in Borneo: A Sketch*. Wallingford, Pa.: privately published, 1899.

Headly, D., "Some Bisaya Folklore," *Brunei Museum Journal*, Vol. 5, No. 2, 1950: 187–192.

Hickling, H. "Brunei Silver," *Corona: The Journal of Her Majesty's Overseas Service*, Vol. 7, August 1955: 294–296.

Saunders, G. E. *Borneo Folktales and Legends.* Kuching: Borneo Literature Bureau, 1976

Shariffuddin, P. M. "The Royal Nobat of Brunei," *Brunei Museum Journal,* Vol. 4, No. 1, 1977: 7–17.

Taha Abdul Kadir. *Cerita Tradisi Brunei Darussalam.* (Brunei Darussalam's Folklore). Petaling Jaya, Selangor, Malaysia: Pelanduk Publications, 1985.

Language

Bakri, Mahmud. "Brunei and the Official Language Issue," S. Takdir Alisjahbana (ed.). *The Modernization of Languages in Asia.* Papers presented at the Conference for the Malaysian Society of Orientalists held in Kuala Lumpur from 29 September-1 October, 1967, Kuala Lumpur: Malaysian Society of Asian Studies, University of Malaya, 1967: 134–139.

Cense, Anton Abraham and E. M. Uhlenbeck. *Critical Survey on Studies of the Languages of Borneo.* The Hague: Nijhoff 1958.

Craig, Shawna and Linda A. Kimball. "The Early Stage Vocabulary and Grammar Acquisition of a Brunei Malay Child," *Borneo Research Bulletin,* Vol. 18, No. 2, September 1986: 131–147.

Haynes, A. S. "A List of Brunei-Malay words," *JSBRAS,* Vol. 34, July 1900: 39–48.

Jones, Mohd Gary. "Planning Language Change: Some Social and Cultural Implications for Negara Brunei Darussalam," Abu Bakar bin Haji Apong, Dato Seri Laila Jasa Awang Haji (ed.). *Sumbangsih UBD, Essays on Brunei Darussalam.* Gadong, Brunei: Akademi Pengajian Brunei, Universiti Brunei Darussalam, 1992: 95–105.

Kimball, Linda Amy. "The First Words of a Brunei Child," *Brunei Museum Journal,* Vol. 2, No. 1, 1970: 67–86.

―――. "Some Language Aspects of Brunei Malay Enculturation," *Borneo Research Bulletin,* Vol. 10, No. 2, April 1978: 3–13.

MacBryan, G. T. "Additions to a Vocabulary of Brunei-Malay," *JSBRAS,* Vol. 86, November 1922: 376–377.

Marshall, H. B. "A Vocabulary of Brunei Malay," *JSBRAS,* Vol. 83, April 1921: 45–74.

Martin, Peter. "Linguistic Research in Brunei Darussalam: A Review," Abu Bakar bin Haji Apong, Dato Seri Laila Jasa Awang Haji (ed.). *Sumbangsih UBD: Essays on Brunei Darusslam.* Gadong, Brunei: Akademi Pengajian Brunei, Universiti Brunei Darussalam, 1992: 106–117.

Ray, Sidney H. "The Languages of Borneo," *Sarawak Museum Journal,* Vol. 1, No. 1, November 1913: 1–196.

Literature

Abdullah Hussain and Muslim Burmat. *Bunga Rampai Sastera Melayu Brunei.* (A Collection of Brunei Malay Literature). Kuala Lumpur: Dewan Bahasa & Pustaka, 1984.

Bahana Rasa: Antologi Cherpen. (Anthology of Short Stories). Bandar Seri Begawan: Dewan Bahasa & Pustaka, 1979.

Ding Choo Ming. *Bibliografi Sastera Kreatif Melayu, Jilid 1: Brunei, Malaysia dan Singapore, 1920–80.* (A Bibliography of Malay Creative Writings, Vol. 1: Brunei, Malaysia and Singapore, 1920–80), Bangi, Malaysia: Perpustakaan Universiti Kebangsaan Malaysia, 1980.

Gunn, Geoffery C. "Brooke, Brunei and the Image of the White Rajah in Joseph Conrad's *The Rescue*," Abu Bakar bin Haji Apong, Dato Seri Laila Jasa Awang Haji (ed.). *Sumbangsih UBD, Essays on Brunei Darusslalam,* Gadong, Brunei: Akademi Pengajian Brunei, Universiti Brunei Darussalam, 1992: 140–147.

Lufti Abas. "Contemporary Brunei Fiction- Some Examples," Abu Bakar bin Haji Apong, Dato Seri Laila Jasa Awang Haji (ed.). *Sumbangsih UBD, Essays on Brunei Darussalam,* Gadong, Brunei: Akademi Pengajian Brunei, Universiti Brunei Darussalam, 1992: 118–127.

Muslim Burmat. *Hadiah Sebuah Impian* (The Prize of Dreams). Bandar Seri Begawan: Dewan Bahasa & Pustaka, 1983.

Wignesan, T. "Writing in Sabah, Sarawak and Brunei," *Journal of Commonwealth Literature,* Vol. 19, No. 1, 1984: 149–152.

Mass Media

Alkin, Glyn. "Broadcasting Development in Brunei," *Combard* (Commonwealth Broadcasting Association), No. 46, January-March 1980: 39–42.

Lent, John A. "Brunei: Television in a Rich Mini State," *BMIE's World Broadcast News,* March-April 1979: 10.

———. "Mass Media in East Malaysia and Singapore," *Gazette: International Journal for Mass Communications,* Vol. 30, No. 2, 1982: 97–108.

Lim Pui Huen, Patricia. *Singapore, Malaysia and Brunei Newspaper, An International Union List.* Singapore: Institute of Southeast Asian Studies, Library Series No. 19, 1992.

Media Directory: The 13th Media Directory Incorporating the Creative Services. Singapore: Association of Accredited Agents, 1987.

Economy

General

Cleary, Mark and Simon Francis. "Brunei: The Search for a Sustainable Economy," *Southeast Asian Affairs 1994,* Singapore: Institute of Southeast Asian Studies, 1994: 59–75.

——— and Shuan Yann Wong. *Oil, Economic Development and Diversification in Brunei.* London: St. Martin's Press, 1944.

Gunn, Geoffrey C. "Rentier Capitalism in Negara Brunei Darussalam," Kevin Hewison, Richard Robinson and Gary Rodan (eds.). *Southeast Asia in the 1990s, Authoritarianism, Democracy and Capitalism*. St. Leonards, Australia: Allen & Unwin, 1993: 109–132.

Hanna, Willard A. "Brunei: Welfare Sultanate- With Capital," *Southeast Asia Series*, New York: American Universities Field Staff Inc., Vol. 5, No. 9, 1957.

Long, Bernard. "Brunei seeks to diversify its economy," *Singapore Trade and Industry*, December 1974: 39–42.

Sritua Arief. *The Brunei Economy*. East Balmain, New South Wales: Rosecons, 1986.

Agriculture and Natural Resources

Beales, Richard W., David Currie and Robert H. Lindley. *Investigations into some fisheries resources in Brunei*. Brunei Museum Journal, Monograph Series No. 5, Kota Batu, Brunei: Brunei Museum, 1980.

Birkenmeier, Elmar. "Fisheries Development in Brunei," *Brunei Museum Journal*, Vol. 1, No. 1, 1969: 192–196.

———. "Notes on some 'coral fishes' in Brunei waters," *Brunei Museum Journal*, Vol. 2, No. 1, 1970: 294–317.

Currie, David J. *Brunei Bay penaeid prawn keys*. Bandar Seri Begawan: Department of Fisheries, 1980.

Flemmich, Charles O. "History of Shifting Cultivation in Brunei," *The Malayan Agricultural Journal*, Vol. 28, No. 5, May 1940: 234–239.

Groome, J. St. J. *Evaluation of Smallholder Farming Enterprises, 1965–1974*. Sinaut, Brunei: Brunei Shell Petroleum Co., 1975

———. "Hedge row pepper production in Brunei," *Singapore Journal of Primary Industries*, Vol. 5, No. 1, 1977: 49–61.

Hewitt, R. B. "The agricultural systems of Temburong District, Brunei in 1972," *Brunei Museum Journal*, Vol. 5, No. 4, 1984: 203–214.

——— and Muhammad bin Yassin. "Rice varieties in the Temburong District of the State of Brunei," *Brunei Museum Journal*, Vol. 2, No. 3, 1971: 138–141.

Janardanan, E. C. "Brunei Malay Rubber Beginnings," *Sarawak Museum Journal*, Vol. 10, Nos. 19–20, 1962: 598–599.

Khoo Soo Hock. "Agricultural land use," Khoo Soo Hock, et al. *Brunei in Transition: Aspects of its Human Geography in the Sixties*. Kuala Lumpur: Department of Geography, University of Malaya, Occasional Paper No. 2, 1976: 74–149.

Lim, J. S. "A short account of sago production in Kuala Balai- Belait," *Brunei Museum Journal*, Vol. 3, No. 2, 1974: 144–155.

Purvis, Malcolm John. *Research report on the food economy of Malaysia and Brunei*. Ithaca, N.Y.: Department of Agricultural Economics, Cornell University, 1965.

Tempany, H. A. "Agriculture in Brunei," *The Malayan Agricultural Journal*, Vol. 20, November 1932.

Williams, C. N. "Effects of lime, drainage, manganese dioxide seedling conditions on rice in acid sulphur soil in Brunei," *Experimental Agriculture*, Vol. 16, No. 3, 1980: 313–320.

Wong Shuan Yang. *The Forgotten Sector in an Oil-Rich Economy: Agriculture in Brunei*. V R F. Series No. 210, Tokyo: Institute of Developing Economies, 1993.

Mineral Resources

Ahmad Hamzah. "Oil and security in Brunei," *Contemporary Southeast Asia*, Vol. 2, No. 2, September 1980: 182–191.

"Brunei Oil," *Corona: The Journal of Her Majesty's Overseas Service*, Vol. 3, No. 6, June 1951.

Brunei Shell Petroleum. Seria, Brunei: Shell Petroleum Co., Public Affairs Department, 1986.

"Country Profile: Brunei," *OPEC Bulletin*, 1984/85: 35–42.

Energy Information Administration. *The Petroleum Resources of Indonesia, Malaysia, Brunei and Thailand*. Washington, D.C.: U.S. Department of Energy, 1984.

Hamzah, B. A. *Oil and Economic Development Issues in Brunei*. Singapore: Institute of Southeast Asian Studies, 1978.

———. *The Oil Sultanate: Political History of Oil in Brunei*. Kuala Lumpur: Mawaddah Enterprise, 1991.

Harper, G. C. *The Discovery and Development of the Seria Oilfield*. Special Publication No. 5, Bandar Seri Begawan: Brunei Museum, 1975.

Horton, A. V. M. "Rajah Charles Brooke and Mining Concessions in Brunei," *JMBRAS*, Vol. 59, Pt. 1, 1986: 49–72.

Lim, J. S. and P. M. Shariffuddin. "Charcoal production in Brunei," *Brunei Museum Journal*, Vol. 3, No. 3, 1975: 201–219.

Matassim Haji Jibah. "Notes on Brunei Coal (1830–1924)," *Brunei Museum Journal*, Vol. 4, No. 4, 1980: 104–118.

Moffatt, J. W. "Brunei as an oil state," *Trade and Industry*, Vol. 17, No. 10, 5 December 1974: 516–518.

Morrison, Hedda. "Brunei and the Seria oil fields," *New Commonwealth Trade and Commerce*, Vol. 21, No. 7, April 1951: 498–501.

Redfield, A. H. "Petroleum in Borneo," *Economic Geology*, Vol. 17, No. 5, August 1922: 313–349.

———. "Promising Oil Reserves in Sarawak and Brunei," *Far Eastern Survey* (American Council, Institute of Pacific Relations), Vol. 8, 1939.

Business and Trade

Brunei: A Guide for Business and Investors. Singapore: Coopers & Lybrand, 1985

Department of Trade and Industry, New Zealand. *Malaysia and Brunei Handbook*. Wellington: Government Printer, 1975.

Voon Phin Keong. "Commerce and international trade," Khoo Soo Hock, et al. *Brunei in Transition: Aspects of its Human Geography in the Sixties*. Kuala Lumpur: Department of Geography, University of Malaya, Occasional Paper No. 2, 1976: 222–260.

"Why Companies Should Investigate Opportunities in Booming Little Brunei," *Business Asia* (Hong Kong), Vol. 6, No. 26, 27 June 1975: 201–203.

Wimalatissa, W. A. "Entrepreneurial Characteristic and Business Performance of Small Business Owners and Managers—A Case Study of Beribi Industrial Complex, Gadong," Abu Bakar bin Haji Apong, Dato Seri Laila Jasa Awang Haji (ed.). *Sumbangsih UBD: Essays on Brunei Darussalam*. Gadong, Brunei: Akademi Pengajian Brunei, Universiti Brunei Darussalam, 1992: 217–236.

Development

Cleary, Mark and Shuan Yann Wong. "Diversification Problems in a Rentier State: The Case of Brunei," *Pacific Viewpoint*, Vol. 34, No. 1, 1993: 69–76.

Colclough, Christopher. "Brunei: Development Problems of a Resource-Rich State," *Euro-Asia Business Review*, Vol. 4, No. 4, October 1985: 29–32.

Franz, Johannes C. *The Sultanate of Brunei: Oil, Wealth and Problems of Development*. M. Schmitz and A. Sharp (trans.), Nurenberg: Wirtschafts und Sozialgeographisches Institut der Friederich-Alexander-Universitaet, 1980.

Zaharah Haji Mahmud. "Trends of Change and Development in the Rural Areas," Khoo Soo Hock, et al. *Brunei in Transition: Aspects of Its Human Geography in the Sixties*. Kuala Lumpur: Department of Geography, University of Malaya, Occasional Paper No. 2, 1976: 150–182.

Industry

Ameer Ali. "Industrialization or Industries? The Vision and the Viability in Brunei Darussalam," Abu Bakar bin Haji Apong, Dato Seri Laila Jasa Awang Haji (ed.). *Sumbangsih UBD: Essays on Brunei Darussalam*. Gadong, Brunei: Akademi Pengajian Brunei, Universiti Brunei Darussalam, 1992: 196–205.

Basu Sharma. "Multinational Corporations and Industrialization in Southeast and East Asia," *Contemporary Southeast Asia*, Vol. 6, No. 2, 1984: 159–171.

United Nations Economic Commission for Asia and the Far East. *Industrial Development: Asia and the Far East, Vol. II- Afghanistan, Australia, Brunei, Burma, Cambodia, Ceylon, Republic of China, Hong Kong, India, Indonesia, Iran, Japan, Republic of Korea*. Selected documents presented to the Asian

Conference on Industrialization, Manila, 6–20 December 1965, New York: United Nations, 1966.

Labour and Employment

Colclough, Christopher and Martin Godfrey. "The Economics of Labour Shortage: Three case studies from northern Borneo," *IDS Bulletin* (Institute of Development Studies), Vol. 17, No. 4, October 1986: 48–56.

Neville, Warwick. "Economy and Employment in Brunei," *Geographical Review*, Vol. 75, No. 4, October 1985: 451–461.

Voon Phin Keong. "Employment and Labour," Khoo Soo Hock, et al. *Brunei in Transition: Aspects of Its Human Geography in the Sixties.* Kuala Lumpur: Department of Geography, University of Malaya, Occasional Paper No. 2, 1976: 184–221.

Land and Settlements

Lee Yong Leng. "Historical aspects of settlement in British Borneo," *Pacific Viewpoint*, Vol. 2, 1961: 187–212.

———. *North Borneo: A Study in Settlement Geography.* Singapore: Eastern Universities Press, 1965.

———. "The City of Many Waters," *Hemisphere*, Vol. 8, No. 6, May 1964: 8–11.

———. "The long house and Dayak Settlement in British Borneo," *Oriental Geographer*, Vol. 6, 1962: 39–60.

Lim Thim Fook. "Urban Settlements," Khoo Soo Hock, et al. *Brunei in Transition: Aspects of Its Human Geography in the Sixties.* Kuala Lumpur: Department of Geography, University of Malaya, Occasional paper No. 2, 1976: 52–75.

Niew Shong Tong. *Demographic Trends in Negara Brunei Darussalam.* Gadong, Brunei: Universiti Brunei Darussalam, 1989.

Zaharah Haji Mahmud. "Spatial prognosis of the rural population," Khoo Soo Hock, et al. *Brunei in Transition: Aspects of its Human Geography in the Sixties.* Kuala Lumpur: Department of Geography, University of Malaya, Occasional Paper No. 2, 1976: 1–51.

Transport and Communications

Beckett, A. H. and S. Marshall. "Design and Construction of Muara Deep Water Port, Brunei (Paper 8649)," *Proceedings of the Institution of Civil Engineers*, Vol. 74, Pt. 1, August 1983: 349–364.

Gibson-Hill, C. A. "The coastal boats of North Borneo and Labuan Bay," *Sabah Society Journal*, Vol. 3, No. 4, March 1968: 190–204.

Goh, H. S., A. S. Rajendra and S. K. Pui. "Coastal problems encountered at the Muara Port area in Brunei," *International Conference on Coastal and Port Engineering in Developing Countries*, Colombo, Sri Lanka, Vol. 1, 20–26 March 1983: 115–129.

Sterling, W. A. D., C. B. Paget, J. M. Eddison and M. C. Earwaker. "Construction of [the] new international airport, Brunei," *Proceedings of the Institution of Civil Engineers*, Vol. 62, Pt. 1, November 1977: 605–622.

History and Historiography

Historiography

Brown, D. E. "Patterns in Brunei History and Culture," *Borneo Research Bulletin*, Vol. 16, No. 1, April 1984.

Nicholl, Robert (ed.). *European Sources for the History of the Sultanate of Brunei in the Sixteenth Century*. Brunei Museum Special Publication No. 9, Bandar Seri Begawan: Brunei Museum, 1975.

———. "Notes on Controversial Issues in Brunei History," *Archipel*, Vol. 19, 1980: 25–42.

———. "Some Problems of Brunei Chronology," *JSEAS*, Vol. 20, No. 2, September 1989.

General

Brown, D. E. *Brunei, The Structure and History of a Bornean Malay Sultanate*. Kota Batu, Brunei: Brunei Museum, 1970.

Fulton, S. J. "Brunei: Past and Present," *Asian Affairs* (London), Vol. 15, 1984: 5–14.

Hughes-Hallett, H. R. "A Sketch History of Brunei," *JMBRAS*, Vol. 18, Pt. 2, 1940: 23–42. See also, *Brunei Museum Journal*, Vol. 4, No. 1, 1981: 1–18 (Reprinted).

Rutter, Owen. *British North Borneo, An Account of Its History, Resources and Native Tribes*. London: Constable & Co. Ltd., 1922.

Saunders, Graham. *A History of Brunei*, Kuala Lumpur: Oxford University Press, 1994.

Wright, L. R. "Brunei; A Historical Relic," *Journal of the Hong Kong Branch of the Royal Asiatic Society*, Vol. 17, 1977: 12–29.

Pre-16th Century

Bellwood, P. and Matussim bin Omar. "Trade patterns and political developments in Brunei and adjacent areas, AD 700–1500," *Brunei Museum Journal*, Vol. 4, No. 4, 1980: 155–179.

Braddell, Ronald. "P'o-li in Brunei," *Sarawak Museum Journal*, Vol. 5, No. 1, 1949: 5–9.

Brown, Carrie C. "An Early Account of Brunei by Sung Lien," *Brunei Museum Journal*, Vol. 2, No. 4, 1972: 219–231.

———. "Two Ming Texts Concerning King Ma-na-je-chia-na of P'o-ni," *Brunei Museum Journal*, Vol. 3, No. 2, 1974: 222–229.

———. "Some Ming Regulations on Provisions for Tributary Delegations," *Brunei Museum Journal*, Vol. 3, No. 2, 1974: 230–231.

Carey, T. F. "Two Early Muslim Tombs at Brunei," *JMBRAS*, Vol. 11, No. 2, December 1933: 183.

Carroll, J. S. "Berunai in the Boxer Codex," *JMBRAS*, Vol. 55, No. 2, December 1982: 1–25.

Chen Da-sheng. "A Brunei Sultan in the Early 14th Century: A Study of an Arabic Gravestone," *JSEAS*, Vol. 23, No. 1: 1–13.

Nicholl, Robert. "Brunei Rediscovered: A Survey of Early Times," *JSEAS*, Vol. 14, No. 1, March 1983: 219–237.

Ongkili, James P. "Pre-Western Brunei, Sarawak and Sabah," *Nusantara*, No. 3, January 1973.

The 16th and 17th Centuries

Angelas, F. Delor. "Brunei and the Moro Wars," *Brunei Museum Journal*, Vol. 1, No. 1, 1969: 119–132.

Blair, E. H. and J. A. Robertson. *The Philippines Islands*. Vols. 4 & 33, Cleveland, 1903–1909.

Brown, D. E. "Antonio Pigafetta's Account of Brunei in 1521," *Brunei Museum Journal*, Vol. 3, No. 2, 1974: 171–179.

———. "Spanish accounts of their expeditions against Brunei, 1578–79," *Brunei Museum Journal*, Vol. 3, No. 2, 1974: 180–221.

Carroll, John S. "Aganduru Moriz' account of the Magellan expedition at Brunei," *Brunei Museum Journal*, Vol. 6, No. 1, 1985: 54–61.

Nicholl, Robert. "Relations between Brunei and Manila, AD 1682–1690," *Brunei Museum Journal*, Vol. 4, No. 1, 1977: 128–176.

Teixeira, M. "Early Portuguese and Spanish Contacts with Borneo," *Da Sociedade De Geografia De Lisboa*, Lisbon, July-December 1964.

The 18th to 20th Centuries

Black, Ian. "The Ending of Brunei Rule in Sabah, 1878–1902," *JMBRAS*, Vol. 41, No. 2, December 1968: 176–192.

Crisswell, Colin N. "The Origins of the Limbang Claim," *JSEAS*, Vol. 2, No. 2, 1971: 218–229.

————. *Rajah Charles Brooke: Monarch of All He Surveyed.* Kuala Lumpur: Oxford University Press, 1978.

————. "M. S. H. McArthur and Brunei, 1904–1908 or 'A Dying Kingdom' Reprieved," *Brunei Museum Journal,* Vol. 6, No. 4, 1988: 1–32.

Crosbie, A. J. "Brunei in Transition," *Southeast Asian Affairs 1981,* Singapore: Institute of Southeast Asian Studies, 1981: 75–92.

Horton, A. V. M. *The British Residency in Brunei, 1906–1959.* Hull: The University of Hull, Centre for South-East Asian Studies, Occasional Paper No. 6, 1984.

————. "Pengiran Indera Mahkota Shahbandar Mohammad Salleh and James Brooke in the History of Brunei," *Brunei Museum Journal,* Vol. 4, No. 3, 1979: 38–51.

Jacob, G. L. *The Raja of Sarawak: An Account of Sir James Brooke, K.C.B., LL.D., Given Chiefly through Letters and Journals,* Vols. I & II, London: Macmillan & Co., 1876.

Keppel, Sir Henry, *The Expedition to Borneo of H.M.S. Dido for the Suppression of Piracy; with Extracts from the Journal of James Brooke of Sarawak,* Vols. I & II, 3rd Ed., London: Chapman and Hall, 1846.

Leigh, Michael. "Independence for Brunei," *Current Affairs Bulletin,* Vol. 60, No. 1, 1983: 19–23.

————. *Brunei—Independence for Whom?,* Parliament of the Commonwealth of Australia Current Issue Brief No. 1, Canberra: Legislative Research Service Department Library, 1984.

Mundy, Captain Rodney. *Narrative of Events in Borneo and Celebes, Down to the Occupation of Labuan: From the Journal of James Brooke, Esq., Rajah of Sarawak and Governor of Labuan together with Narrative of the Operations of H.M.S. Iris.* Vols. I & II, 2nd Ed., London: John Murray, 1848.

Saunders, Graham. "James Brooke's Visit to Brunei in 1844: A Reappraisal," *Sarawak Museum Journal,* Vol. 17, No. 34–35, 1969: 294–314.

Sidhu, Jatswan S. *Sejarah Sosioekonomi Brunei, 1906–1959* (Socioeconomic History of Brunei, 1906–1959). Kuala Lumpur: Dewan Bahasa & Pustaka, 1995.

Stubbs, R. E. "Two Colonial Office Memoranda on the History of Brunei," *JMBRAS,* Vol. 41, No. 2, December 1968: 83–116.

Tarling, Nicholas. "British Policy in the Malay Peninsula and Archipelago, 1824–1871," *JMBRAS,* Vol. 30, No. 3, October 1957: 1–228.

Treacher, W. H. "British Borneo: Sketches of Brunei, Sarawak, Labuan and North Borneo," *JSBRAS,* Vol. 20, 1889: 13–74.

Treggoning, K. G. "American Activity in North Borneo, 1865–1881," *Pacific Historical Review,* Vol. 23, November 1954.

————. "Steps in the Acquisition of North Borneo," *Historical Studies: Australia and New Zealand,* Vol. 5, No. 19, 1952: 234–243.

———. "The Partitioning of Brunei," *Journal of Tropical Geography*, Vol. 11, April 1958: 84–89.

Warren, James. "Slave Markets and Exchange in the Malay World: The Sulu Sultanate, 1770–1878," *JSEAS*, Vol. 8, No. 2, 1977: 162–175.

———. *The Sulu Zone*, Singapore: University of Singapore Press, 1981.

Wright, L. R., *The Origins of British Borneo*. Hong Kong: Hong Kong University Press, 1970.

Post-Independence, 1984–

Abu Bakar Hamzah. "Brunei Darussalam, Continuity and Tradition," *Southeast Asian Affairs 1990*. Singapore: Institute of Southeast Asian Studies, 1991: 91–104.

Clarita, Carlos R. "Brunei: From Protectorate to Independence," *Monograf Sejarah* (Journal of the Historical Society, University of Malaya, Kuala Lumpur), No. 1, 1984/85: 128–132.

Leake, David, Jr. *Brunei, The Modern Southeast-Asian Islamic Sultanate*. Kuala Lumpur: Forum, 1990.

Mani, A. "Negara Brunei Darussalam in 1992: Celebrating the Silver Jubilee," *Southeast Asian Affairs 1992*. Singapore: Institute of Southeast Asian Studies, 1992: 95–112.

Menon, K. U. "Brunei Darussalam in 1986: In Search of a Political Kingdom," *Southeast Asian Affairs 1987*. Singapore: Institute of Southeast Asian Studies, 1987: 85–101.

———. "Brunei Darussalam in 1988: Ageing in the Wood," *Southeast Asian Affairs 1988*. Singapore: Institute of Southeast Asian Studies, 1988: 140–144.

Ong Teck Meng. "Modern Brunei: Some Important Issues," *Southeast Asian Affairs 1983*. Singapore: Institute of Southeast Asian Studies, 1983: 71–84.

Pushpa Thambipillai and Hamzah Sulaiman. "Brunei Darussalam: After a Decade of Independence," *Southeast Asian Affairs 1995*. Singapore: Institute of Southeast Asian Studies, 1995: 111–123.

Ranjit Singh, D. S. "Brunei in 1985: Domestic Factors, Political and Economic Externalities," *Asian Survey*, Vol. 26, No. 2, February 1986: 168–173.

———. "Brunei Darussalam in 1987: Coming to Grips with Economic and Political Realities," *Southeast Asian Affairs 1988*. Singapore: Institute of Southeast Asian Studies, 1988: 63–70.

Sharon Siddique. "Brunei Darussalam in 1985: A Year of Nation Building," *Southeast Asian Affairs 1986*. Singapore: Institute of Southeast Asian Studies, 1986: 45–51.

———. "Brunei Darussalam in 1991: The Non-Secular State," *Southeast Asian Affairs 1992*. Singapore: Institute of Southeast Asian Studies, 1992: 91–100.

Tilak Doshi. "Brunei, The Steady State," *Southeast Asian Affairs 1991*. Singapore: Institute of Southeast Asian Studies, 1992: 71–80.

Politics

Law and Constitution

Chiew, James. "Brunei Darussalam: Abode of Peace," Carmelo V. Sison (ed.). *Constitution and Legal Systems of ASEAN Countries*, Manila: The Academy of ASEAN Law and Jurisprudence, University of the Philippines, 1990: 1–17.

Maxwell, W. G. and W. S. Gibson. *Treaties and Engagements Affecting the Malay States and Borneo*. London: Jes. Truscott, 1924.

Ranjit Singh, D. S. "Executive Power and Constitutionalism in ASEAN States: The Brunei Experiance," Carmelo V. Sison (ed.). *Constitution and Legal Systems of ASEAN Countries*. Manila: The Academy of ASEAN Law and Jurisprudence, University of the Philippines, 1990: 18–44.

Politics and Political Parties

Hamzah, B. A. "Political History of Brunei" (Part I & II), *Asian Defence Journal*, No. 3, May-June 1980: 70–74 and; No. 4, July-August 1980: 18–22.

Matassim Haji Jibah. "Political development in Brunei with reference to the reign of Sultan Omar Ali Saifudin III (1950–1967)," M.A. Thesis, University of Hull, 1983, Hull: The Library Photographic Services, 1984.

Ranjit Singh, D. S. "Brunei," Haruhiro Fukui (ed.). *Political Parties of Asia and the Pacific, Afghanistan-Korea (ROK)*. Westport, Conn.: Greenwood Press, 1985: 93–98.

———. "The Internal Politics of Brunei in the 1950's and 1960's," *Proceedings of the 8th Conference of the International Association of Historians of Asia (IAHA), August 25–29, 1980*, Kuala Lumpur: IAHA, 1980.

Sopiee, M. N. *From Malayan Union to Singapore Separation, Political Unification in the Malaysian Region, 1945–1965*. Kuala Lumpur; University of Malaya Press, 1974.

Zaini Haji Ahmad. *Pertumbuhan Nasionalisme di Brunei, 1939–1962*. (The Growth of Nationalism in Brunei, 1939–1962). Kuala Lumpur: ZR Publications, 1989.

———. *The Brunei People's Party: Selected Documents*. Petaling Jaya: Institute for Social Analysis, 1987.

Government and Administration

Braighlinn, C. *Ideological Innovation under Monarchy: Aspects of Legitimation Activity in Contemporary Brunei*, Amsterdam: VU University Press, 1992.

Horton, A. V. M. "British Administration in Brunei, 1906–1959," *Modern Asian Studies*, Vol. 20, Pt. 2, April 1986: 353–374.

Hussainmiya, B. A. "Residents Versus Rulers in Brunei Darussalam," *International Seminar on Brunei Malay Sultanate in Nusantara, Proceedings, Vol. 2.* 13–17 November 1994, Bandar Seri Begawan: Yayasan Sultan Haji Hassanal Bolkiah and Akademi Pengajian Brunei, Universiti Brunei Darussalam, 1996: 637–651.

Leys, Peter. "Observations on the Brunei Political System, 1883–1885," *JMBRAS*, Vol. 14, No. 2, December 1968: 117–130.

Wijeweera, Bernard. "Administrative Development in Brunei Darussalam, 1950–90: A Survey in Historical Perspective," Abu Bakar bin Haji Apong, Dato Seri Laila Jasa Awang Haji (ed.). *Sumbangsih UBD: Essays on Brunei Darussalam*. Gadong, Brunei: Akademi Pengajian Brunei, Universiti Brunei Darussalam, 1992: 183–195.

The Monarchy

Bartholomew, James. *The Richest Man in the World: The Sultan of Brunei*. London: Viking, 1989.

Brown, Donald E. "Elites in the Sultanate of Brunei from the 19th Century to the Eve of Independence," *International Seminar on Brunei Malay Sultanate in Nusantara, Proceedings, Vol. 2.* 13–17 November 1994, Bandar Seri Begawan: Yayasan Sultan Haji Hassanal Bolkiah and Akademi Pengajian Brunei, Universiti Brunei Darussalam, 1996: 666–688.

———. "The Coronation of Sultan Muhammad Jamalul Alam, 1918," *Brunei Museum Journal*, Vol. 2, No. 3, 1971: 74–80.

Chalfont, Alun. *By God's Will: A Portrait of the Sultan of Brunei*. London: Weidenfeld & Nicolson, 1989.

Crisswell, Colin. "Pg. Anak Hashim's Role in Brunei Affairs Prior to His Accession to the Throne in 1885," *Sarawak Museum Journal*, Vol. 25, No. 46, 1977: 41–54.

Hussainmiya, B. A. *Sultan Omar Ali Saifuddien III and Britain, The Making of Modern Brunei*. Kuala Lumpur: Oxford University Press, 1995.

Kraar, Louis. "The World's Richest Man: Brunei's free-spending Sultan of oil," *Fortune*, Vol. 116, No. 8, 12 October 1987: 132–133.

Low, Hugh. "Selesilah (Book of Descent) of the Rajas of Bruni," *JSBRAS*, No. 5, June 1880: 1–35.

Mohd Taib Osman. "The Malay Sultanate: Past and Present Functions with Particular Reference to Negara Brunei Darussalam," *International Seminar on Brunei Malay Sultanate in Nusantara, Proceedings, Vol. 2.* 13–17 November 1994, Bandar Seri Begawan: Yayasan Sultan Haji Hassanal Bolkiah and Akademi Pengajian Brunei, Universiti Brunei Darussalam, 1996: 472–483.

Orendain, Joan. *The Sultan of Brunei.* Manila: Filipinas Foundation Inc. for Ayala International, 1983.

Shariffudin, P. M. and Abd. Latif Haji Ibrahim. " 'Batu Tarsilah': The Genealogical Table of the Sultans of Brunei," *JMBRAS*, Vol. 47, No. 1, July 1974: 87–95. (See also *JMBRAS* Reprints 4, 1977: 343–349).

———. "The Royal Wedding," *Brunei Museum Journal*, Vol. 1, No. 1, 1969: 1–14.

Simon, Francis. *Pictures of the Palace: Traveller's Accounts of the Brunei of Sultan Abdul Momin and Sultan Hassan Between 1881 and 1906.* Hull: University of Hull, Centre for South-East Asian Studies, Occasional Paper No. 23, 1993.

Sweeny, P. L. Amin. "Silsilah Raja-raja Berunai" (Genealogy of Brunei's Sultans), *JMBRAS*, Vol. 41, No. 2, December 1968: 1–82.

Treacher, W. H. "Genealogy of the Royal Family of Brunei," *JSBRAS*, Vol. 15, June 1885: 79–80.

International Relations and Defence

Barton, Bruce. "Brunei—Newest and Richest in Asia," *International Perspectives: The Canadian Journal on World Affairs*, January-February 1984: 27–29.

Burley, T. M. "Brunei: ASEAN's reluctant independent," *Insight: Asia's Business Monthly*, December 1981: 38–40.

Hamzah, B. A. "Brunei joins ASEAN: Its expectations," *Asian Pacific Community: A Quarterly Review*, No. 24, Spring 1984: 1–13.

Huxley, Tim. "Brunei's Defence Policy and Military Expenditure." Working Paper No. 166, Canberra: Research School of Pacific Studies, The Australian National University, September 1988.

———. "Defending a Mini State," Chin Kin Wah (ed.). *Defence Spending in Southeast Asia.* Singapore: Institute of Southeast Asian Studies, 1987: 224–251.

Irwin, Graham. *Nineteenth Century Borneo: A Study of Diplomatic Rivalry.* Singapore: Donald Moore Books, 1965.

Keith, H. G. *The United States Consul and the Yankee Raja.* Brunei Museum Journal Monograph No. 4, Bandar Seri Begawan: Brunei Museum, 1980.

Leifer, M. "Decolonization and International Status: The Experiance of Brunei," *International Affairs*, Vol. 54, No. 2, April 1978: 240–252.

Pushpavathi Thambipillai. "Brunei in ASEAN, The Viable Choice?," *Southeast Asian Affairs 1982*, Singapore: Institute of Southeast Asian Studies, 1982: 105–112.

———. "Diplomacy and the Small State: Brunei Darussalam and the International System," Abu Bakar bin Haji Apong, Dato Seri Laila Jasa Awang Haji (ed.). *Sumbangsih UBD: Essays on Brunei Darussalam*. Gadong, Brunei: Akademi Pengajian Brunei, Universiti Brunei Darussalam, 1992: 279–289.

Ranjit Singh, D. S. "Brunei in International Cross-Currents, 1946–1963," *International Relations Journal*, Kuala Lumpur: Department of History, University of Malaya, Vol. 2, 1974/75: 95–109.

———. "Brunei and the Malaysia Negotiations," *International Relations Journal*, Kuala Lumpur: Department of History, University of Malaya, Vol. 3, 1975/76: 19–34.

———. *Brunei 1839–1983, The Problems of Political Survival*. Singapore: Oxford University Press, 1984 (Reprinted 1991).

Rayner, Leonard. "Brunci and Britain," *Round Table*, No. 290, April 1984: 153–158.

Tarling, Nicholas. *Britain, the Brookes and Brunei*. Kuala Lumpur: Oxford University Press, 1971.

Weatherbee, Donald. "Brunei: The ASEAN Connection," *Asian Survey*, Vol. 23, No. 6, 1983: 723–735.

Zainal Kling. "The Changing International Image of Brunei," *Southeast Asian Affairs 1990*. Singapore: Institute of Southeast Asian Studies, 1990: 89–100.

Sciences

Geography

Cleary, M. C. "An Historical Geography of Brunei in the Early Residency period, 1906–1941," Abu Bakar bin Haji Apong, Dato Seri Laila Jasa Awang Haji (ed.). *Sumbangsih UBD: Essays on Brunei Darussalam*. Gadong, Brunei: Akademi Pengajian Brunei, Universiti Brunei Darussalam, 1992: 258–268.

Hewitt, Bernard Robert. "The Geography of the State of Brunei with Special Reference to Agriculture and Agricultural Systems." M.A. Thesis, Hull: University of Hull, 1975.

Khoo Soo Hock, et al. *Brunei in Transition: Aspects of Its Human Geography in the Sixties*. Kuala Lumpur: Department of Geography, University of Malaya, Occasional Paper No. 2, 1976.

Sirinanda, K. U. "Biophysical Environment of Brunei," Abu Bakar bin Haji Apong, Dato Seri Laila Jasa Awang Haji (ed.). *Sumbangsih UBD, Essays on Brunei Darussalam*. Gadong, Brunei: Akademi Pengajian Brunei, Universiti Brunei Darussalam, 1992: 237–257.

Stewart, M. B. *A Geography of Negara Brunei Darussalam*. Bandar Seri Begawan: Dewan Bahasa & Pustaka Brunei, 1986.

Geology

Bronnimann, Paul, et al. "Bruneica Clypea N. Gen. N. Sp., A Recent Remaneicid (Foraminiferida: trochamminacea) from brakish waters of Brunei, Northwest Borneo," *Revue de Paleobiologie*, Vol. 2, No. 1, May 1983: 35–41.

Eckert, H. R. "Planktonic Foraminifera and Time-stratigraphy in well ampa-2," *Brunei Museum Journal*, Vol. 2, No. 1, 1970: 320–327.

James, D. M. D. (ed.). *The Geology and Hydrocarbon Resources of Negara Brunei Darussalam.* Bandar Seri Begawan: Muzium Brunei, 1984.

Jones, R. E. and G. Thorp. "Method of Analyzing Performance of Gravel-Pack Completions in Seria Field, Brunei," *Journal of Petroleum Technology*, Vol. 32, No. 3, 1980: 496–504.

Liechti, P. *Geology of Sarawak, Brunei and the western part of North Borneo.* Kuching, Sarawak: Government Printing Office, 1962, 2 Vols.

Mahmood, D. N. P. "Scanning Electron Microscope Studies of Selected Foraminifera from the Seria Formation, Penanjong, Brunei," *Brunei Museum Journal*, Vol. 3, No. 2, 1974: 271–284.

Tate, R. B. *Gravel in Temburong District and Its Suitability as Concrete Aggregate.* Kuala Belait: Geological Survey Department, Government of Brunei, 1968.

———. "Longshore Drift and Its Effect on the New Muara Port," *Brunei Museum Journal*, Vol. 2, No. 1, 1970: 238–252.

———. "Paleo-environmental Studies in Brunei," *Brunei Museum Journal*, Vol. 3, No. 2, 1974: 285–305.

Willford, G. E. *The Geology and Mineral Resources of Brunei and Adjacent Parts of Sarawak.* Brunei: Brunei Press, 1960.

Medicine

de Zulueta, Julian. "Malaria in Sarawak and Brunei," *Bulletin of the World Health Organization*, Vol. 15, Nos. 3–5, 1956: 651–671.

Horton, A. V. M. "The Brunei Smallpox Epidemic of 1904," *Sarawak Museum Journal*, Vol. 33, No. 54, 1984: 89–99.

Kimball, Linda Amy. *Borneo Medicine: The Healing Art of Indigenous Brunei Malay Medicine.* Ann Arbor, Michigan: University Microfilms International, 1979.

———. "The Concept of Malaria in Brunei Malay indigenous medicine," *Borneo Research Bulletin*, Vol. 7, No. 1, April 1975: 5–11.

Rahman, B. H. A. "Determination of SMA 12/60 reference values as the basis for diagnostic evaluation of biochemical profiling of the rural community in Brunei," *Brunei Museum Journal*, Vol. 4, No. 4, 1980: 238–250.

Wolf, Stewart and Thomas D. Wolf. "A preliminary study in medical anthropology in Brunei," *Pavlovian Journal of Biological Science*, Vol. 13, No. 1, 1978: 42–54.

Woodcock, A. A. and A. M. Cunnington. "Allergenic importance of house dust and storage mites in asthmatics in Brunei, S.E. Asia," *Clinical Allergy*, Vol. 10, No. 5, 1980: 609–616.

Flora and Fauna

Allen, B. C. St. G. "Notes on the Vegetation at a Variety of Habitats in Brunei," *Brunei Museum Journal*, Vol. 5, No. 3, 1983: 200–221.

Ashton, P. S. *Ecological Studies in the mixed Dipterocarp forests of Brunei State*, Oxford: Clarendon Press, 1964.

———. *Manual of Dipterocarp tress of Brunei State*. London: Oxford University Press, 1964.

Banks, Edward. "Mammals of Borneo," *Brunei Museum Journal*, Vol. 4, No. 2, 1978: 165–241.

Birkenmeier, Erika. "Notes on the order Mantodea with reference of Brunei State," *Brunei Museum Journal*, Vol. 1, No. 1, 1969: 225–233.

———. "Observations on Amantis reticulata (Haan) in Brunei (Dictyoptera-Mantidae)," *Brunei Museum Journal*, Vol. 2, No. 3, 1971: 147–159.

Brunei Ministry of Development. *Potential Tree Species for Negara Brunei Darussalam*. Bandar Seri Begawan: Ministry of Development, Town and Country Planning Department, 1985.

Cassidy, Alan C. "An Annotated Checklist of Brunei Butterflies, including a new species of the genus Catapaecilma (Lycaenidae)," *Brunei Museum Journal*, Vol. 5, No. 2, 1982: 202–272.

———. "An Enlarged Checklist of Brunei Butterflies (Lepidoptera: rhopalocera) including descriptions of one new species and two new subspecies," *Brunei Museum Journal*, Vol. 6, No. 1, 1985: 135–168.

Currie, David. "Settlement and Growth of the oyster 'Saccostrea cucullata' in Brunei waters," *Brunei Museum Journal*, Vol. 4, No. 3, 1979: 182–198.

Eden, Sharon. "Some Freshwater Aquarium Fish of Brunei," *Brunei Museum Journal*, Vol. 5, No. 4, 1984: 181–202.

Gauld, Ian D. "A Preliminary Survey of the Ophioninae (Hymenoptera, Ichneumonidae) of Brunei," *Brunei Museum Journal*, Vol. 6, No. 1, 1985: 169–188.

Harrison, Tom (ed.). *Borneo Jungle: An Account of the Oxford University Press Expedition of 1932*. Singapore: Oxford University Press, 1988 (Originally 1938).

Ho Kiam Fui. "Distribution of Recent Benthonic Foraminifera in the 'inner' Brunei Bay," *Brunei Museum Journal*, Vol. 2, No. 3, 1971: 124–137.

Kern, James A. "Observations on the habit of the Proboscis monkey, Nasalis larvatus (Wurmb), made in the Brunei Bay area, Borneo," *Zoologica*, Vol. 46, No. 11, 1964: 183–192.

Kidd, Eric. "Some notes on the Birds of Brunei," *Brunei Museum Journal*, Vol. 4, No. 2, 1978: 115–164.

——— and Richard Beales. "A Study of Lowland Rainforests Birds in Brunei," *Brunei Museum Journal*, Vol. 4, No. 1, 1977: 197–225.

Moulton, J. C. "Hand-list of the Birds of Borneo," *JSBRAS*, Vol. 67, 1914: 125–191.

Smith, Anthony P. "Observations of Birds in Brunei," *Sarawak Museum Journal*, Vol. 25, No. 46, 1977: 235–269.

Smythies, Bertram E. "An Annotated Checklist of the Birds of Borneo," *Sarawak Museum Journal*, Vol. 7, No. 9, 1957: 532–818.

———. *The Birds of Borneo*. Edinburgh: Oliver & Boyd, 1968.

St. John, Spencer. *Life in the Forests of the Far East*. Vol. II, London: Smith Elder & Co., 1862.

Society

Education

Abdul Razak bin Haji Muhammad. "A Critical Examination of Brunei's Higher Education Needs." M.Ed. Thesis, Birmingham: University of Birmingham, 1970.

Abu Bakar Haji Apong. "The Development of Education in Brunei During Self Government Period, With Special reference to Primary Education." M.A. Thesis, Lancaster: University of Lancaster, 1980.

Abu Hanifah bin Mohd. Salleh. "Curriculum Innovation in Brunei since 1970, With Special Reference to the introduction of Scottish Integrated Science." M.Ed. Thesis, Hull: University of Hull, 1980.

Chong, Nelson C. T. "An Examination of the Dysfunctional Role and Problems of Education in National Unity and Development with Special Reference to Brunei." M.Ed. Thesis, Hull: University of Hull, 1979.

Education in Brunei Darussalam: An Outline. Bandar Seri Begawan: Ministry of Education and Health, 1985.

Education System of Negara Brunei Darussalam. Bandar Seri Begawan: Jabatan Pelajaran, Kementerian Pelajaran dan Kesihatan, Negara Brunei Darussalam, 1985.

Goodman, Norman G. "Recent Development in International Education Indonesia, Malaysia and Brunei," *Regional Education Profile: Asia: China, Hong Kong, Macau, Thailand, Indonesia, Malaysia, Brunei*. New York: Institute of International Education (IIE), 1986.

Hill, Guy. "English in Brunei: Second Language or Foreign Language?," *World Language English*, Vol. 1, No. 4, August 1982: 240–242.

Jamaludin bin Saman. "Problems of Education in Rural Societies with Special Reference to Brunei." B.Ed. Thesis, Hull: University of Hull, 1982.

Laporan Surohanjaya Pelajaran Brunei. Report of the Education Commission, Brunei. Bandar Seri Begawan: Jabatan Setia Usaha Kerajaan, 1972.

Mustapha P. Metasan. "Educational Policy in Brunei: With Special Reference to the National Language." B.A. Thesis, Birmingham: Faculty of Education, University of Birmingham, 1979.

Sidhu, Jatswan S. "Pengenalan dan Perkembangan Sistem Pendidikan Inggeris di Brunei, 1906–1959" (The Introduction and Development of English Education in Brunei, 1906–1959), *Sejarah* (Journal of the Department of History, University of Malaya), No. 3, 1994/95: 111–128.

———. "Pengenalan dan Perkembangan Sistem Pendidikan Vernakular Melayu di Brunei, 1906–1959" (The Introduction and Development of Malay Vernacular Education in Brunei, 1906–1959), *Malaysia in History* (Journal of the Malaysian Historical Society). Kuala Lumpur: Malaysian Historical Society, Vol. 23, 1995: 90–102.

Zainidi bin Haji Sidup. "An Examination of Disparity in Educational Provision with Special Reference to Brunei." M.A. Thesis, Hull: University of Hull, 1979.

Population

Austin, Robert F. "Some Demographic Characteristics of the Iban Population of Brunei" (Part I & II), *Brunei Museum Journal*, Vol. 3, No. 4, 1976: 64–69; & Vol. 4, No. 1, 1977: 1–6.

Brunei: The Land and Its People. Seria, Brunei: Brunei Shell Petroleum Co. Ltd., 1978.

Harrisson, Thomas H. "The Chinese in Borneo," *International Affairs*, Vol. 26, No. 3, July 1950: 354–362.

Jones, Laurence Walter. *The Population of Borneo: A Study of the Peoples of Sarawak, Sabah and Brunei*. London: Athlone Press, 1966.

Lee Yong Leng. "Population of British Borneo," *Population Studies*, Vol. 15, 1962: 226–243.

———. "The Chinese of Sarawak (and Brunei)," *Sarawak Museum Journal*, Vol. 11, Nos. 23–24, 1964: 516–532.

Mani, A. "A Community in Transition: Indians in Negara Brunei Darussalam," in K. S. Sandhu and A. Mani (eds.). *Indian Communities in Southeast Asia*. Singapore: Institute of Southeast Asian Studies & Times Academic Press, 1993: 1–30.

Neville, Warwick. "The Population Composition of Brunei," *Singapore Journal of Geography*. Vol. 11, No. 1, 1990: 27–42.

Sandin, Benedict. *The Sea Dayaks before the White Rajah Rule*. East Lansing: Michigan State University Press, 1968.

Shariffuddin, P. M. "The Kedayans," *Brunei Museum Journal*, Vol. 1, No. 1, 1969: 15–23.

Religion

Awang Haji Mohd. Jamil, Pehin Orang Kaya Amar Diraja Dato Seri Utama Dr. "Islam in Brunei," *Brunei Museum Journal*, Vol. 4, No. 1, 1977: 35–42.

Federspiel, Howard M. "Islam and Development in the Nations of ASEAN," *Asian Survey*, Vol. 25, No. 8, August 1985: 805–821.

Harrisson, Tom H. "The Advent of Islam to West and North Borneo," *JMBRAS*, Vol. 45, Pt. 1, January 1973: 10–20.

Hooker, Michael B. *Islamic Law in South-East Asia*. Singapore: Oxford University Press, 1984.

Matussin, Omar. "Islam di Brunei: Dari Perspektif Arkiologi" (Islam in Brunei: From an Archaeological Perspective), *Karya*, Vol. 1, No. 1, May 1979: 7–13.

Milner, A. C. "Islam and Malay Kingship," *Journal of the Royal Asiatic Society of Great Britain and Ireland*, No. 1, 1981: 46–70.

Mohd, Jamil Al-Sufri. "Islam in Brunei," *Brunei Museum Journal*, Vol. 4, Pt. 1, 1977.

Pameran Sejarah Perkembangan Islam di Brunei. (An Exhibition on the History of Islam's Development in Brunei). Bandar Seri Begawan: Dewan Bandaran, 1979.

Rooney, John. *Khabar Gembira (The Good News): A History of the Catholic Church in East Malaysia and Brunei, 1880–1976*. Turnbridge Wells, England: Burns & Oates, 1981.

Social Services

Davidson, J. A. "Postal Services in Brunei's Water Town," *Brunei Museum Journal*, Vol. 3, No. 4, 1976: 87–95.

Lim, J. S. "The Postal History of Brunei, 1906–1937," *Brunei Museum Journal*, Vol. 4, No. 1, 1977: 112–127.

Mohd, Jaman bin Mohamed. "An Estimate of Brunei's Housing Needs, 1980–2000," *Brunei Museum Journal*, Vol. 5, No. 3, 1983: 187–199.

———. "Brunei Housing Needs, 1986–2000," *South East Asian Economic Review*, Vol. 6, No. 3, December 1985: 149–163.

Sidhu, Jatswan S. "Proses Perbandaran di Brunei: Kelahiran dan Perkembangan Bandar Brunei, Kuala Belait dan Seria, 1906–1959" (The Proses of Urbanisation in Brunei: The Growth and Development of Brunei Town, Kuala Belait and Seria, 1906–1959), *Purba, Kuala Lumpur: Journal of the Malaysian Museum Association*, No. 12, 1993: 83–93.

Appendix A

Genealogy of the Sultans of Brunei Darussalam, c. 1363–1995*

1. SULTAN MUHAMMAD: 1363–1402
2. SULTAN AHMAD: 1408–1426
3. SULTAN SHARIF ALI: 1426–1432
4. SULTAN SULAIMAN: 1432–1485
5. SULTAN BOLKIAH: 1485–1524
6. SULTAN ABDUL KAHAR: 1524–1535
7. SULTAN SAIFUL RIJAL: 1535–1581
8. SULTAN SHAH BRUNEI: 1581–1582
9. SULTAN MUHAMMAD HASSAN: 1582–1597
10. SULTAN ABDUL JALILUL AKBAR: 1597–1659
11. SULTAN ABDUL JALILUL JABBAR: 1659–1660
12. SULTAN HAJI MUHAMMAD ALI: 1660–1661
13. SULTAN ABDUL HAKKUL MUBIN: 1661–1673
14. SULTAN MUHYIDDIN: 1673–1690
15. SULTAN NASRUDDIN: 1690–1710
16. SULTAN HUSIN KAMALUDDIN: 1710–1730; 1737–1740
17. SULTAN MUHAMMAD ALIUDIN: 1730–1737
18. SULTAN OMAR ALI SAIFUDDIN I: 1740–1795
19. SULTAN MUHAMMAD TAJUDDIN: 1795–1804; 1804–1807
20. SULTAN MUHAMMAD JAMALUL ALAM I: 1804
21. SULTAN MUHAMMAD KANZU ALAM: 1807–1826
22. SULTAN MUHAMMAD ALAM: 1826–1828
23. SULTAN OMAR ALI SAIFUDDIN II: 1828–1852
24. SULTAN ABDUL MUMIN: 1852–1885
25. SULTAN HASHIM JALILUL ALAM AQAMADDIN: 1885–1906
26. SULTAN MUHAMMAD JAMALUL ALAM II: 1906–1924
27. SULTAN AHMAD TAJUDDIN: 1924–1950
28. SULTAN OMAR ALI SAIFUDDIEN III: 1950–1967
29. SULTAN HASSANAL BOLKIAH: 1967–

*Many dates are still in dispute and this list has undergone subsequent alteration.

Appendix B

British Residents, 1906–1959

Jan. 1906–May 1907 : M. S. H. McArthur
May 1907–Dec. 1907 : H. Chevalier
Jan. 1908–April 1908 : M. S. H. McArthur
Apr. 1908–Sept. 1909 : J. F. Owen
Sept. 1909–Nov. 1909 : B. O. Stoney
Nov. 1909–Nov. 1913 : H. Chevalier
Nov. 1913–Dec. 1914 : F. W. Douglas
Jan. 1915–May 1916 : E. B. Maundrell
May 1916–March 1921 : G. E. Cator
March 1921–March 1923 : L. A. Allen
March 1923–Feb. 1926 : E. E. F. Pretty
March 1926–May 1927 : O. E. Venables
May 1927–May 1928 : E. E. F. Pretty
May 1928–Jan. 1929 : P. A. B. McKerron
Jan. 1929–Aug. 1929 : R. J. F. Curtis
Aug. 1929–Sept. 1931 : P. A. B. McKerron
Sept. 1931–Oct. 1934 : T. F. Carey
Nov. 1934–Jan. 1937 : R. E. Turnbull
Jan. 1937–Dec. 1939 : J. Graham Black
Jan. 1940–Dec. 1941 : E. E. Pengelley

* * * *
Interregnum
(Japanese Occupation)
* * * *
July 1946–Jan. 1948 : W. J. Peel
Jan. 1948–Aug. 1948 : L. H. N. Davis
Aug. 1948–June 1951 : E. E. F. Pretty
July 1951–June 1953 : J. C. H. Barcroft
June 1953–July 1954 : J. O. Gilbert

July 1954–Oct. 1954 : D. H. Trumble
Oct. 1954–June 1956 : J. O. Gilbert
June 1956–Dec. 1956 : D. C. White
Dec. 1956–July 1958 : J. O. Gilbert
July 1958–Sept. 1959 : D. C. White

Appendix C

THE STRUCTURE OF GOVERNMENT*

As Head of the State of Brunei Darussalam, the Sultan is vested with supreme executive authority under the Constitution of 1959. He presides over a full ministerial government system and is personally advised as Head of State by the following councils:

The Religious Council: As head of the Islamic faith, the Sultan receives advice from this council on Islamic matters. Members of this council are appointed by the Head of the State.

The Privy Council: The main function of the Privy Council, over which the Sultan presides, is to advise on constitutional matters, the exercise of the prerogative of mercy, and the awarding of honorary titles. Members of this council are also appointed by the Head of the State.

The Council of Cabinet Ministers: Since 1 January 1984, the Council of Ministers is known as the Council of Cabinet Ministers. Appointed by the Head of the State, the council advises him on all executive matters.

The Council of Succession: Should the need arise, this council is empowered to determine the succession to the throne subject to the Constitution and the Succession and Regency Proclamation of 1959. Its members are drawn mainly from the royal family and are appointed by the Sultan.

---

*Prior to 1984, there was also the Legislative Council which introduced bills, passed legislation and scrutinized government policies. It was presided over by a Speaker who was appointed by the Sultan. However, on 13 February 1984, this council was dissolved by the Sultan and since then legislation is enacted through Royal Proclamations under the 1959 Constitution.

Appendix D

The Present Cabinet

Ministers

Sultan: Yang Di-Pertuan Negara Brunei Darussalam; Prime Minister; Minister of Defence; Minister of Finance and President of the Cabinet: His Majesty Paduka Seri Baginda Sultan Haji Hassanal Bolkiah Mu'izzaddin Waddaulah.

Minister of Foreign Affairs: His Royal Highness Paduka Seri Pengiran Perdana Wazir Sahibul Himmah Wal-Waqar Pengiran Muda Haji Mohamed Bolkiah @ Prince Mohamed Bolkiah.

Minister of Home Affairs and Special Adviser to His Majesty The Sultan and Yang Di-Pertuan in the Prime Minister's Office: Yang Berhormat Pehin Orang Kaya Laila Setia Bakti Diraja Dato Laila Utama Haji Awang Isa bin Pehin Datu Perdana Menteri Dato Laila Utama Haji Awang Ibrahim @ Pehin Dato Haji Isa.

Minister of Education: Yang Berhormat Pehin Orang Kaya Laila Wijaya Dato Seri Setia Haji Awang Abdul Aziz bin Begawan Pehin Udana Khatib Dato Seri Paduka Haji Awang Umar @ Pehin Dato Haji Abdul Aziz.

Minister of Law: Yang Berhormat Mulia Pengiran Laila Kanun Diraja Pengiran Haji Bahrin bin Pengiran Haji Abbas @ Pengiran Bahrin.

Minister of Industry & Primary Resources: Yang Berhormat Pehin Orang Kaya Setia Pahlawan Dato Seri Setia Awang Haji Abdul Rahman bin Dato Setia Haji Awang Mohammad Taib @ Pehin Dato Haji Abdul Rahman.

Minister of Religious Affairs: Yang Berhormat Pehin Jawatan Luar Pekerma Raja Dato Seri Utama Dr. Ustaz Haji Awang Mohammad Zain bin Haji Serudin @ Pehin Dato Dr. Haji Mohammad Zain.

Minister of Development: Yang Berhormat Pengiran Dato Seri Laila Jasa Dr. Haji Ismail bin Pengiran Haji Damit @ Pengiran Dato Dr. Haji Ismail.

Minister of Culture, Youth & Sports: Yang Berhormat Pehin Jawatan Luar Pekerma Raja Dato Seri Paduka Haji Awang Hussain bin Pehin Orang Kaya Digadong Seri Diraja Dato Laila Utama Haji Mohd. Yusof @ Pehin Dato Haji Hussain.

Minister of Health: Yang Berhormat Dato Paduka Dr. Haji Johar bin Dato Paduka Haji Noordin @ Dato Dr. Haji Johar.

Minister of Communications: Yang Berhormat Dato Seri Laila Jasa Haji Awang Zakaria bin Datu Mahawangsa Haji Awang Sulaiman @ Dato Haji Zakaria.

Deputy Ministers

Deputy Minister of Defence: Yang Amat Mulia Pengiran Sanggamara Diraja Major-General (Res) Pengiran Haji Ibnu bin Pengiran Datu Penghulu Pengiran Haji Apong @ Major-General Pengiran Haji Ibnu.

Deputy Minister of Foreign Affairs: Yang Mulia Dato Haji Paduka Haji Awang Haji Mohd. Ali bin Haji Mohd. Daud @ Dato Haji Mohd. Ali.

Deputy Minister of Finance: Yang Mulia Dato Paduka Seri Laila Jasa haji Awang Ahmad Wally Skiner @ Dato Haji Ahmad Wally Skinner.

Deputy Minister of Home Affairs: Yang Mulia Dato Paduka Haji Awang Abidin bin Orang Kaya Perwara Abdul Rashid @ Dato Haji Abidin.

Deputy Minister of Education: Yang Mulia Dato Seri Laila Jasa Haji Awang Ahmad bin Haji Jumat @ Dato Haji Ahmad Jumat.

Deputy Minister of Religious Affairs: Yang Dimuliakan Pehin Siraja Khatib Dato Paduka Seri Setia Ustaz Haji Awang Yahya bin Haji Ibrahim.

Deputy Minister of Culture, Youth and Sports: Yang Mulia Dato Paduka Haji Awang Selamat bin Haji Munap @ Dato Haji Selamat.

Appendix E

The Ministries and their Responsibilities

PRIME MINISTER'S OFFICE: Royal Brunei Police; *Adat Istiadat* (Malay Customs); Public Service Commission; Audit; Privy Council; Council of Ministers; Council of State; Establishment; Detention Center; Anti Corruption Bureau (ACB); Petroleum Unit; Broadcasting and Information; and Narcotics Control Bureau.

MINISTRY OF DEFENCE: Royal Brunei Armed Forces (RBAF) and Gurkha Reserve Unit (GRU).

MINISTRY OF FOREIGN AFFAIRS: Foreign Affairs Office.

MINISTRY OF FINANCE: Treasury; Brunei Investment Agency (BIA); Customs; States Stores; Economic Development Board (EDB); and Economic Planning Unit (EPU).

MINISTRY OF HOME AFFAIRS: District Offices; Immigration; Labour; Prisons; Municipal; Government Security; Cooperative Development; Weights and Measures; and Fire Brigade.

MINISTRY OF COMMUNICATIONS: Postal Services; Civil Aviation; Marine; Telecommunications; Ports; and Land Transport.

MINISTRY OF LAW: Law; Judicial; and Printing.

MINISTRY OF EDUCATION: Education.

MINISTRY OF RELIGIOUS AFFAIRS: Religious Affairs.

MINISTRY OF DEVELOPMENT: Agriculture; Fisheries; Forestry; Public Works; Electrical; Town and Country Planning; Survey; Housing Development; and Land.

MINISTRY OF CULTURE, YOUTH AND SPORTS: Language and Literature Bureau; Welfare, Youth and Sports; Museum; and Historical Center.

MINISTRY OF HEALTH: Medical and Health.

Tables

Table 1: Population Estimates, 1981, 1986 and 1990

	1981	1986	1990
Total Local Population	147,900	171,000	193,000
Citizens	127,700	148,000	166,600
Permanent Residents	20,200	23,400	26,400
Temporary Residents	44,900	56,900	62,800
Total Population	**192,800**	**227,900**	**255,800**

Source: Fifth National Development Plan, 1986–1990. Bandar Seri Begawan: Economic Planning Unit, Ministry of Finance, 1986: 14.

Table 2: Area and Population Density by District, 1986

	All Districts	Brunei/Muara District	Belait District	Tutong District	Temburong District
Area (sq. km.)	5,765	571	2,724	1,116	1,304
Total Population	226,300	136,100	53,600	28,100	8,500
By Sex:					
Male	116,800	69,400	28,200	14,600	4,600
Female	109,500	66,700	25,400	13,500	3,900
By Race:					
Malay	155,600	102,500	23,900	23,300	5,900
Other					
Indigenous	11,400	2,600	5,600	1,900	1,300
Chinese	41,400	21,300	17,200	2,100	800
Others	17,900	9,700	6,900	800	500

Source: Brunei Darussalam in Profile. Bandar Seri Begawan: Government of Brunei, 1989: 111.

Table 3: Selected Macroeconomic Indicators, 1980–1990

Source/Year	1980	1985	1990
Government revenue (B$ million)	6,266	7,533	2,706
Government expenditure (B$ million)	1,142	4,117	2,790
Oil-related GDP (%)	83.7	72.8	62.9
Non-oil related GDP (%)	16.3	27.2	37.1
Exports (B$ million)	9,852	6,532	4,316
Imports (B$ million)	1,230	1,348	1,847

Note: Beginning in 1986 government revenues from investments were excluded from the national account.

Source: The table above was first published as "Table 1: Selected Macro-Economic Indicators, 1980–90" in 1994 in the article "Brunei: The Search for a Sustainable Economy" by Mark Cleary and Simon Francis in Southeast Asian Affairs 1994 (p. 69). Reproduced here with kind permission of the publisher, Institute of Southeast Asian Studies, Singapore.

Table 4: Imports by Product, 1984–1986

	Million Brunei Dollars		
	1984	1985	1986
Machinery and transport	465.93	456.30	550.80
Manufactured goods	270.61	289.88	305.70
Food and live animals	204.78	196.12	209.12
Misc. manufactured articles	119.17	145.28	153.05
Chemicals	102.12	95.09	101.46
Beverages and tobacco	70.25	70.51	84.88
Crude material (fertilizer, rubber, wood, etc.)	11.65	16.60	17.36
Mineral fuels: crude petroleum, refined and related materials	21.16	23.94	14.60
Misc. transactions and commodities	56.44	46.74	7.94
Animal and vegetable oils and fats	9.39	7.93	5.51
Total imports	**1,331.50**	**1,348.39**	**1,450.42**

Source: Brunei Darussalam in Profile, 112.

Table 5: Exports by Product, 1984–1986

	Million Brunei Dollars		
	1984	*1985*	*1986*
Mineral fuels: petroleum, refined and related materials	6,729.53	6,435.62	3,877.70
Machinery and transport equipment	32.07	55.31	55.29
Food and live animals	8.30	10.04	17.66
Manufactured goods, classified chiefly by materials	9.89	10.77	14.05
Misc. manufactured articles	21.08	10.86	13.19
Beverages and tobacco	4.20	3.70	5.40
Crude materials (fertilizer, rubber, wood, etc.)	1.60	1.54	2.61
Chemicals	4.95	3.27	2.49
Misc. transactions and commodities	2.05	1.64	1.66
Animal and vegetable oils and fats	0.27	0.14	0.04
Total Exports	**6,813.94**	**6,532.89**	**3,990.10**

Source: Brunei Darussalam in Profile, 112.

Table 6: Imports by Countries of Origin, 1984–1986

	Million Brunei Dollars		
	1984	*1985*	*1986*
Singapore	322.05	328.50	373.32
Japan	265.83	267.00	256.48
U.S.A.	202.47	209.95	177.25
United Kingdom	115.81	124.25	114.67
Germany (F.R.)	24.97	51.90	87.66
Malaysia, West	64.24	61.07	75.65
Other Countries	74.91	55.46	65.82
Netherlands	34.31	23.73	48.44
Thailand	33.85	41.74	45.16
Australia	43.77	36.86	37.31
Taiwan	39.24	36.74	34.16
Italy	10.53	15.89	32.62
China	26.53	26.78	27.45
France	23.98	15.49	22.76
Hong Kong	19.48	20.15	19.59
Korea, Rep. of	12.98	13.79	12.87
Denmark	8.82	9.76	9.52
Sabah	5.65	4.56	5.76
Sarawak	2.08	4.77	3.95
Total	**1,331.50**	**1,348.39**	**1,450.41**

Source: Brunei Darussalam in Profile, 113.

Table 7: Exports by Countries of Destination, 1984–1986

	Million Brunei Dollars		
	1984	*1985*	*1986*
Japan	4,662,54	4,000.79	2,667.87
Thailand	442.59	692.85	323.93
Korea, Rep. of	370.16	458.98	293.57
Singapore	490.03	568.85	266.68
U.S.A.	377.38	479.03	243.18
Taiwan	146.96	229.11	67.13
Sarawak	36.07	30.89	40.55
Australia	0.16	0.23	33.28
Philippines	117.29	34.50	29.29
Sabah	9.24	10.70	10.00
Malaysia, West	1.00	0.58	4.70
United Kingdom	3.09	2.58	3.62
New Zealand	0.62	0.29	1.83
Hong Kong	0.37	0.31	1.50
Indonesia	1.03	21.51	1.31
Germany (F.R.)	0.09	1.03	0.80
France	154.89	0.14	0.52
Other Countries	0.38	0.43	0.25
Netherlands	0.05	0.09	0.09
Total	**6,813.94**	**6,532.89**	**3,990.10**

Source: Brunei Darussalam in Profile, 113.

Table 8: Expenditure Allocations for National Development Plans (NDP) 3, 4 and 5

	NDP3 1975–79	NDP4 1980–85	NDP5 1986–90
Total Value (B$ thousand)	533,544	1,749,814	2,610,000
Percentage Allocations			
Industry/Agriculture (%)	6.6	2.2	10
Transport/Communications (%)	33.6	23.3	20
Social Services (%)	36.6	28.2	29
Utilities (%)	20.9	14.3	20
Public Buildings (%)	2.9	16.4	10
Security (%)	n.a.	15.5	10
Others (%)	n.a.	0.1	1

Source: The table above was first published as "Table 2: Expenditure Allocation for NDP3, NDP4, and NDP5" in 1994 in the article "Brunei: The Search for a Sustainable Economy" by Mark Cleary and Simon Francis in *Southeast Asian Affairs 1994* (p. 72). Reproduced here with the kind permission of the publisher, Institute of Southeast Asian Studies, Singapore.

Table 9: Expenditure for 6th National Development Plan, 1991–1995

Total Budget	*B$5,509,000*	
Industry		10.0%
Industrial Fund	1.8%	
Agriculture/Forestry	1.5%	
Commerce	1.0%	
Industrial Estates	3.1%	
Transport and communications		20.0%
Roads	8.9%	
Telecommunications	7.1%	
Aviations/Ports	3.2%	
Social services		29.3%
Housing	14.2%	
Education	7.0%	
Public Facilities	4.5%	
Religious Affairs	1.0%	
Public utilities		20.0%
Electricity	10.7%	
Water	5.8%	
Drainage	1.9%	
Public buildings		10.0%
Security		7.0%
Army	6.3%	
Police	0.7%	
Others		3.7%

Source: Sixth National Development Plan, 1991–1995.

Table 10: Working Population by Industry and Sector, 1981

	Private Sector	Public Sector
Agriculture, Forestry and Fishery	2,248	1,187
Mining & Quarrying	3,843	20
Manufacturing	2,649	134
Electricity & Water Supplies	187	1,774
Wholesale & Retail	5,207	65
Restaurant & Hotel	2,065	26
Construction	9,986	2,658
Transport, Storage and Communication	2,878	1,651
Finance, Insurance and Business Services	1,663	347
Community, Social and Personal Services	5,429	28,853
Unknown	247	11
Total	**36,402**	**36,726**

Source: *Brunei Darussalam in Profile*, 111.

Table 11: Consumer Price Index (Average), 1985–1986 (1977 = 100)

	1985	1986
All Commodities	146.4	149.0
Food	154.8	155.7
Clothing and Footwear	147.4	150.5
Gross Rent, Fuel and Power	155.2	156.4
Furniture, Furnishing and Household Equipment and Operation	128.9	133.7
Transport and Communication	139.0	143.5
Recreation, Entertainment, Education and Cultural Services	133.5	133.6
Miscellaneous Goods and Services	142.3	150.5

Source: *Brunei Darussalam in Profile*, 113.

Table 12: Exports of Oil/Gas, 1993 (B$ millions)

Crude Petroleum	
Japan	522.1
South Korea	390.6
Thailand	359.9
Singapore	291.2
Taiwan	106.4
Philippines	81.6
Australia	28.9
Total	**1,780.7**
Gas	
Japan	1,591.4
Petroleum Spirit	
Japan	102.5
South Korea	15.0
U.S.A.	4.7
Total	**122.2**

Source: The table above was first published as "Table 1: Exports of Oil/Gas, 1993" in 1995 in the article "Brunei Darussalam, After a Decade of Independence" by Pushpa Thambipillai and Hamzah Sulaiman in *Southeast Asian Affairs 1995* (p. 118). Reproduced here with the kind permission of the publisher, Institute of Southeast Asian Studies, Singapore.

Glossary

adat	custom
agama (ugama)	religion
agar-agar	jelly
akademi	academy
amanah	sacred oath
Awang	traditionally, a title for aristocrats; now a respectful term of address equivalent to the English "Mr"
ayer (modern spelling: air)	water
bahasa	language
bandar	town; city; port
barisan	front
Bendahara	the principal official in a kingdom, often likened to a Prime Minister; senior wazir (vizier)
bersatu	united
bin	son of; for Muslims only
binti	daughter of; for Muslims only
bumiputera	son of the soil; indigenous person; native
buruh/buroh	labourer
cheteria/ceteria	noble officials, ranked below the wazir
cikgu	teacher
dakwah	to "call" or "invite", i.e. the duty of Muslims to call all mankind to Islam
Darussalam	Abode of Peace
Dato or Datuk	a title often used with a great non royal chief; now equivalent to the English "Sir"

daulat	the divinity of a ruler; majesty
Dayang	the feminine of Awang; now a respectful term of address for non-noble women
guru	teacher
haji	a title used by a Muslim who has performed the hajj
Hajj	pilgrimage to Mecca that all devout Muslims should make at some point in their lives if they possibly can
hamba	literally, slaves; subjects; inhabitants
hikayat	narrative, story, tale in prose
istana	palace of the Sultan
isteri	wife
jajahan	dependencies
jalan	road
kampung/kampong	a village; a compound of houses usually under the authority of an important individual
kaum ibu	women's organisation; literally, mother's group
kerajaan	government; appanage of the Sultan
kesatuan	union; association
kuala	estuary
kuripan	appanage of an official other than the Sultan
masjid	mosque
Menteri (mentri)	Minister
Menteri Besar	Chief Minister
merdeka	independence
minyak	oil
mukim	district; subdistricts
murid	pupil; student
nahkoda	a trading sea captain or merchant adventurer
negara	state; country

padi	rice
Pehin	a title given to non-noble officials of high rank
Pemancha	a traditional title
pengajian	studies
penghulu	headmen; head of village; district head
pengiran	a noble
Pengiran Bendahara	traditionally, the first-ranking wazir
Pengiran Di Gadong	traditionally, the second-ranking wazir
Pengiran Indera	a noble title, as in "Pengiran Indera Mahkota"
Pengiran Isteri	the title given to Sultan Hassanal Bolkiah's second wife
Pengiran Muda	the title given to the heir to the throne, Sultan Hassanal Bolkiah's eldest son
Pengiran Pemancha	traditionally, the fourth-ranking wazir
Pengiran Temenggong	traditionally, the third-ranking wazir
persatuan	association
raja/rajah	king; one who is of royal blood
Raja Isteri	royal wife; queen; the title of Sultan Hassanal Bolkiah's first wife
rakyat	subjects; commoners; people
Seri Begawan	Seri Begawan Sultan; the retired Sultan
shaer/syair	a poetic form used for storytelling
shahbandar	harbourmaster
sharif	a descendant of the Prophet Muhammad
Sheikh	a Muslim title
silsilah	chronicle; genealogy
sungai	river; dependency
surau	a Muslim prayer house
syarikat/sharikat	company; association

Temenggong	Malay minister in charge of defence, justice and palace affairs
tua	old
Tuanku	the title applied to a noble of royal descent
tulin/tulen	literally, pure; hereditary appanage
universiti	university
wazir	vizier; minister; the four highest noble officials under the Sultan
Yang Di Pertuan	He who is made King; Paramount Ruler
zakat	tithe; religious contribution applied to charitable purposes

About the Authors

D. S. RANJIT SINGH (Cert. Ed., Malayan Teachers College; B.A., M.A., Ph.D. University of Malaya) is currently an Associate Professor at the Department of History, University of Malaya in Kuala Lumpur, having served there for about 24 years. He has taught courses on Malaysian and Southeast Asian History. His area of specialization includes the history of British Borneo and Contemporary Southeast Asia. He was also consultant to the Ministry of Foreign Affairs, Malaysia, on border issues. Between 1994–1996, he served as Deputy Dean of the Faculty of Arts and Social Sciences, University of Malaya.

JATSWAN S. SIDHU (B.A., M.A. University of Malaya; M.A. University of Leeds) is currently a Lecturer at the International Studies Programme, Faculty of Arts and Social Sciences, University of Malaya in Kuala Lumpur. Prior to this, he was a tutor at the Department of History, University of Malaya between 1989 to 1992. In addition to teaching at the University of Malaya, he was also a visiting lecturer at the University of Malaysia Sarawak (UNIMAS) between 1994 and 1995. His area of specialisation includes the history of Brunei and Burma as well as International Relations.